A
Purpose Driven
GOD

A
Purpose Driven
GOD

Bo Kirkwood

Published by Selah Publishing Group, Bristol, TN.

Printed in the United States of America.

ISBN: 978-1-58930-326-3

Praise for *The Evolution Delusion* by Dr. Bo Kirkwood

"Dr. Kirkwood has done an expert job succinctly explaining the salient points of the major creationist and intelligent design literature. All Christians and believers alike should read this book." Josh Gurtler, PhD, senior research scientist, USDA, Agricultural Research Service

"Neo-Darwinian evolution arrogantly claims to be the only scientific explanation for origins. Bo Kirkwood falsifies that proposition by showing that when the objective mind follows sound scientific principles, it will necessarily conclude the theory is totally inadequate because it is built upon the crumbling foundation of unscientific suppositions." Craig Thomas, PhD in animal science, retired from Michigan State University

"An excellent read. The book was very informative." Kathleen L.

"Dr. Kirkwood is highly regarded in his study on the subject of evolution. His objectiveness on the subject, and pure scientific approach to address the theory of evolution, is refreshing." M.S.C.

"My husband heard of this book on the radio and asked me to get it for him. He says it is one of the best books he has read." Linda L.

"Excellent book! Will be ordering more by this author!" Don V.

"The best book on the delusion of evolution!!! A must-read for all truth seekers." Fran R.

"Personally know him and heard him speak on this on this subject. Amazing job." D.C.

"Excellent. Well-thought-out and developed. The author makes a compelling case that everyone should read. Although the author is not reticent about expressing his own personal opinion with regards to the various options, he does not do it in an overbearing way. This is a book that everyone who is remotely interested in the origin of life should read." Dr. T.L.

"In *The Evolution Delusion*, Dr. Bo Kirkwood offers an honest and fair comparison of molecules-to-man evolution and intelligent design. Dr. Kirkwood indicates that he has a great deal of respect for Charles Darwin, even to the point of saying that Charles Darwin was a man of great integrity. I recommend this book to anyone who can approach this subject with an open mind. Stephen F.

"This is an excellent treatment of the subject. A very fair and balanced presentation of the pros, cons of evolution and intelligent design by an author who has obviously studied these areas deeply and has a great bit of knowledge to impart." D.S.

"Amazing! A magnificent refutation of Darwin's evolutionary theory, presented from well scientific methods, not complete Christian doctrine. This book has the ability to change scientific views on not just human evolution, but the foundations of many so-called scientific theories, through the diligence of real scientific research. A must-read for scientists and Christians alike!" Paula B.

"It makes sense to me." S.A.

ABOUT THE AUTHOR

Dr. Bo Kirkwood is a retired family physician who now serves as a hospice director for Heart-to-Heart Hospice in southeast Texas. He graduated from the University of Houston with a bachelor's degree in biology, from the University of Houston of Clear Lake with a master's degree in behavioral science, and a medical degree from the University Health Science Center, Fort Worth, Texas, College of Osteopathic Medicine, North Texas University. After his internship at Garden City Hospital in Michigan, he practiced family medicine in Pasadena, Texas, for over thirty-six years. He was a professor of medicine for Lincoln Memorial University Medical School, as well as an adjunct professor of medicine at McGovern Medical School in Houston, Baylor Medical School in Houston, and the University of Texas Medical Branch in Galveston, Texas.

Dr. Kirkwood has a special interest in Christian apologetics and intelligent design and has lectured on these topics for many years, with many of his lectures available on YouTube. He is the author of three books—*Unveiling the Da Vinci Code*, *The Evolution Delusion*, and *The Purpose-Driven God*, and, co-authored with his brothers, Dr.

Ron Kirkwood and Dr. John Kirkwood, *Christian Ethics and Medical Science*. He has contributed articles to *Truth* magazine, as well as other publications, and he has spoken about evolution on *Coast to Coast* AM Radio and other radio shows.

He is passionate about his Houston Cougars and beloved Houston Astros, and he is an avid golfer. With his wife, Cherry, he has three sons, three daughters-in-law, and nine cherished grandchildren. He and his wife now reside on a small farm in Navasota, Texas, where they raise registered Quarter Horses and AKC-registered white Labradors.

Quotes

"When scientist read nature rightly, nature discloses herself in new and surprising ways, like a rich and multifaceted text to the patient interpreter. A proper reading creates new lines of research and exploration. Herein lies a virtue in seeing the correlation between life friendliness and discovery as a sign of purpose rather than mere coincidence : we should expect to find this correlation elsewhere, and we should expect to keep making discoveries because of it."[1]
—Guillermo Gonzalez

"For we are His workmanship, created in Christ Jesus for good works, which God prepared beforehand that we should walk in them."[2]
—The Apostle Paul

TABLE OF CONTENTS

Acknowledgements

Writing this book has been a labor of love, but it has not occurred in a vacuum. I have had much help along the way.

I would like to thank Larry Dickens and Wayne Scott for their initial review and comments on my book in its infancy. I would also like to thank those who reviewed my book in its later state and rendered advice: my son, Dr. Toby Kirkwood; Dub Simpson; and Craig Thomas. Thank you all so much. For technical support, especially in finding charts and photographs, thank you, Jonathon Kern. I would like to thank Christy Phillippe for her expert editing. Thanks to Garlen Jackson at Selah Publishing for his guidance and support. April Mitchel was also very helpful in revising the early versions of this manuscript.

A special thank-you is in order for Dr. Tom Winkler of the Discovery Institute for his introduction to Dr. James Tour and Eric Metaxas on one particular autumn night.

Finally and most importantly, I would like to thank my wife of fifty years, Cherry, for her love and support, and especially for her indulgence through the many rewrites and corrections in getting to the final version of this book. I could not have done it without her.

Thank you.

For Cherry

Introduction

I am very astonished that the scientific picture of the real world is very deficient. It gives a lot of factual information, puts all our experience in a magnificently consistent order, but it is ghastly silent about all and sundry that is really near to our hearts, that really matters to us. It cannot tell us a word about red and blue, bitter and sweet, physical pain and physical delight, knowing nothing of beautiful and ugly, good or bad, God and eternity. Science sometimes pretends to answer questions in these domains, but the answers are very often so silly that we are inclined to not take them seriously.

—Erwin Schrödinger

Science cannot deal with non-quantitative aspects of life.

—David R. C. Deane

WHY? IT'S THE BIG QUESTION OF THE UNIVERSE: WHY IS THERE anything? Why is there something as opposed to nothing? Why is the grass green; why is the sky blue? Why does two plus two equal four? Why does gravity exist? Why should matter attract matter? Why doesn't matter repel matter? Why does the speed of light exceed that of anything else we know of so far? Why is relativity a thing, and why does quantum theory posit a dual reality of particle and wave as it pertains to light? Secularists generally hate "why" questions, primarily because they know they cannot answer them, but also because these questions are not considered that important to them. In a conversation with astronomer Fred Hoyle, wondrously retained for posterity on YouTube, Richard Feynman indicated that he hated to contemplate "why" questions because he was "afraid of the dark." For Feynman, "The chessboard has been set up [referring to the physical laws of nature], but we have no idea how or why the physical laws are what they are." Also for Feynman, one of the most prominent theoretical physicists of the twentieth century, trying to explain *why* was virtually impossible; therefore, he thought, we should ignore it.[1] In trying to explain quantum mechanics, Feynman wrote, "I am describing to you how nature works. You won't understand why nature works that way. I can't explain why nature behaves in this particular way. I hope you can accept nature as she is—absurd."[2] Nonetheless, "why" questions are important to humans, and have been asked since men have been able to communicate by the written words, all the way back to the ancient Summerians of 3,000 B.C. or before.[3]

Scientists will pursue "how" questions, but usually not the "why" questions, even though "why" explanations are foundational to the descriptions of "how." Stephen Hawking, in his seminal work, *A Brief History of Time*, purposely avoids the "why" questions. For example, when it comes to what existed before the so-called Big Bang, or what Hawking called a "singularity," he admits you cannot know and will never know the answer to that question, so why ask it at all? The question is better explained by philosophers, not scientists, according to Hawking.

John Lennox, imminent Irish mathematician and Christian apologist, likens the "why" question to a cake made by Aunt Matilda. With apologies to Dr. Lennox, I'm going to change his story slightly for my readers and call it Aunt Margaret's peach cobbler—myself being a Texan. Aunt Margaret makes a peach cobbler for cousin Jimmy's birthday. Without knowing this, we asked nutritional scientists, as well as biochemists, physicists, and mathematicians, to tell us why Aunt Margaret made a peach cobbler. I would argue that without asking Aunt Margaret, it is impossible for them to know the answer to this question. They can analyze the cobbler from a scientific point of view, discover its ingredients, and make a number of deductions—such as the fact that the cobbler has sugar, flour, peaches, et cetera—but they will never come to the answer of "why" on their own. Similarly, we might ask a scientist why the water is boiling. He or she can describe the thermokinetics of how increased temperature causes the water molecules to become agitated and boil, but the answer might have been simply to boil an egg! This does not mean "why" questions are unimportant. "It is one thing to suggest that science cannot answer questions of ultimate purpose. It is quite another to dismiss purpose as an illusion because science cannot deal with it," writes Lennox.[4]

Richard Dawkins, in the first page of his popular book *The Blind Watchmaker*, wrote, "Biology is the study of complicated things that give the appearance of having been designed for a purpose." Any appearance of design is, therefore, an "illusion," as is a belief in purpose for Mr. Dawkins.[5]

But why avoid the "why" questions? Primarily it's because "why" questions always fall back on philosophical or religious thought, areas most scientists wish to avoid assiduously. They want nothing to do with seeking primary cause. Furthermore, teleology, or the study of purpose, is also eschewed for the same reasons. To assign purpose is to imply design, and to imply design is to imply a designer, which must be avoided at all costs, even if the evidence clearly points to one. Scientists wrongly deduce that because many of the mechanisms of the universe are understandable, there is no need to bring God into the question!

Lennox calls this a categorical mistake. For example, let's pretend an alien being comes to earth and finds a working motor vehicle. Initially, they may deduce that the vehicle is working because it has a god inside it, making it work. Later, however, the alien discovers the mechanism by which the car works and realizes there is no god inside; therefore, they dismiss how the engine got there to begin with, that it was designed by an intelligent being capable of doing so.

David R.C. Deane, Australian engineer and author, believes the "how" and "why" questions are categorically different. He wrote, "Only if we suppose that the how designation and the why explanation are of the same category or kind will we be faced with a contradiction and therefore press to choose between alternatives (which is what scientism does) by categorically confusing science with truth, absorbing or dissolving the why of purpose by the how of process."[6] Deane also wrote, "Science descriptions do not explain the ultimate fact of existence; rather they presuppose it."[7] Further, "Science cannot be the only means of acquiring truth as this very statement cannot be obtained from scientific research."[8]

Winston Churchill once said, "They must indeed have a blind soul who cannot see that some great purpose and design is being worked out here below, of which we have the honor to be the first servants."[9] Carl Baugh, in his book, *Against All Odds,* writes that most people, at some point in their lives, ask four fundamental questions: Who am I? Where did I come from? What is my purpose here? And where am I going?[10]

The materialists primarily have no use for these questions. *Who am I?* The secularist would say we are just a collection of atoms and molecules, here by chance—randomly and by chance alone. *Where did I come from?* From the stardust initially produced by a singular event, currently known as the Big Bang. *What is my purpose?* There is no purpose to life unless one can say that seeking pleasure and avoiding pain is a purpose. *Where am I going?* Nowhere—except to the grave and eventually back to the elemental particles of which we are made. Certainly, for the materialist, there is no afterlife, and some would even argue that to believe in an afterlife is "poisonous" because it takes away the joy of life, having to worry about what occurs hereafter. In other words, if one has to worry about accountability, the joy of life is supremely affected. Is it surprising, therefore, to hear the secularist say that humans "are nothing but a big fly";[11]

"the worm represents a very simple human";[12] and humans are only "slightly remodeled chimpanzee-like apes."[13]

Unfortunately, for many in the Western world, the meaning of life has ceased to stand for anything loftier than the pursuit of happiness. It is a sad individual who thinks his or her life has no purpose. "Vanity of vanities" is how a very wise person put it many, many years ago. A purposeless life with no meaning, where life is accidental, where thoughts and beliefs are predetermined, where there's no free will or inspiration, is void, and it leads to a "firm foundation of unyielding despair," as English philosopher Bertrand Russell once posited. This, of course, has its consequences, that is this un-purposefulness. "With the basic assumption that man is alone in the universe, man's reason tells him that he has no ultimate value. But he cannot live like that. He cannot put his new view into practice. The only logical conclusion seems to be suicide, which at the same time seems to be the ultimate absurdity, the ultimate denial of his own humanity," so says Denis Alexander in his book, *Beyond Science*.[14]

We are left with Nietzsche's nihilism, the idea that there is no aim and there is no answer as to the "why" questions of the universe. Man has thus lost all dignity, and nothing remains. Dr. Alexander, emeritus fellow at St. Edmunds College at Cambridge, relays the words of a suicide note left by a student years ago: "To anyone in the world who cares—Who am I? Why am I living? Where am I going? Life has become stupid and purposeless . . . The questions I had when I came to college are still unanswered, and now I'm convinced that there are no answers. There can only be pain, guilt, and despair in this world. My fear of death and the unknown is far less terrifying than the prospects of the unbearable frustration, futility, and hopelessness of continued existence."[15] What a tragic ending to such a young life.

I believe, on the contrary, that the universe, the biologic world, logic, even mathematics itself shout, *There is purpose in this life!* In the following pages, I hope to give evidence of this. Everything our senses can experience has a purpose. How can someone look up into the night sky and not see purpose or design? How can one view the pictures of the Crab Nebula from the Hubble Space Telescope, or consider the beauty of a lily, or hear the sound of a mockingbird, and not appreciate purpose? The world—yes, the universe—does, indeed, demonstrate exquisite design. The psalmist has written, "The fool has said there is no God.""[16] The materialist chooses to avoid the vast amount of evidence—sadly to their peril, I believe. The apostle Paul wrote in his Roman letter that they are "without excuse,"[17] because the evidence is so obvious and easily seen.

We must not let science define us as a species. William Dembski has written, "The invocation of science must not become a wand for magically giving credence to claims, especially for special interest who want certain things to be true and who use science to make it seem that they are true. Science in today's culture often becomes an idol."[18] *The great Russian dissident and author Aleksendr Solzhenitsyn, in his 1983 Templeton Prize acceptance speech, said, "All attempts to find a way out of the plight of today's world are fruitless without a repentant return of our consciousness to the creator of all. Without this, no exit will be illuminated, and we shall be unable to find our way. Our entire earthly existence is but a transitional stage in the movement towards something higher, and we must not stumble and fall, nor must we linger fruitlessly on one rung of the ladder.* I believe that God created the universe with man in mind to fulfill His purpose and to give us purpose for our existence. Science can never address these issues of why and purpose. I hope that by the end of this book, I will have adequately defended such a statement.

Chapter
1

WILLAIM WILBERFORCE

*"To what or whom do we owe our existence? We cannot rest without
the answer, because absolutely everything of importance is riding on it.
To know where everything came from is to know where we came from,
and where we came from has everything to do with who we are, and
who we are has everything to do with how we ought to live.*

—*Douglas Axe*

*We human beings can overcome our natural predilections with a
spiritual transformation that infuses life with incalculable meaning—
incalculable because it is a life found in the infinite beatitude of God
himself, in Jesus Christ.*

—*David R.C. Deane*

"SOME ARE BORN GREAT, SOME ACHIEVE GREATNESS, AND SOME
have greatness thrust upon them." So wrote William Shakespeare in
his comedy *Twelfth Night*, almost four centuries ago. In this chapter,
we will examine the lives of several people who achieved a form
of greatness by finding their purpose in life and actively pursuing
it. One in particular was William Wilberforce, who was not born
into greatness, but who changed his life and thus found meaning
and purpose. Although I doubt Wilberforce would have considered
himself "great" in his lifetime, history has preserved for us his efforts,
and I for one would certainly consider his achievements "great,"
as Wilberforce was one of the chief forces behind the abolition of
slavery in Great Britain.

It is the wee hours of the morning of February 24, 1807, in London, and the House of Commons is about to pass one of the most important pieces of legislation ever passed in the history of this august body, which will abolish a most disgusting, heinous practice that had been around almost thirty years. That practice is the African Atlantic slave trade, a practice that involuntarily translocated more people—some twelve and a half million—than in the history of the planet. First introduced by Ferdinand II of Spain in 1510, the then-current practice was perpetuated by two major factors: greed and the insatiable need for tea by European subjects, tea sweetened by sugar from the sugarcane plantations of the West Indies. Long before the cotton fields of Georgia, Alabama, and Mississippi, African slaves were utilized to grow, harvest, and—worst of all—process sugarcane to satisfy the needs of Great Britain and Europe. It was a brutal, savage, but lucrative endeavor, and not one that would be easily squelched.

The great Alexander Hamilton, former aide to George Washington and eventual secretary of the treasury of the United States, witnessed this horrific, inhumane practice firsthand. Having been raised on the island of Nevis, what he saw would stay with him and influence him for the rest of his life. In the sugar lands of the British Indies, Hamilton saw fellow human beings being treated like animals, subjected to horrible living conditions and wretched working conditions, people poorly fed and dressed with a life expectancy of only decades. Many, in fact, died during the processing of the cane due to the intense heat generated by the boilers and the prolonged working hours. Per Ron Chernow, "It is hard to grasp Hamilton's later politics without contemplating the raw cruelty he witnessed as a boy and that later deprived him of the hopefulness so contagious in the American milieu. On the most obvious level, the slave trade at St. Croix generated a permanent detestation

Alexander Hamilton

of the system and resulted in his later abolitionist efforts."[1]   How could it not have?

Traveling to the West Indies or America—sometimes referred to euphemistically as the "middle passage," an eight-week voyage from the west coast of Africa to the West Indies or America, was almost unimaginable in its brutality and repugnance. Slaves were packed into small ships, shackled at the arms and legs, sleeping virtually on top of each other with disease and putrefaction indescribable.

An unlikely firsthand witness to this was John Newton, the great Anglican minister who wrote arguably the greatest spiritual hymn of all time, "Amazing Grace." As a young man, Newton was envious of Amos Clow, a buccaneering slave trader noted for his cruelty. Newton saw slaves separated from families, "stripped naked, branded, tethered and whipped into submission before being dragged off in terror to the ships that would carry those who survived into slave markets of the West Indies or America."[2] One in ten would not survive the voyage. At this time, though, Newton was more interested in the profits Amos Clow was generating for himself than any of the cruelty he was witnessing, and after a tumultuous time as an apprentice, including being shipwrecked himself, Newton eventually would gain his own ship to captain, the *Duke of Argyle*.[3] "The best that can be said about Newton's intentions at this time is that they were in a state of confusion and conflict between his slave trading and his spiritual conscience," says Jonathan Aiken, in his excellent biography on Newton.[4] Unlike Clow, the evidence shows that Newton at least cared for the health and welfare of his captives, and his mortality rates were quite low compared to that of other captains of the time. Contrary to popular belief, there was not one specific event that changed Newton, but rather multiple experiences, both on the *Greyhound*

John Newton

as a youth and later on the *Argyle* and then the *African*. In any event, on his last slave trading voyage, Newton met Scotsman Alexander Clunie, who would have an immense impact on Newton's life for the better. Clunie reinforced Newton's faith, taught him how to better pray, how to speak with fellow believers, how to study the Bible, and how to witness based upon his personal testimony.[5] When sipping tea with his wife, Polly, one day, Newton suffered a stroke, causing temporary paralysis. After this medical crisis, Newton was to give up his slave trading, no doubt because of advice from his doctor, but also due to his growing doubts over the inhumane aspects of his duties.

Eventually Newton would come to decry the African American slave trade and become a staunch abolitionist, joining the ranks of many in England who were finally waking up to the inhumanity of slavery, not a little caused by the testimony of Newton himself. Of course, there were others who gave their testimonies, including the writings of Olaudah Equiano from 1745 to 1797, who offered a rare firsthand account of slavery, having been captured as a child in what is now called Nigeria. Equiano eventually earned his freedom and wrote of his exploits in English, which, in turn, would be published and widely circulated. In his writings, he told of his own kidnapping, his separation from his sister, and the brutal treatment he received.

Equiano wrote regarding the conditions of the ship, "The closeness of the place, and the heat and the climate, added to the number of the ship being so crowded that each had scarcely room to turn himself, almost suffocated us. This produced perspirations so that the air soon became unfit for respirations from a variety of loathsome smells and brought on a sickness among the slaves of which many died. The shrieks of the women and the groanings of the dying rendered it a scene of horror almost inconceivable."[6]

Evidence of the brutality was also witnessed by Alexander Falconbridge. Falconbridge was a surgeon on a slave ship and would offer Parliament an account of his experience. Of course, it was to the slave traders' advantage to keep their captives in some degree of health, but during voyages that were rough, slaves were kept below deck, and Falconbridge explained how movement against the wooden planks would "rub skin off shoulders, elbows, and hips to render the bones in these areas quite bare. As a result, the floors would be covered with the blood and mucus and would resemble a slaughterhouse." Said Dr. Falconbridge, "It is not in the power of human imagination to picture a situation to more dreadful or disgusting."[7]

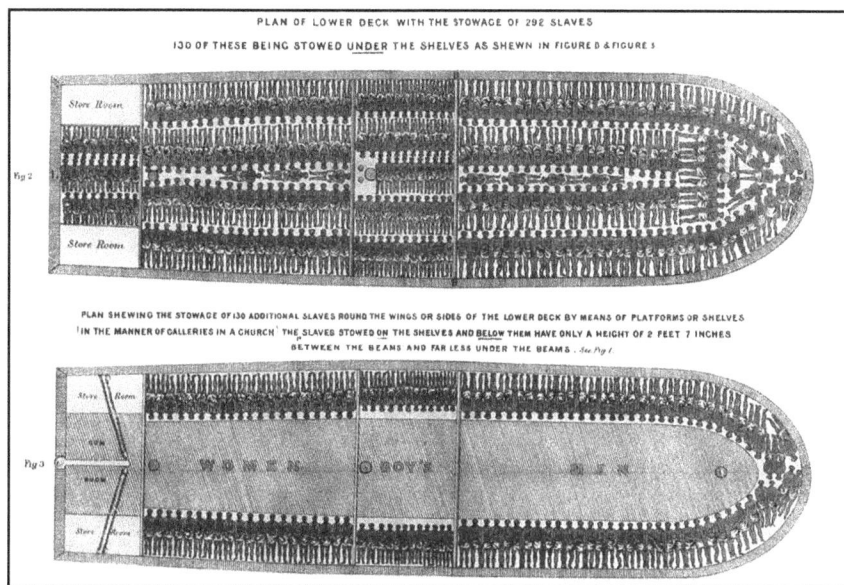

Slave Ship

By the middle of the eighteenth century, more and more people were beginning to ask for the abolishment of the Atlantic African slave trade, both in Great Britain and America, but it was the Quakers who led the way in setting out Christianity against slavery. Anthony Benezet, a Quaker, began to realize the incompatibility of slave trading with Christianity. Benezet was an American who wrote in 1767, "Nothing can more clearly and positively militate against the slavery of the Negroes than the declarations lately published that 'all men are created equal, that they are endowed by their creator with certain unalienable rights.'"[8] In 1784, London Quaker James Ramsey published two powerful pamphlets denouncing the slave trade. These pamphlets were based on twenty-two years of living in the West Indies, and they provided information and ammunition for the abolitionist movement, which was then just beginning to take hold. His arguments were both powerful and convincing.

By this time, Thomas Clarkson, an abolitionist and acquaintance of Ramsey's, brought William Wilberforce his essay, "Is It Right to Make Slaves of Others Against Their Will," in 1787. The abolitionist movement was, indeed, gaining momentum, but it needed someone in Parliament to take up the cause. That someone would be Wilberforce, and from that time onward, this would become his passion and calling. Ironically, Wilberforce's seat in Parliament had been occupied by David Hartley, one of the few MPs (members of Parliament) to attack the slave trade in the House of Commons whose seat Wilberforce unseated in 1780. At the time, Wilberforce was not yet a Christian, but shortly after his election, he became a devoted evangelical Christian. He would denounce his prior life of debauchery and likened his conversion to "waking from a dream and recovering the use of my reason after a delirium."[9] He went on to write, "I quite forgot that I was an accountable being; that I was hereafter to appear at the bar of God." As an evangelical Christian, Wilberforce believed in the providence of God, that Christian principles should be applied to all areas of life, and in the overpowering sense of accountability and a responsibility to God for one's actions. After his conversion, Wilberforce became a driving force to mobilize the country's moral and social leaders in a nationwide struggle against vice. The so-called Proclamation Society was formed to denounce drunkenness, prostitution, lewdness, thievery, and basically sin in general. It was an ambitious task, to say the least, unlikely to be successful, but it was his meeting with

Clarkson in 1787 that would change the trajectory of his life forever and cement his legacy.

Wilberforce began educating himself about the slave trade. Later in his life, he would write, "It was the condition of the West Indian slaves, which drew my attention, and it was in the course of my inquiry that I was led to Africa and the abolition."[10] Wilberforce was no doubt also highly influenced by many others, including John Newton, someone with whom he was well acquainted and whom he saw a lot of during this time. In fact, Newton was someone Wilberforce had known as a child. With the help of Newton, Ramsey, Clarkson, and others, Wilberforce had now found his calling—to abolish the slave trade. In fact, it is safe to say that his decision to deconstruct the slave trade became his single-most purpose in life. The reports of the high death rate of slaves during the Atlantic crossing really clinched it for him. Wilberforce would write, "Let the consequences be what they would. I would from this time determine that I would never rest until I had affected its [the slave trade] abolition."[11]

William Wilberforce

In May 1787, sitting under an oak tree with Prime Minister William Pitt and William Greenville, Pitt's cousin and a future foreign secretary, Wilberforce informed Pitt of his decision to introduce a bill to Parliament to abolish the slave trade. All three men were twenty-seven years of age. It would take some time, but on May 12th of 1789, Wilberforce rose from his seat to give a three-and-a-half-hour speech to introduce his new proposal to abolish the slave trade. But even with the prime minister's backing, it would not prove to be an easy task. By all accounts, his speech was masterfully delivered, and his case was compelling, but when money and fortune is at stake, it takes more than just a good speech. Unfortunately, Pitt did not have a united cabinet, and there was no reliable majority in Wilberforce's favor. Hence, his proposal failed, coming to a grinding stalemate that would last considerably longer than Wilberforce could ever have imagined.[12]

In the meantime, history intervened. The French Revolution began and had a powerful effect on British politics. News of the Revolution, as well as news from the French-owned plantations of revolt by slaves in the West Indies, produced fear among the Brits, especially those who held lands in the West. In fact, abolition was no longer on the table. Nonetheless, Wilberforce pressed on, only to be rejected time and time again. Some, such as Clarkson, would temporarily leave the cause for the time being, yet Wilberforce maintained his own resolution in the determination to keep it alive. "Wilberforce's work for the abolition of the slave trade could well be compared to a quest for gold, but the refining required to achieve it was an arduous business," writes Jonathan Aitken.

But Wilberforce was a man, and men do get tired, frustrated, and disillusioned. In July 1796, he wrote to John Newton that he was considering retiring from public life, which would, of course, have had a devastating effect on the abolitionist cause. Newton, as you can imagine, was strongly opposed to this. In a comparison to Daniel, Newton wrote to him, "You live in the midst of difficulties and snares, and you need a double guard of watchfulness and prayer. But since you know both your need of health and where to look for it, I may say to you, as Darius to Daniel, 'thy God, whom thou servest continually, is able to preserve and deliver you'."[13] Daniel, likewise, was a public man and in critical circumstances. But he trusted in the Lord, he was faithful in his departments, and therefore, though he had enemies, they could never prevail against him. It worked. Wilberforce stayed in Parliament and published his manifesto, "A Practical View," which was a bestseller of the time, and in which Wilberforce elucidated his views on true Christianity, including his view on slavery. Wilberforce's book was widely praised—and not just by friends.

One key component of the book was Wilberforce's belief that the teachings of Christianity, "if they are true, must be taken to a logical conclusion in terms of human behavior.".[14] Further, he called on Christians "specifically to believe in the doctrines, imbibe the principles, and practice the precepts of Christ."[15] Wilberforce also asked Christians "to assert the cause of Christ in an age when so many who bear the name of Christians are ashamed of him and let them pray continually for their country in this season of national difficulty," words well applicable today, I might add.[16]

As we can see, for Wilberforce, being a politician had a purpose; it was not just about a position. He wanted to advance a cause, and that cause was to stop the horrible practice of slavery. He was still a very young man at this time, only thirty-seven years old, and the task was still yet incomplete.

Finally, by 1806, the tide was turning in favor of Wilberforce's cause. William Pitt had died, and a new government was formed. Pitt had always been sympathetic to Wilberforce and his cause, but the job of prime minister carried with it many duties, especially that of directing war, with which it seems Britain was perpetually involved. In other words, Pitt had other priorities to address. His successor, Lord Grenville, was likewise sympathetic to abolitionists, and he started maneuvering behind the scenes to abolish the slave trade. In order not to alarm pro-slavers, Wilberforce opted to stay quietly behind the scenes.

In 1806, Grenville called for new elections, and afterward a bill was again introduced to abolish the slave trade. Interestingly, America had already voted, under the leadership of President Thomas Jefferson in December 1806, to make it illegal from January 1st of 1808 to bring to the United States "any negro, mulatto or person of colour as a slave." Though Britain was unaware of its passage, the Brits, no doubt, were aware of its likely success.

By the night of February 23, with the triumph of the House of Lords repeated in the House of Commons, and with tears streaming down Wilberforce's cheeks and the eulogies of his colleagues ringing in his ears as even the recalcitrant recognized the inevitable, the bill carried by 280 votes to 16 to abolish slave trading in great Britain forever.[17] It was the end of a glorious struggle for the elimination of "the most execrable and inhumane traffic that ever disgraced the Christian world," exclaimed Bishop Proteus at the time.[18]

John Newton would live to see the Abolition Act passed in his eighties, but only barely. He died just months later, almost totally blind, partially deaf, and forgetful, but he was nonetheless aware of its passage. One can only imagine how delighted Newton must have been.

It would be a gross understatement to say that the passage of the Abolition Act, as it was called, was an achievement for William Wilberforce. Ever the humble, Wilberforce was all too ready to give credit to others. It was not until 1811 that the British slave trade was truly eradicated, but within the continent of Africa, slaves were still being rounded up, and illicit trading persisted despite the laws to the contrary in both the United States and Britain. In fact, in the United States, there was no diminution in demand for slaves in the Deep South. Some estimates are that at least fifty thousand slaves were imported to the States between 1807 and 1861, the start of the Civil War. Of course, abolishing the slave trade did not abolish slavery. Thus, a new campaign began for Wilberforce. In his new manifesto, now at the age of sixty-four, Wilberforce called for further measures to abolish slavery. Wilberforce was in favor of a gradual dissolution of slavery, but by the summer of 1824, with his health failing, he could no longer carry the torch. As he put it, he became "a bee which has lost its sting." He thus left Parliament without fanfare after forty-four consecutive years of service.[19]

In May 1833, slavery was finally abolished in Great Britain and its colonies. William Wilberforce had lived just long enough to see his lifelong work finally accomplished. Though frail and dying, he rejoiced nonetheless, his Christianity never wavering. Finally, on August the third of 1833, he was laid to rest in Westminster Abbey, among such luminaries as Isaac Newton, thus solidifying his legacy.

What do you think motivated Wilberforce and so many others to dedicate their lives to rid the world of slavery's pernicious blight on humanity? For Wilberforce, it would take two decades of hard work—work met along the way with frustration and disappointment, only to be endured to win the battle. It would have been so very easy to give up, and some did, but not Wilberforce. So again, what do you suppose was his motivation? Was it greed? No. There was nothing materially to be gained in the fight for the freedom of the African slaves. Was it glory for which Wilberforce was looking? Again, it is very unlikely. And as we have seen when legislation was finally passed abolishing slavery, Wilberforce stayed on the sidelines. Yes, he would get recognition for his fight, but even then, there were those who tried to belittle his role as an abolitionist, including Thomas Clarkson, who, as we have seen, at one time, had given up the cause himself. Was it to help some personal acquaintance? No, Wilberforce was never personally acquainted with any of the people whom he sought to help.

The primary motivation for Wilberforce seemed to be the application of the Golden Rule: "Do unto others as you would have done to yourself," to paraphrase. Wilberforce sought the good of individuals he would never meet. His motivation was a strong personal desire to see the inhumanity of slavery squelched and to obey his Lord and Savior. "Everyone should know Wilberforce," reflected Abraham Lincoln, one of the great emancipators of all time.[20] He would have been a good man to know! Wilberforce was, indeed, a remarkable figure, but at the same time, a bit of an enigma. He was a conservative in disposition, yet he led the greatest progressive cause of his time. Few ever questioned his integrity or sincerity, not even his foes.

The reason for including him and others in the first chapter of this book is to demonstrate purpose. Who could deny these individuals led a purposeful life? For Wilberforce, his purpose was twofold, a theme that will be revisited later in this book. His primary purpose was to serve his Lord and Savior, Jesus Christ. His secondary purpose was that toward his fellow man. One can imagine Wilberforce citing Mark 12:30–31: "'And you shall love the Lord your God with all your heart, with all your soul, with all your mind, and with all your strength.' This is the first commandment. And the second, like it, is this, 'you shall love your neighbor as yourself,' There is no other commandment greater than these." Wilberforce epitomized these commandments, in my opinion.

"The opportunity for individuals to change history is shaped by the great social and intellectual forces of their time. Yet it is also true that such forces can only act through agency of enterprising individuals," writes author and past leader of the conservative party in Great Britain William Hague.[21] No doubt slavery would have been abolished without Wilberforce and his colleagues, but it would not have happened when it did without these brave women and men.

After the abolishment of slavery in Great Britain, it would take several more decades before it would also be abolished in the United States through Abraham Lincoln's Emancipation Proclamation, and even then, only after a great civil war that would result in the death of over seven hundred thousand people. Of course, there were many heroes of the abolitionist movement in the United States besides Lincoln, including Frederick Douglass, Harriet Beecher Stowe, and, in particular, Harriet Tubman, a former slave who worked through the

Underground Railroad and risked her own life and bodily harm to help free many enslaved people from the South—heroism for which she received very little in return.

Abraham Lincoln

Most of us will never have the opportunity to change the history of the world, but certainly there are those who will. Nonetheless, we can all lead a life of purpose. The materialists say there is no purpose in life. I would disagree. Everyone has a purpose in their lives, either for good or evil, and even those who see no purpose in life, in fact, have chosen *that* as their purpose. The world would be much better if there were more William Wilberforces in it.

Over the next several chapters, we will examine the universe, the solar system, and our very own earth, and see whether purpose does not seem to be evident. We will then look at nature and eventually the human body itself for evidence of purpose. We will even take a deep dive into evolution to see if there is purpose to be found there. We will then turn our attention to mathematics. Does mathematics imply a mind, and therefore a designer? Also, finally, we will turn our attention back to mankind. Is there a purpose for our existence? Or are we just here taking up space? I for one do not think so. I think we will find purpose.

Chapter
2

THE SWERVE

There's only the natural world, no spirits, no deities or anything else, there is a chain of explanations concerning things that happen in the universe, which ultimately reaches to the fundamental laws of nature and stops.

—Sean Carroll

There are not many options—essentially just two. Either human intelligence ultimately owes its origins to mindless matter; or there is a creator. It is strange that some people claim it is their intelligence that leads them to prefer the first to the second.

—John Lennox

ASK ANYONE, ANYONE, WHAT THEIR WORLDVIEW IS, AND YOU are likely to get the deer-in-the-headlight look, or a comeback question such as, "What is wrong with you?" You see, most people have no clue what that question even means. Yet, I promise you, everyone has a worldview, and it is fundamentally important to how one views the universe, the world, and their fellow man—as well as how one feels about his or her own purpose. As a result, one's worldview will determine how one interprets data and how one views the evidence that surrounds them, or even if one is open at all to examining the evidence and hence questioning their own worldview. So, what do I mean by *worldview*? A *worldview* is how one attempts to answer the "big questions" proposed in the opening of this book, that is: *Who am I? Why am I here? How did I get here, and where am I going?* And it's important to understand that a person's worldview can certainly change.

There are many worldviews, but there are only two major categories into which they fall: 1) deism or theism, both of which assume a superior being that transcends time and space, or 2) natural materialism, which postulates there is no superior intellect and all we know and see came about by purely undirected naturalistic forces.

In this book, I will use *materialism* to mean "methodological naturalism," also known as "methodological materialism." Incorporated in materialism is *scientism*, or the view that only science constitutes legitimate knowledge, which William Dembski calls "self-referentially incoherent."[1]

One must be careful in evoking the term *science* as an explanation for something. People throw around phrases like "science has proven . . ." or "the consensus of science . . ." or "the settled science . . ." almost like religious dogma, and thus they squelch any counteractive questioning or arguments. We shall see later in this book that science is in a perpetual state of flux. Dembski notes, "Whenever I hear the words 'consensus science' or 'settled science,' I reach for my wallet because I know I'm about to be scammed."[2] A truly settled scientific claim requires

William Dembski no debate!

Needless to say, there are significant differences between these two worldviews. The theistic worldview will see exquisite design in the universe; the materialist will say design is just an illusion. The theist will note the high improbability of the existence of the universe in which we live; the materialist will say we are just extremely lucky. The theist will see purpose in life; the materialist will see life as utterly purposeless. The theists will acknowledge accountability; the materialist will not.

So, it becomes vitally important as to which worldview an individual adheres, whether they can articulate that view or not. Both worldviews have been around for thousands of years, and one could argue the theistic worldview has been around since the beginning of man. The theistic worldview certainly has predominated mankind for much of this time, but it would be a mistake to believe naturalistic materialism is a "new" concept.

The eminent twentieth-century philosopher, mathematician, logician, and avid materialist Bertrand Russell described the "modern" materialistic viewpoint succinctly: "Man is a part of nature, not something contrasted with nature. His thoughts and his bodily movements follow the same laws that describe the motion of the stars and the atoms."[3] For Russell, "Whatever knowledge is attainable, must be attained by scientific method; and what science cannot discover, man cannot know."[4] Clearly, Russell was describing scientism. Materialists see no intrinsic value in human life, no more so than that of any animal. David Hume, eighteenth-century empiricist, said, "The life of a man is of no greater importance to the universe than that of an oyster."[5]

Bertrand Russell

Life for the materialist becomes very deterministic, or, in other words, there is no free will. All that we do, and for that matter, all that we think, is biochemical in nature. Friedrich Nietzsche believed human beings are, thus, "determined by their bodies and are subject to its passions, impulses, and instincts."[6] More recently Richard Dawkins would write, "DNA neither cares nor knows. DNA just is. And we dance to its music."[7]

As one views current events in the world, it seems to me the materialistic worldview is winning out. In fact, author Stephen Greenblatt argues that materialism is "modern" and may have

Stephen Greenblatt

been propagated in the first century BC by a poet of the name Titus Lucretius Carus. In Greenblatt's Pulitzer Prize and National Book Award–winning book, *The Swerve: How the World Became Modern,* he describes how fifteenth-century bibliophile-scribe Poggio Bracciolini's discovery of Lucretius's poem "On the Nature of Things," changed the world forever into the modern, scientific, materialistic world in which we now live.

This seems like a very ambitious conclusion of Mr. Greenblatt's, but certainly Lucretius's poem contains a robust amount of fodder for the materialist. Borrowing from fourth-century-BC philosopher Epicurus, Lucretius, in his epic poem, writes that the universe is made up of an infinite number of atoms, which are moving randomly through space with no master plan, no divine architect, and certainly no intelligent designer.

Furthermore, there is no reason that humans should be held to a higher regard than animals, and there is certainly nothing special about mankind, per Lucretius. Any thoughts of life after death are delusional, and therefore, the key to happiness on this earth is to be found only in the pursuit of pleasure while one is still alive. Death, therefore, has no sting, as there will be no accountability in the afterlife; hence, there will be no punishment because sin does not exist.

Mr. Greenblatt sees this as a very good thing because it frees us from the fear of death, a problem that, apparently, Mr. Greenblatt's own mother had. For Greenblatt, all religions of the world feed on this fear, and as a result, true happiness is impossible unless one can "live an ethical life without reference to postmortem rewards and punishments; to contemplate without trembling the death of the soul." [8] Greenblatt contends that Lucretius's poem "On the Nature of Things" changed the trajectory of mankind, and its discoverer, Poggio, became the "midwife of modernity."[9]

I would posit that our world is becoming more and more materialistic; however, I doubt very seriously it had anything to do with Lucretius's poem. In fact, the seeds of materialism were planted long before Lucretius ever penned his work. The concept of atomism was formulated in the fifth century BC by Leucippus, and it was further expounded on by his pupil, Democritus. Writing in the fourth century AD, Aristotle also alludes to atomism.

Also, as previously noted, Lucretius's poem is basically Epicurean. Epicurus was a philosopher who lived in the fourth and fifth centuries BC—well before Lucretius. For Epicurus, the function of the human mind was to "not seek higher things," but to maximize pleasure and to "minimize pain." Epicurus was also an atomist, believing all matter was made up of discrete, "solid, indivisible atoms" plus empty space. Even the soul was made up of "atoms," and it was too delicate to survive outside the body; thus, it also died when the physical body died. For Epicurus, when death occurred, that was it: "Death is nothing to us."

The atomic theory has certainly been verified by modern science, but much still needs to be explained! We now know, for example, that atoms are *not* indivisible, and that they contain protons, electrons, and neutrons. Furthermore, protons are made up of "quarks" with various properties of spin, but if you can find someone who can truly tell you what a "quark" is made of, please let me know! Also, quantum theory has shown that most of matter (atoms) is, in fact, empty space (99.9 percent!)—a concept difficult to grasp, but true, nonetheless.

In fact, our universe is essentially made up of electrons and quarks, which are, in essence, tiny clouds (standing waves) of energy; these clouds are immaterial and indestructible, woven together by information-processing laws. The inner core, or nucleus, of an atom is made up of protons and neutrons, which are fermions and defined by their mass and spin. The orbiting electron is referred to as a lepton, and its distance from the nucleus is relatively very far, being 5.3 x 10-11 Bohr radius. To understand the distance from the proton by comparison, think of it this way: If we have a basketball that we are going to call the nucleus, the electron is spinning approximately two miles away, but yet it is held together by electromagnetic force. As an example, iron is made up of 99.9999999999999 percent vacuous space from the nucleus to the electrons. When you think about it, that's a lot of space. The protons themselves are held together by incredibly strong forces—in fact, this is referred to as the "strong force."

What we perceive as mass, then, is almost illusory, which certainly makes us understand how incredibly powerful the "strong force" is. In essence, protons, neutrons, and electrons represent energy, and yet "No one can describe in any comprehensible way what the fundamental essence of energy is," so says author and electrical engineer Ken Pederson. [10]

Epicurus felt that atoms moved about in random motion, but on occasion, they might "swerve" in their forward course—exhibiting a change in direction, if you will. The universe then came about as a result of this "swerve"; hence the title of Greenblatt's book. This "swerve" explains the cosmological problem for Epicurus, but notice that Epicurus does not explain where atoms originated, nor, for that matter, where time and space came from. Further, no explanation is given for what caused this "swerve," if there was a cause at all.

Epicurus

The cosmology of Epicurus may sound familiar to us, as it is not much different from the "Big Bang" cosmology. The "Big Bang" supposedly began with a "singularity"—that is, matter and energy so densely packed as to be unseen, with gravity unmeasurable.

This "singularity" expanded very rapidly, 10^{43} seconds, and then over 14.7 billion years, the stars, galaxies, planets, and life itself came into existence, all due to random acts obeying the fundamental laws of nature, so says the materialist. The materialist cannot say where the singularity came from, although some are now ascribing quantum fluctuations as the "cause" for the singularity, but here again, where did quantum fluctuations come from, and for that matter, why are there "laws" of nature to begin with?!

This all seems to take us back to the steady state theory, which is that all matter has always existed, a theory held by Sir Fred Hoyle and others, but rejected by virtually all cosmologists now. Why? There is just too much evidence for an expanding universe—and an expanding universe must have a beginning!

Let me reiterate. Naturalistic materialism is the belief that all there is in the universe is matter. Matter explains energy per Einstein's equation, $E=MC^2$, thus there is no intelligent design and any evidence of such is illusory. We live, we die, and that is all there is. Everything we see in the universe, including our own lives, has occurred by random chance, and it all began with the so-called Big Bang. What occurred before the Big Bang is of no importance to the materialist, and Stephen Hawking admitted as much in his book *A Brief History of Time*. Hawking wrote, "As far as we are concerned, events before the Big Bang can have no consequences and so should not form part of a scientific model of the universe. We should therefore cut them out of the model and say that the Big Bang was the beginning of time. This means that questions such as who set up the conditions for the Big Bang are not questions that science addresses."[11] Seems like a bit of a cop-out, doesn't it? Clearly, as a result, natural materialism purports there are no consequences to our lives, and that is clear. But it fails to address a major objection and logic flaw.

This flaw is that there is no answer to the question, where does "good" come from? First of all, "good" can be very difficult for the materialist to define, other than to say that each society determines what is "good." But this has its own set of problems, doesn't it!

This is not to say that evolutionists and materialists have not tried to explain from a naturalistic point of view why there is morality and kindness, because they have. It's just that their stories are just that—stories and conjectures—and are not based on anything you or I would call "scientific." You see, there is an entity called the evolutionary psychologist, and from his or her point of view, there is no human behavior that cannot be accounted for by evolution.

Compassion and sacrifice are renamed *altruism*, and EPs (evolutionary psychologists) look to ants to explain where humans learned this behavior. Mindless worker ants sacrifice their lives to the queen ant, passing on their genetics in order for the entire tribe of ants to perpetuate. The EPs call this "inclusive fitness," and while such altruism may not benefit the individual ant, maybe it increases the fitness of the whole.[12] Richard Dawkins believes there is a "selfish gene," which seems like a misnomer, where humans, bacteria, and viruses "share gene products and behave in a way that can't be described as anything but generous."[13] What a bunch of nonsense. First, "natural selection" selects only for the individual organism. Why would an individual animal care whether or not his or her species continues? Furthermore, Dennis Noble, an Oxford psychologist, observes that "selfish genes have no empirical basis in science."[14]

Denyse O'Leary has written, "EP simply doesn't have enough grounding and evidence to be a science."[15] It sounds "scienc-y," and it has the word *evolution* in its description, but science it isn't! Man's ability for abstract thought, morality, and reason is set aside by evolutionary psychologists.

Certainly, kindness and compassion are frequently demonstrated by humans, but the question remains: Why? Evolution cannot explain it "scientifically." We live in an eat-or-be-eaten world.

Many people elevate themselves by pulling others down. And yet we commonly observe little acts of kindness in our society—or at least I do. These range from someone opening a door for an elderly individual or infirm person, to buying a stranger lunch, to donating time and funds to the needy, to coming to the rescue of those ravaged by tornadoes or hurricanes, to helping someone stranded beside the road. We see kindness all around us. But is man innately kind, or does that come from a higher source, even if that person doesn't acknowledge that higher source?

David Berlinski believes, "Men are not by nature good. Quite often, quite to the contrary. And for this reason they must be restrained by threats if possible, by force if necessary." [16] The eminent atheist Richard Dawkins believes to the contrary, writing, "Perhaps I am a Pollyanna to believe that people would remain good when unobserved and unpoliced by God."[17]

I believe kindness comes from being taught to be kind. Watch small children at play. It is not natural for them to share, yet many will do so because they were taught to by their parents or grandparents or some other individual. I believe the ultimate source of kindness comes from above. The German poet Goethe once wrote, "Let man be noble, generous and good; for that alone distinguishes him from all living beings we know. Only mankind can do the impossible. He can distinguish, he chooses and judges he can give permanence to the moment." The prophet Jeremiah said many years ago, "O Lord, I know that the way of man is not in himself. It is not in man who walks to direct his own steps."[18]

For Epicurus, "Living justly helped to eliminate anxiety. Someone who is incapable of living prudently, honorably and justly cannot live pleasurably and vice versa!"" [19] Why not? What is the cause of such anxiety? Epicurus placed a premium on friendship and said, "Good friends feel the fortune of his friend like his own." But why? To the theist, and let me say, more specifically those of a

Judeo-Christian ethic—good comes from one source, that source being God. The most fundamental command, "Love your neighbor as yourself," is second only to, "Love your God with all your mind and with all your soul and with all your might."[20] If anxiety occurs, it is because we do not follow these commands.

Mr. Greenblatt, in *The Swerve*, devotes many pages to the bad behavior of the "church." Like most materialists, Mr. Greenblatt makes the generic mistake of lumping all of religion into one big pot, so to speak. As a result, any bad conduct by any religion is an indictment on all religions. So, when he discusses the atrocities of the Catholic Church, for example, such as the selling of indulgences, the Crusades, the Spanish Inquisition, etc., this is, in essence, an accusation toward all religions. In his poem "On the Nature of Things," Lucretius addresses this issue as well, an argument likely borrowed by Greenblatt. For Lucretius, all religions are evil. It would seem that humanism and materialism are then superior to religion. But I ask, even in view of the religious atrocities mentioned, as well as many others that have occurred, which I do not deny, I would very much argue they are not the results of practicing pure Christianity, but rather an adulteration of Christianity. Which belief system do you suppose has done more good for society: the naturalistic materialistic, or the theistic? There has certainly been a lot of good done in the name of religion, especially as seen from a benevolent side, but what good has come from materialism? Does seeking pleasure, avoiding pain, and living lives that are devoid of consequences produce anything good?

To be clear, I'm not saying all materialists are evil people. Many, in fact, are very humane and supportive of benevolent works. But overall, which belief system has *the power* to do more good and which has led to more evil? It seems to me that Greenblatt's conclusion concerning theism does not fit with reality.

Maybe we should compare the two worldviews. Materialists, for example, will refer to the scientific method and the birth of science as a consequence of its philosophy, but this is not supported by the truth. One can argue that the greatest minds that have ever existed in the world were believers in a supreme God, and John Lennox argues that science flourished because of a belief in God.

A prime example is Sir Isaac Newton, the discoverer of the fundamental laws of motion and co-discoverer of calculus. He was arguably one of the most brilliant minds to ever live, with his book *The Principia* being either one of the most or the most important scientific book, in history. Also, James Clarke Maxwell, Scottish scientist and discoverer of the fabulous electromagnetic equations still used today, was a devout believer. In fact, on a placard above the door of his lab at Cambridge, James Clarke Maxwell had placed the words from Psalm 11:2: "The works of the Lord are great, sought out of all them that have pleasure therein." Johannes Kepler, the discoverer of the elliptical orbits of the planets, was also a believer in God. This list of believers includes also Nicholas Copernicus, Francis Bacon, Galileo Galilei, William Harvey, René Descartes, Robert Boyle, and many, many more.[21] Also, today there are many astute scientists from various fields of astrophysics, biology, chemistry, and mathematics, who are believers in intelligent design and practice good science based on their belief.

Some have said good science cannot be practiced unless one holds to materialism, but as we have observed, this simply is not true. Good science has been, and continues to be, practiced by believers in a supreme being. Furthermore, bad science can certainly be produced by the materialist, and it has been in the past. To be clear, then, whether one is a deist or a materialist does not define whether one practices good science or bad science, but rather in the methodology one chooses to use.

Origin-of-life research today begins with the premise set forth by Charles Darwin in 1859 in his book *On the Origin of Species*, that life began on earth, undirected by purely random naturalistic processes. Natural selection and the survival of the fittest explains it all! But does it? We now know natural selection can help explain the survival of the fittest, but not the arrival of the fittest. Neo-Darwinism is totally inept in explaining the origins of life, and so far, origin-of-life experiments have miserably failed to produce even the most simple, rudimentary forms of life. Further discussion on this topic will occur later in this book, but for now we can safely say that all origin-of-life experiments require some intelligent input, and even with that, no "life" has ever remotely been created in the laboratory.

We have been told we have been brought into the modern world by the burgeoning belief in materialism, as if it is a good thing—the modern era ostensibly starting in the 1500s and the Industrial Revolution beginning in the 1700s. But modernity would exponentially begin in the twentieth century.

The twentieth century ushered in tremendous new technological and biological discoveries. Antibiotics—the first true one being penicillin, discovered by Alexander Fleming in 1928—changed the world and has saved millions of lives. Vaccines have virtually eliminated many diseases that once killed untold numbers, such as smallpox, polio, and measles. The Human Genome Project has now mapped out the complete genetic blueprint for human DNA, with potential cures for genetic diseases on the way. Radio, television, computers, and space travel highlight the technological discoveries of the twentieth century. This century also took us into the nuclear age with Einstein's discovery of relativity and then the discovery of quantum mechanics.

Some would argue that these discoveries have negated any need for religion, and Steven Weinberg takes it even further, affirming, "Religion is an insult to human dignity. With it or without it you would have good people doing good things and evil people doing evil things. But for good people to do evil things, it takes religion.[22]

Psychologist Steven Pinker has stated, "Something in modernity and its cultural institutions has made us more noble." In Pinker's 2011 book, *The Better Angels of Our Nature*, the author spends 832 pages trying to convince us that mankind has been growing gentler and less violent since the Middle Ages. Pinker's book was well-received, with billionaire Bill Gates calling it one of the most important books he has ever read, and many others lauding it for its scholarship. One review doubled down on Pinker's thesis, blaming the media for the illusion of how violent things really are. Oh, if only that were true! Mr. Pinker goes on to say, "Comprehensive data again and again paints a shockingly happy picture."[23] Really?

Steven Pinker

David Berlinski, in his brilliant book *Atheism and Its Scientific Pretensions: The Devil's Delusion*, would argue that modern man is anything but more noble. For example, who was responsible for the inventions of poisonous gases, hyper-explosives, experiments in eugenics, the formula of Zyklon B gas, heavy artillery, cluster bombs, napalm, intercontinental ballistic missiles, nuclear weapons, military space platforms, and so on? The Nazis, under Adolf Hitler, were especially evil, removing gold teeth from murdered concentration camp victims, making lampshades of their skin, and even manufacturing soap from the fat of their flesh. It certainly wasn't the Vatican or any other religious group that invented these things.

Human sacrifice, slavery as a labor-saving device, genocide, the death penalty for misdemeanors, rape as a tool of war, homicide as a major form of conflict resolution—such things are supposedly rare or nonexistent today, per Pinker. Maybe Pinker reads or listens to news from other sources than me, but all those things listed above are not only still present, but they are even running rampant in our modern world. Human slavery certainly still exists today, especially in sex trafficking and human bondage. Murder and rape have certainly not left us. And genocide is still occurring. Take, for example, the Uyghurs in Northwestern China; eleven million people, mostly Muslim and Turkic-speaking, have been and currently are being brutally treated by the Chinese government, deprived of their basic human rights, abused, and in many cases, outright killed. We will look further at such atrocities later in this book, but it seems evident that humankind is not aspiring to some newfound nobility.

Furthermore, the twentieth century has been the most murderous century in human history. Berlinski gives a summary of what he calls, "Excessive deaths of the 20th century," of which I will give only a partial list here to consider. Excessive deaths are listed as: twenty million under Stalin's regime; forty million under Mao's People's Republic of China; fifteen million in the First World War; twenty million in the Second World War,[24] nine million in the Russian civil war; 2.5 million in the Chinese civil war; 3.8 million in the Kinshasa Congo; and on and on. Berlinski, in his book *Human Nature*, states that 231 million men, women, and children "died violently in the 20th century, shot over open pits, murdered in secret police cellars, asphyxiated in Nazi gas ovens, worked to death in arctic mines or timber camps, the victims of deliberately contrived famines or lunatic industrial experiments, whole populations ravaged by alien armies, bombed to smithereens, or sent to wander in their exiled millions across the violated borders of Europe and Asia." Per Berlinski, "In considering Pinker's assessment of the times in which we live, the only conclusion one can profitably draw is that such an excess of stupidity is not often found in nature."[25]

Do you know any hospitals or benevolent institutions named after Stalin, Mao, or Pol Pot? I don't. Eric Metaxas put the number at 150 million of those executed by atheistic regimes in his book *Is Atheism Dead?* He notes, "The special wickedness of atheism in this arena cannot easily be escaped."[26] Solzhenitsyn said, "Within the philosophical system of Marx and Lenin, and at the heart of their psychology, hatred of God is the principle driving force, more than all their political and economic pretensions." Under the aegis of communism, Metaxas stated this might be the "single most disgusting fact in the history of the human species." In 1937 alone, 106,300 clergymen were murdered by the Soviets, per Metaxas.[27]

My point in all this is to say that those who want to blame religion for the woes of the world and the loss of humankind would do well to take a better look at history. The true number of the murdered in the name of God is almost laughable compared to the same caused by natural materialism, and therefore atheism, when one seriously examines the facts.

Scientific atheism, and hence naturalistic materialism, is a bankrupt worldview. Mankind has not been made better off because of it. Much more good has been accomplished through a theistic worldview, and that is hardly debatable. Even science itself had its rise from Christian thought. As Metaxas writes, esteemed historian Alfred North feels that civilization owes Christianity a lot of gratitude because "certain habits of thoughts, such as the lawfulness of nature, emanated from them and came directly from Christian doctrine of the world of creation.[28] Metaxas argues, and I believe rightfully so, that hospitals and the practice of caring for the sick came from a Christian worldview, as historically it is known that hospitals were started by Christians.[29]

A Christian worldview sees value in human life. John Lennox, countering the new atheist rites, "We thought we could get rid of God and retain value in human beings. We were wrong. We destroyed both God and man.[30] Once again, Berlinski writes in *The Devil's Delusion*, "And as far as we can tell, very few of those carrying out the horrors of the 20th century worried over much that God

David Berlinski

was watching what they were doing. That is after all the meaning of secular society.[31] It would seem that mankind has lost his sense of purpose, and if you think the twenty-first century is starting off any better, think again (a topic we will expand on in chapter 11).

A PURPOSEFUL UNIVERSE

A commonsense interpretation of the facts suggests, that a super intellect has monkeyed with physics, as well as chemistry and biology, and that there are no blind forces worth speaking about in nature. The numbers one calculates from the facts seem to me so overwhelming as to put the conclusion almost beyond question."

—Fred Hoyle

That we came from (God's) workshop should astound us all the more. Among all the wonders that make earth their home we alone are compelled to stop and stare, to take this whole spectacle in—five parts inspiration to one part troubling—and to ponder it, knowing that none of it is accidental.

—Douglas Axe

"IN THE BEGINNING, GOD CREATED THE HEAVENS AND THE EARTH." So begins the book of Genesis, the first book of the Old Testament Bible. The Bible offers few details, but from the first verse, it tells us that everything we see today had its origins "in the beginning," including time, matter, energy, and all the physical laws and constants scientists have discovered thus far. The "beginning" in the book of Genesis thus represents the beginning of everything, including our own universe. But was there a purpose in the beginning, and was our universe created for this purpose? The answer is yes. It would seem God had human beings in mind from the very beginning. Dr. Michael Denton, physician, geneticist, scientist, and author of

Evolution: A Theory in Crisis, a book instrumental in launching the intelligent design movement, says the universe seems to be uniquely designed, and designed specifically for humankind. This is a very bold and ambitious statement; so, what are his arguments?

Denton refers to the "prior environmental fitness of nature" in his book *The Miracle of Man.*[1] What does Denton mean by this? He is referring to the finely tuned nature of the universe, which enables our biologic design, our ability to make fire, our ability to develop metallurgy, and our advancement in technology to be part of this prior fitness. "It is as if, in an act of extraordinary prescience that was built into nature from the beginning, a suite of priorities finally calibrated for beings of our physiological nature and anatomic design, and for our ability to follow the path of technological enlightenment from the Stone Age to present,"[2] writes Denton.

Dr. Michael Denton

Our universe would seem, then, to be a very unique place. You might say, of course, it's a unique place, as it's the only one we have. But not so fast! The prevailing cosmological theory today is the multiverse, or the multi-universe. This theory, if it can really be called a theory, is not born out of any great scientific discovery, but rather it is an attempt to answer the fine-tuning argument observed and not doubted by scientists, instead of opting for an intelligent designer. Sean Carroll, Harvard-trained physicist, says that the multiverse theory is a prediction of string theory and inflation theory, both far from being proven themselves.[3]

Even the most ardent atheistic scientists cannot help but appreciate the exquisite fine-tuning found throughout our universe. So, to avoid the "design" implications of this fine-tuning, the idea of the multiverse was invented. You see, if there are an infinite number of universes, there must be at least one like ours that would have had all the properties in place necessary for life.

The multiverse theory has been called "fantasy," "intellectually bankrupt," a "cheap way out," and "lacking evidential support," and this by scientists, especially by string theorists.[4] Furthermore, the multiverse theory leads to interesting absurdities, with universe models similar but slightly different than our observable universe. Physicist Alan Guth, the father of inflationary theory, even admitted, "There is a universe where Elvis is still alive."[5] This has caused some to even speculate we may be living in a computer-simulated universe, sort of a "Matrix-like"" environment, and this idea is even gaining momentum, endorsed by popular physicist Neil deGrasse Tyson.[6],[7]

Neil deGrasse Tyson

"The inflationary multiverse would render all scientific reasoning, explanation and perception unreliable, undermining any basis for accepting the multiverse hypothesis or any scientific hypothesis or conclusion whatsoever. It would be hard to invent a more self-refuting hypothesis than that!" writes Stephen C. Meyer in his brilliant book *Return of the God Hypothesis*. Richard Swinburne has said, "To postulate a trillion-trillion universes rather than the one God in order to explain the orderliness of our universe, seems the height of irrationality."

Of course, what is missing from the multiverse argument is the question, Who or what created this multiverse-generating mechanism that keeps popping out universes like popcorn? If we are actually living in a computer simulation, then who created the computer program and simulator? Stephen C. Meyer writes that if there were a multiverse-generating mechanism, it itself would require unbelievable, exquisite fine-tuning. Myers quotes from Robin Collins, physicist and philosopher, who likens physicists "who attempt to explain fine-tuning solely by referring to universe-creating mechanisms, without intelligent design, to a hapless soul who denies any ingenuity in the making of a freshly baked loaf of bread simply because the baker used a bread-making machine."[8]

The multiverse argument is, therefore, a default theory. It explains nothing and allows for everything. It is in no way scientific, and it could best be characterized as philosophical. From this point of view, we are therefore simply very lucky to be living in the one universe suitable for human life.One might even say the multiverse is the materialist version of "god-of-the gaps".

In a bit of irony, Stephen Hawking launched his career by proving the universe had a beginning, then spent the rest of his career trying to disprove himself. Why? The implication of a beginning purports a cause, with the most likely cause being that of an intelligent being, or God. Stephen Meyer says that many scientists are beginning to disavow the multiverse idea and regard it as "speculative metaphysical".

Dr. Meyer once again has noted that theoretical physicists Sean Carroll and Heywood Tam present a "vanishing small ratio of approximately 1 to 10 to the 66000000th power for any one universe to allow for a life."[9] Pause for a moment and let that number sink in. Ten to the 66th-million power is an extraordinarily large number, even for cosmologists! And yet the materialistic cosmological physicist would rather accept that number for the likelihood of us existing in a multiverse than to believe in an intelligent designer.

Let's turn the tables. What if those who believed in God said there was one-in-66th-millionth chance of His existence, yet they believed in Him, nonetheless. Believers would be ridiculed and branded as "irrational," or worse yet, "delusional," which I suppose is exactly what the materialist does. Richard Dawkins has even said as much, referring to those who do not believe in evolution as "ignorant, stupid or insane (or wicked, but I'd rather not consider that)."[10] And yet it is the materialist who is sane and intelligent in accepting this very, very highly unlikely event of the multiverse!

Here's where the word *infinity* comes into play. These gargantuan improbabilities, in essence, represent infinity. So, in other words, there must be an infinite number of universes for one such as ours to exist. When one resorts to an infinite number of anything, you are no longer relying on logic. Bernard Carr, a University of London theoretical physicist, says, "To the hardline physicist, the multiverse may not be entirely respectable, but it is at least preferable to evoking a creator."[11] I would say, to Dr. Carr's credit, he is at least being honest.

This harkens back to the famous quote of Richard Lewontin in 1997, in the *New York Review of Books*, where he admitted that scientists must accept some claims that might seem absurd, "And we have to accept unsubstantiated stories because of a prior commitment to materialism, and after all, we cannot allow a divine foot in the door."[12]

Astrophysicist Hugh Ross has called our universe "just the right universe". Roger Penrose commented in a film from 1992, "I would say the universe has a purpose. It is not there just some by chance."[13] Even Hawking himself, in his book *A Brief History of Time*, stated, "It would be very difficult to explain why the universe should have begun in just this way, except as an act of God who intended to create beings like us."[14]

Dr. Ross has identified thirty-five carefully defined characteristics of the universe that require exquisite fine-tuning and narrowly defined values that must be what they are for life of any kind to exist. These include the strong nuclear force, the weak nuclear force, the gravitational constant, the electromagnetic force constant, the ratio of the electromagnetic force constant to the gravitational force constant, the ratio of electron to proton mass, the ratio of numbers of electrons to protons, the expansion rate of the universe, the entropy level of the universe, the baryon or nucleon density of the universe, the velocity of light, the age of the universe, the initial uniformity of creation, the fine structure constant, the average distance between galaxies, the average distance between stars, the decay rate of the proton, the carbon-to-oxygen energy level ratio, the brown state energy level of helium, the decay rate of beryllium, the mass excess of the neutron over the proton, the initial excess of nucleons over the anti-nucleons, the polarity of the water molecule, supernovae eruptions, white dwarf binaries, the ratio of exotic to ordinary matter, galaxy clusters, the number of effective dimensions in the early universe, the number of effective dimensions in the present universe, the mass of the neutrino, Big Bang ripples, the total mass density, the space energy density, the size of the relativistic dilation factor, and the uncertainty magnitude of Heisenberg's uncertainty principle.

Dr. Hugh Ross

Using these thirty-five factors, Dr. Ross has calculated the improbability of life, and as you can imagine, the number is astronomical. In fact, just four factors requiring such fine-tuning yields an unlikelihood in the part of 1:10 to the 37th power for life of any kind to exist.

When one extrapolates from the universe to life, the problem gets even bigger for the materialist. For carbon-based life to exist, sixty-six factors or parameters must be fine-tuned. This fine-tuning is extraordinary and rises to a 10 to the 145th power.[15] In longhand, that would be written as one in a trillion, trillion, trillion, trillion, trillion, trillion, trillion, trillion, trillion, trillion, trillion. English physicist Paul Davies, in the BBC series *Horizon*, said it this way: "The really amazing thing is not that the life on earth is balanced on a knife-edge, but the entire universe is balanced on a knife-edge and would be total chaos if any of the natural 'constants' were off even slightly."

Getting back to Dr. Denton's prior fitness concept, Lawrence Henderson in 1913 published the classic *The Fitness of the Environment*, which alludes to this prior fitness. In his book, Henderson espoused the belief that the natural environment was particularly fit for carbon-based life.

Denton, in *The Miracle of Man*, points to the hydrologic cycle, the aerobic cycle of our planet, the respiratory mechanism, the circulatory system, and multiple parameters of life that point to a fine-tuning and design. For example, he discusses the properties of water and its ability to exist in three forms—solid, liquid, and gas—at ambient temperatures as crucial for life to exist. No other substance on earth exhibits these qualities. As a liquid, water acts as a universal solvent, dissolving rock and distributing essential minerals to terrestrial organisms. Water's low viscosity and high mobility enhances this action, as does the freezing and fracturing of ice. Minerals delivered by water are essential for plant life. "It is hard to imagine any ensemble of fitness more indicative of design than the way the many diverse properties of water work together in the hydrological cycle to enable terrestrial life," says Dr. Denton.[16]

Denton, in his chapter on aerobic life, states, "All complex advanced animals on earth, where there are high energy requirements, use oxidation to produce energy. There are no exceptions."[17] This is expressed in the simple formula CH (sugar-fat) plus $O_2 \rightarrow CO_2$ plus water plus energy (ATP and heat). This formula clearly requires oxygen, which fortunately we have plenty of, our atmosphere containing 20 percent of it. Photosynthesis generates oxygen as well as sugar and the fats that we eat, for which the energy comes from the sun. This fitness of the sun's radiation for life cannot be overestimated and depends on several improbable "coincidences of nature."

Light from the sun is an electromagnetic spectrum of radiation. Our sun produces visible and infrared light primarily. For photosynthesis, it is the visible wavelengths that are responsible to activate chemical reactions, again, a fortunate thing for us, as we have plenty of it. One must keep in mind that the wavelength of visible light along the electromagnetic spectrum are minuscule, between 380 to 750 nanometers in length.[18] Understanding that the entire spectrum of solar radiation encompasses 4,000 nanometers, it is very fortunate that visible life incorporates such a high proportion of that spectrum for us.

Ian Campbell has called the number of coincidences listed above as staggering in his book, *Energy and the Atmosphere*. He states, "Hence visible light, as it may be termed generally, has exactly the right scale of energy per light quantum or photon to give rise to the possibility of photochemistry, that is chemical reactions driven by the energy of sunlight."[19]

It is also important that our atmosphere absorbs significant amounts of infrared radiation, or else our earth would be intolerably hot during the day and likewise cold at night with temperatures of less than zero, and carbon-based life would not exist. It is also fortuitous that the atmospheric gases of nitrogen (N_2), oxygen (O_2), ozone (O_3), carbon dioxide (CO_2), and water vapor (H_2O) exist in just the right proportions or life could not exist on earth. It is also good that CO_2 plus H_2O plus greenhouse gases are stable in the presence of oxygen; otherwise the whole atmospheric system and global heat balance would collapse.

And referring back to our formula, the three atmospheric gases are indispensable to photosynthesis; hence, our very existence ($6CO_2 + 6H_2O + light + heat \rightarrow C_6H_{12}O_6 + 6O^2$). "It is as if CO_2, H_2O, and O_2 are deliberately colluding to incorporate themselves into the stuff of living matter," writes Michael Denton.[20]

A key fact to keep in mind is that scientists to date are not sure why there is so much oxygen in our atmosphere. "There is no precise explanation for earth's value of O_2 atmospheric abundance," say Sara

Seager and William Barnes in a paper written in 2015 and published in the periodical *Science Advances*. Of course, we know that O_2 is our oxygen produced by photosynthesis, but what gets us to the precise level is unknown.

One might ask, with all this oxygen in the atmosphere, why are there not more forest fires than we currently see? No doubt, recent history has seen plenty of forest fires, in both Canada and California especially, but nonetheless, with as much oxygen as we see in our atmosphere, our planet should be perpetually engulfed in flames. The answer as to why there are not more fires lies in the molecule of nitrogen. It turns out nitrogen acts as a fire retardant—and fortunately, we have significant levels of nitrogen in our atmosphere to both retard fire and prevent the oceans from evaporating. Also, fortuitously, nitrogen is not a greenhouse gas.

The ensemble of atmospheric factors that make life on earth possible is absolutely unbelievable. Dr. Denton summarizes these: "The energy release when oxygen combines with reduced carbon supplies us with copious amounts of metabolic energy, the gaseous nature of oxygen allows us to extract it via our lungs, the low solubility of oxygen which prevents its loss in the oceans, all allow for life on earth."[21]

Then there is this: the sun, and its light, which is just right for photochemistry, coupled with the transparency of the atmosphere to visual light, plus the absorption of infrared radiation that allows the warming of the earth to ambient temperatures, are, once again, just right for life. There are even more qualities of our atmosphere we could discuss that allow for life, but suffice it to say, "nature" is clearly set for life to abound on earth.

Again, from Denton, "It is now widely acknowledged that carbon-based life embedded in a water matrix is the only type of life permitted by the laws of nature."[22] With that being said, Denton would argue that if life is found outside our earth, it would be in the form of oxygen-hungry beings with biologic design much like our own.[23]

Lawrence Henderson says, in essence, that Darwin had it backward. Darwin concentrated on the adaptation to the environment, foregoing the prior environmental fitness that enables "the actualization of the adaptations." Henderson states, "How for example could man adapt his civilization to waterpower if no waterpower existed within his reach?"[24]

For me, it is clear that we humans are not here by some giant accident or afterthought. Planning and purpose are found on our planet that allows for life to exist, and the exquisite fine-tuning of all the "ensembles" allows for our existence and surely could not have occurred by sheer chance. To be extremely clear, what I am not saying is that the fine-tuning necessitates the origin of life, but rather, its perpetuation. In fact, even with this fine-tuning, it is extremely unlikely that life could have arisen spontaneously undirected. Atoms are "populations of identical particles whose properties were not acted on by natural selection and whose properties determined whether life could exist," wrote the great James Clarke Maxwell in 1873.[25] In other words, molecules have no desire to "live," or create life, as Dr. James Tour likes to say. Tour, a brilliant chemist and professor at Rice University, has written, "The proposals offered thus far to explain life's origins make no scientific sense. Beyond our planet, all the others that have been probed are lifeless, a result in accord with our chemical expectations. The laws of physics and chemistry's periodic table are universal, suggesting that life based upon amino acids, nucleotides, saccharides, and lipids is an anomaly. Life should not exist anywhere in our universe. Life should not even exist on the surface of the earth."[26]

I believe, as Dr. Denton does, that nature is exquisitely fit for "intelligent, technologically capable organisms," very much like us, to occupy a very privileged place in the order of the universe.[27] One might ask at this point, are there other explanations for this fine-tuning we observe other than the multiverse theory, which we have seen is no explanation at all. There are, but they are ridiculously weak arguments. For example, in 1974, Brandon Carter proposed what has come to be known as the weak anthropic principle. Carter said, "What we can expect to observe must be restricted by the conditions necessary for our presence as observers."[28] In other words, we should not be at all surprised to find ourselves in a unique universe suited for life, because if we weren't here, we couldn't observe it! Basically, the fine-tuning requires no explanation at all from this argument. Dr. Stephen Meyer explains the flow of this concept in this way, "Stating a necessary condition for the observance of an event is as if it eliminated the need for a causal explanation of conditions that made the event possible is like an insurance investigator blaming the cause of a warehouse fire on the presence of oxygen in the atmosphere.[29]

In a similar vein, we have what is described as the strong anthropic principle, which states that the universe had to be fine-tuned to produce human observers to observe it. The universe may depend on an observer for its very existence, a sort of "collapse of the wave phenomenon" seen in quantum physics first espoused by Schrödinger. Once again, this is no explanation at all, plus it requires the observation of the observer of this fine-tuning to see it many years afterward and not before. Martin Gardner, in the *Scientific American*, called the strong anthropic principle (SAP) *CRAP*: "The completely ridiculous anthropic principle."[30] Finally, some scientists say this fine-tuning of the universe represents or emanates from the laws of physics themselves. They require no explanation because they are part of the "logical structure" of these laws. Meyer rightly points out that it is simply circular reasoning to say that the laws of physics explain themselves.

The fine-tuning of the universe is due to physical necessity, chance, or design. I know of no other possibilities. The chemical reactions for life are clearly not due to a physical necessity. Left alone, they are simply not going to form the molecules necessary for life. Chance is further preposterous, and as we have noted, there are ridiculously high improbabilities for the fine tuning we observe. That leaves design, doesn't it?! As we have noted, some claim that this is an argument based on ignorance or gaps in information, but that is not so. The design argument is based on what we *do* know, which is that the origin of information-rich structures testify to the information-generative power of an intelligent designer.

It is obvious to me that the fine-tuning we observed in this chapter requires a fine-tuner! Some would say this would be a "super-intellect," but I would call it "God." William Dembski, in his groundbreaking book, *The Design Inference*, states that systems that exhibit two characteristics at the same time—extreme improbability and specification—indicate intelligent activity. Mankind has observed this phenomenon forever. We see a special kind of pattern, and we understand intelligence.

Let me illustrate. When I was a boy, my brother and I would visit our cousins in East Texas, and we would go into the woods searching for Indian arrowheads. I'm sure you have seen these, and they are, or at least they were, quite ubiquitous in Texas, home to many Indian tribes, not the least of which were the Comanches. Taking rocks or stones, Comanches would sculpt them into sharp, pointed objects with which we are familiar. When placed on the end of an arrow, these objects could penetrate an animal or an enemy quite effectively. When we stumbled on these relics in the forest, it was obvious to us that at one time, Indians had been here. Now, it is certainly possible that some of these arrowheads could come about naturally by forces of wind, erosion, etc., and sometimes we would have trouble identifying a rock versus an

Arrowhead

Indian arrowhead, nonetheless when we found one, it was certainly indicative of design.

But let's take this one step further. Suppose you were walking through a dense forest and came upon a clearing, then ahead of it you saw a large rock mountain with the likenesses of Abraham Lincoln, Thomas Jefferson, Theodore Roosevelt, and George Washington projecting from it. I am pretty sure your first thought would not be, *Wow, what a remarkable thing nature has produced on this mountainside.* No, you and every rational person would realize it is impossible for wind, rain, or erosion to produce such a distinctive feature as the one described, which is obviously Mount Rushmore in South Dakota. Mount Rushmore was completed in 1941 under the direction of sculptor Gutzon Borglum and his son Lincoln. It took fourteen years to complete, with four hundred workers using the best technology at the time, blasting 450,000 tons of rock from the mountainside. The point here is that humans usually have no problem at all recognizing design when they see it!

Mount Rushmore

Again from Dr. Stephen Meyer: "In any case, in our experience, a small-probability event that exhibits a pattern recognized from independent experience or a set of functional requirements reliably indicates intelligent design."[31] As a result, we can safely say a cosmological fine-tuning is the expected activity of a designing mind, much more than some random chance, mindless, purposeless process. This fine-tuning as it regards the universe cannot be overstated, even if one accepts a Big Bang cosmology, which I do not.

Robert Collins has written extensively about this fine-tuning, but for him the most important factor is the cosmologic constant, which poses a problem for the materialistic cosmologist, admitted to by materialistic physicist Sean Carroll. The cosmologic constant, the energy density of empty space, is not at all what scientists would have guessed using first principles. It is a very small number, and fortunately so. If it were a large positive number, matter could not clump together; if it were a large negative number, it would act as an attractive force, reversing expansion, thus causing the universe to collapse. This unexpected small number is both very precise and counterintuitive, and it is widely regarded as the single greatest problem facing physicists and cosmologists today, so says Collins.[32]

This calculated number versus the measured difference of the vacuum energy is not small. The difference is by a factor of 10 to the 120th power, which is one followed by 120 zeros and is absurdly large, especially when there are only 10 to the 90th particles in the entire observable universe. This "cosmologic problem" at present is unsolvable by physicists, says Sean Carroll.[33] For now, the only explanation for this discrepancy is some "unknown symmetry or other law of physics as yet undiscovered." Nonetheless, this fine-tuning of the cosmologic constant is exquisite and conservatively estimated to be one part in 1 in 10^{53} or a hundred million billion, billion, billion, billion, billion—that is 10 followed by 53 zeros. To illustrate, Collins likens this probability of hitting a bull's-eye the size of an atom on earth with a dart from outer space. For Collins, "If the cosmologic constant were the only example of fine-tuning, and if there were no natural explanation for it, then this would be sufficient by itself to strongly establish design."[34]

Finally, Oxford physicist Sir Roger Penrose calculated quantitatively the unimaginable fine-tuning required for galaxies, stars, and planetary systems to form to be 10^{123}.[35] In a colossal understatement, Paul Davies stated, "The present arrangement of matter indicates a very special choice of initial conditions."[36]

Conceptualizing the high numbers seen in this chapter is almost impossible; our minds just don't deal with large numbers like these.

To illustrate, let's review for just a moment how to conceive of high numbers. Ten to the first power (10^1) is 10 X 1 = 10. Ten to the second power (10^2) is 10 X 10 = 100. Ten to the third power (10^3) is 10 X 10 X 10 = 1,000. Ten to the fourth power (10^4) is 10 X 10 X 10X 10 = 10,000. One million is 10^6, one billion is 10^9, and one trillion is 10^{10}. As you can see, once you get to 10^{10}, you are looking at very large numbers that are hard to express verbally.

To imagine what 10^{40} is, astronomist Hugh Ross likens it to this: Cover America with coins in a column reaching to the moon (236,000 miles away), then do the same for a billion other countries the same size. Paint one coin red and put it somewhere in one of the billion piles. Blindfold a friend and ask her to pick it out. These odds are about 1 in 10^{40} that she will.[37] There are an estimated 10^{80} particles in the universe, though I have no clue how this estimate is derived. You can see then what 10^{123} represents.

This represents fine-tuning that defies any word in the English language. When one couples this huge degree of fine-tuning plus specification, design becomes not only the likely explanation for our existence, but the only one. The universe, our earth, is finely tuned for our existence, and it was purposely fine-tuned. But why? Stay tuned!

Chapter
4

A STRANGE UNIVERSE: RELATIVITY, QUANTUM MECHANICS, AND DARK ENERGY

"The most incomprehensible thing about the universe is that it is comprehensible."

—*Albert Einstein*

"It is the glory of God to conceal things, but the glory of kings is to search things out."

—*Proverbs 25:2*

THE BEGINNING OF EVERYTHING SPOKEN OF IN GENESIS 1 INCLUDES the beginning of the physical laws and constants, as mentioned in the previous chapter. These laws and constants are not mentioned in these verses specifically, and even if they were, early man would likely not have had the capacity to understand them. Verse 6 of Genesis 1 says man was created in God's image. I believe this likeness includes the sentient man, possessing a mind along with the desire and the ability to discover the physical laws that make up the fabric of our universe. It would take multiple millennia, but finally, in the beginning of the twentieth century, mankind—with the help of one particular genius—began to uncover the most basic processes that govern our universe.

The year 1905 was magical. That year, a twenty-six-year-old patent office clerk with no academic position or standing completed six astounding scientific papers, one of which would change forever how physicists viewed the universe and its inner workings. That twenty-six-year-old was, of course, Albert Einstein. His first paper introduced the photon, or quantas of light energy, and it helped launch the field of quantum physics. His fifth paper that year introduced us to the equation $E=MC^2$, but it was the fourth paper that was probably the most revolutionary. The paper, modestly titled, "Electrodynamics of Moving Bodies," with simplicity and clarity resolved previous contradictions on the motion of the earth, but more importantly, Einstein elucidated the principle of relativity. Einstein proposed that the laws of physics are the same in all uniformly moving reference time frames. This is relativity.

Albert Einstein

Five years earlier, physicist Max Planck renounced previous physics and introduced the concept of "quanta of energy," small packets that hold certain, prescribed amounts of energy. Niels Bohr expanded on Planck's theory with his calculations on positions of spectral lines. After 1905, with Einstein's impetus, quantum theory gained momentum. What became evident, with the contributions of Schrödinger, Heisenberg, and Dirac, is that quantum theory can only predict or approximate outcomes, but never with absolute certainty

Relativity and Newtonian mechanics seem to describe how the world works on a large scale. Quantum mechanics describes how the world works on a very small, subatomic scale, and the mathematics do not jibe for both. Both present and demonstrate some very weird things, and they do not necessarily follow our common sense. The strange things we find in relativity are not contradictory; they follow logically once you understand that the laws of physics are the same in any uniformly moving reference frame. This is not so with quantum mechanics. Things seem to occur in the quantum world that defy logic and common sense, and even seem contradictory. We will expand on this shortly, but as far as we can tell, our world, our universe, seems to function based on these mega-laws.

Relativity

The basic concept of relativity was not original with Einstein, but dates as far back as the early seventeenth century with Italian astronomer Galileo Galilei, and further expanded later in that century by Isaac Newton. Galileo understood that the state of uniform motion requires no explanation. What requires explanation is a change in motion. Forces therefore do not cause motion; they cause changes in motion. Galileo knew, for example, that a ball dropped on a moving ship in water moving uniformly will drop straight down onto the deck of the ship. That is relativity. Newton, born in 1642, the year of Galileo's death, expounded on Galileo's concept. With the famous drop of the apple, Newton realized the motion of the apple and the motion of the moon are the same motion, both, of course, influenced by the earth's gravity. Newton went on to claim that every object in the universe attracts each other. Newton expressed his belief in his three laws of motion, published in his famous book *Philosophiae Naturalis Principia Mathematica*, arguably the most important scientific work ever published. These laws stated: 1) An object at rest remains at rest, and an object in motion remains in uniform motion unless subject to another force; 2) The change of acceleration or rate of change of motion is larger for a larger force and smaller for an object of larger mass, expressed force = mass times acceleration; 3) "For every action, there is an equal and opposition reaction."

Isaac Newton

"At the heart of Galileo's and Newton's new understanding of motion is the idea of uniform motion as a natural state, needing no further explanation,"[1] states Richard Wolfson in his excellent book, *Simply Einstein*. Galilean relativity explains why an attendant in a jet airplane going four hundred miles an hour can toss you a pack of peanuts without it smacking you upside the head. Relative to the ground, the peanuts are traveling four hundred–plus miles per hour, but for you in the plane it is much less. As a result, there is no conceivable experiment that can answer the question: Am I moving? All motion becomes relative then. We know this empirically. Our plane provides another example. When you are traveling at uniform motion, the only way you can tell you are moving is to look out the window of the plane because the plane is moving relative to the earth. The same principle applies to us while on terra firma, the earth. Although the earth is spinning at a rapid speed, approximately 1,000 miles per hour, we have no sense of this. This seems remarkable, and a point I want to emphasize is this: there is no reason it has to be this way other than it just is. There is no such thing as absolute motion or absolute rest, and this is baked into the fabric of our reality.

Notice that throughout this discussion, I have used the term *uniform motion*. Newton's laws don't hold in the non-uniform frame of reference, such as at takeoff or landing, or in turbulence while on a plane, or during rough seas while on a ship. This is because the motions in these cases are changing. So, playing tennis at sea during rough weather is going to be very difficult.

So, what is different about Einstein's theory of relativity? The quick answer is light. By the time Einstein began his work—primarily through thought experiment, I might add—physicists had a much better idea how light worked and that made all the difference. The double-slit experiment in 1801 by Thomas Young showed light primarily acts in waves. Scottish physicist James Clarke Maxwell proposed that light was propagated through space in electromagnetic waves and what we know as visible light is only a very small portion of the spectrum of electromagnetic waves, the speed being equal to 186,000 miles per second, but defined by wavelength. With very short wavelengths or very high frequencies, we have dangerous x-rays and gamma rays; for longer waves with low frequencies, we have radio waves. They are all part of the electromagnetic spectrum.[2]

Finally, in 1880, Prussian-born American Albert A. Michelson collaborated with Edward Morley to perform an experiment that would shape the foundations of physics in the late nineteenth century. Without going into great detail, their experiment demonstrated for the first time that the earth was not moving through a proposed medium called "aether," a concept held by virtually all physicists at the time. Their experiment was met with skepticism, but eventually it came to be accepted that there simply is no aether permeating the universe.

Now enters Einstein. His so-called Special Theory of Relativity grew out of contradictions arising through Maxwell's revelation that light consists of electromagnetic waves moving at a speed of light, or "C." Einstein proposed that the laws of physics are the same in all uniformly moving reference frames, with the added caveat that the speed of light is the same in all uniformly moving reference frames, a caveat not really needed as it flows from relativity and is therefore superfluous. Light, therefore, requires no medium, unlike sound waves or ocean waves, and this turns out to be critical in Einstein's theory. Light propagates through empty space and requires no aether.

Conclusions drawn from Einstein's theory of relativity will seem strange and contrary to our common sense; but they follow logically, and as we have said, are never contradictory. They follow the simple fact that the laws of physics are the same in any uniformly moving reference frame. Period!

As a result of relativity, our concept of time and space was turned upside down. It turns out there is no universal clock running somewhere with hours and seconds ticking by at the same pace everywhere in the universe. There is no favored reference frame, in other words. Time is not absolute; it is always local. This is difficult for us to grasp, and that is because of our provincialism. We are stuck here on earth, if you will, and therefore we are limited by speeds far less than the speed of light. Our personal experience leads us to believe time is absolute, but it simply isn't.

For example, as we achieve speeds near the speed of light, time dilates. We measure events by time and space. I was born, for example, at a specific time and place. From relativity, the time interval between two events cannot be the same for two observers in motion relative to each other. Many thought experiments have been conducted to show this, but I will demonstrate with one example taken from Dr. Wolfson.[3]

In our example, a space traveler boards a ship going to a distant star twenty light-years away, traveling at 0.8c. This will be a one-way trip for our example, and there is a clock on earth, on the star we're going to, and inside the spaceship. The question is, how long does this trip take? The formula is quite simple, T = 20 light-years divided by 0.8 light-years = 25 years, from the earth's clock. That formula becomes a bit more complicated when calculating the time on the spaceship. That formula is $T1 = T \times \sqrt{1 - V^2} = 25$ years $\times \sqrt{1 - 0.8^2} \times 25$ years $\times \sqrt{1 - 064} = 25$ years $\times \sqrt{0.36} = 25$ years $\times 0.6 = 15$ years. Don't worry about the details of the formula—they have been substantiated

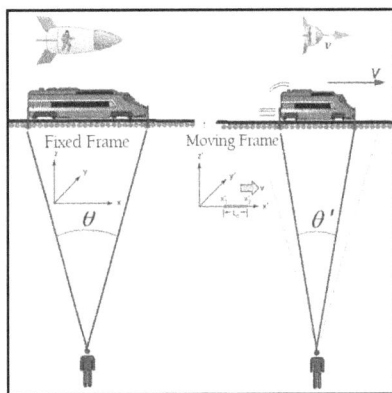

Relativity

by past experimentation—but as you can see, the difference between the time on earth and the time on the spaceship is ten years. This difference, it should be pointed out, is not due to the clock's ship running slower. It's about time itself. As a result, the astronaut who remains on earth would have aged twenty-five years compared to the astronaut on the ship, who would have aged only fifteen years. To be clear, the astronaut who is on the ship does not experience anything different physiologically and would not be aware of this difference until he or she arrived at their destination on the star or when they come back to earth, when now that difference will be even greater, twenty years. I understand this seems implausible, and there are those who may not believe the above scenario, but time dilation has been proven using atomic clocks in high-speed aircraft.[4]

Now, if you think time dilation is strange, another phenomenon predicted by relativity is space contraction. As an object approaches the speed of light, its apparent mass also increases, and its length contracts. Also, as its mass increases, it will take more and more force to produce less and less acceleration; therefore, relativity predicts that no particle can travel faster than the speed of light. It is important to understand here, it is not the fact that time actually moves slower or that objects actually shrink, but rather, it is what two observers will measure based on their frame of reference.

One of Einstein's successors at Princeton, theoretical physicist Freeman Dyson, summarized relativity this way: "There was no absolute space and time and there was no aether. All the complicated explanations of electric and magnetic forces as elastic stresses in the aether could be swept into the dust bin of history, together with the famous old professors who still believed in them."[5] Science was and still remains provisional!

There are many permutations of relativity and proposed paradoxes, such as the concept of simultaneity and the so-called twin paradox, but for our discussion, we will forgo those topics. Einstein also saw light as more than a wave and came to understand that energy is carried by "photons," or particles that make up light, hence the equation E (energy) = M (mass) x C (the speed of light),[2] or $E=MC^2$, a profound concept that seems to hold true. What this equation is saying is that matter is energy in its condensed form.

Physicist Gerald Schroeder calls this "intuitively ridiculous," but true nonetheless.

Ten years after his paper on special relativity, Einstein proposed general relativity, which removed special relativity's restriction to uniform motion and described gravity as a curvature of time and space. Once again, to emphasize, Einstein did not invent relativity, either special or general. If these principles are true, and so far they seem to be, then they are part of our reality and have no particular cause other than *they are what they are!* For me, relativity seems to speak of a grand purpose in the universe.

Quantum Mechanics

If relativity has you shaking your head, quantum theory will make you question your sanity, which it apparently did with Erwin Schrödinger, one of its founders. Findings in the quantum world are very strange and bizarre, and as mentioned, they cannot be deduced by logic or common sense.

This strangeness of quantum mechanics was not lost on one of its early contributors, the bongos-playing genius from Cal Tech who served with Robert Oppenheimer on the Manhattan Project, Richard Feynman. Feynman once said, "I think I can safely say that nobody understands quantum mechanics." This might have

been said with a little sarcasm, but it does point to the mysteriousness of quantum mechanics, and even Einstein, whose early work supported quantum mechanics, would eventually reject it, famously explaining, "God does not play with dice." Even Niels Bohr acknowledged the enigma of quantum mechanics, saying, "If you were not completely confused by quantum mechanics, you do not understand it."

Richard Feynman

Before we explain the above comments, first understand that Newtonian mathematics and quantum mechanics do not jibe with each other, as mentioned earlier. The former does a good job explaining the workings of the universe on a grand, macro level; the latter better explains the workings on a subatomic or micro level. Yet both seem to be correct. Since Einstein's time to the present, a grand unifying theory has been sought to "marry the two," but so far none has been found. String theory has been proposed, but it has its own drawbacks, not the least of which is its need for ten, eleven, or twenty-six dimensions, depending on which version you choose to accept, plus, as David Berlinski has written, "It was an idea that possessed every advantage except clarity, elegance, and a demonstrated connection to reality."

Quantum theory, at its most basic, is the concept of energy being packaged in discrete bits of information, or quanta, a theory, as we have seen, was first proposed by Max Planck. But quantum mechanics is so much more than that. Unlike relativity, developing quantum theory was much more of a collaborative endeavor. Max Planck, Einstein, and Bohr are given credit as its "fathers," but very early on, quantum mechanics would become even more defined by Erwin Schrödinger, Werner Heisenberg, and Paul Dirac. Schrödinger would become known for his wave equations, and Heisenberg for the uncertainty principle, topics we will discuss subsequently.

Quantum mechanics, as we have seen, can be difficult to understand, but I believe the essence of it can be found in the double-slit experiment. I shall not go into great detail here, nor will I present mathematical equations, which are really fairly simple, but I will give a general overview since it is critical to our understanding.[6]

The first double-slit experiment, as we have mentioned, was conducted a century before the birth of quantum mechanics by British Polymath Thomas Young to demonstrate the wave behavior of light. The experiment was rather simple: shine light through a screen with two slits on it and capture the light on the other side with an "absorber." If light passes through the slits in a wave, an interference pattern, much like you would get with two waves of water propagating simultaneously side by side, will be seen. This is what Young found: light went through the slits, and an interference pattern was seen on the other side.

So, for one hundred years, the question seemed to be answered: light exists as waves of electromagnetism, defined later by Maxwell. Einstein, however, was not so convinced, and he proposed that light also exists in particle form, with those particles called photons.

Later, with a vast increase in technology, the double-slit experiment could be done using photons. In this case, individual photons are directed to our screen through the double-slit. As you might imagine, they will randomly go through the slits, and we will observe a pattern on the "absorber" afterward. What we find is an interference pattern—not what we would expect. It is almost as if each individual photon is going through both slits at one time.

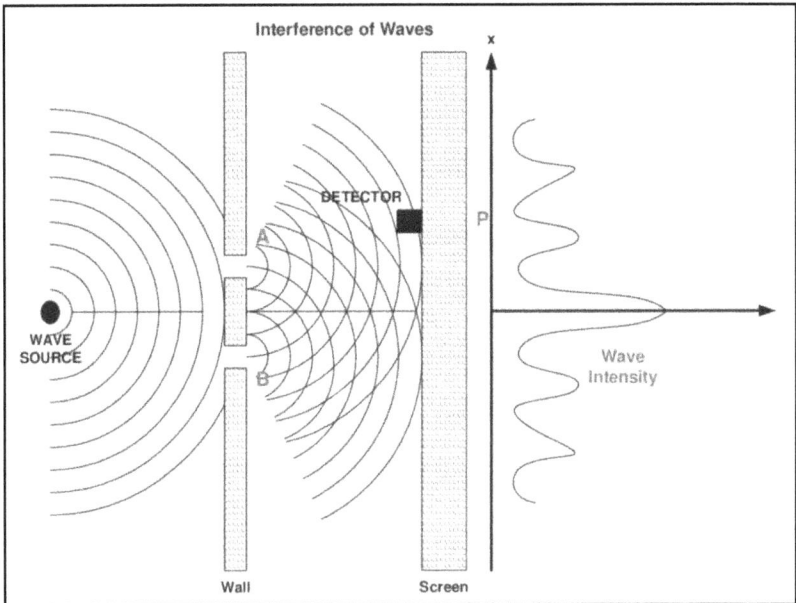

Double-slit

The conclusion is, photons arrive through the slit in lumps, like particles, but distributed like a wave. Again, essentially sometimes photons act like a particle and sometimes like a wave; hence, the wave-particle nature of the photons.

The above phenomena are strange, but things get even stranger. If we add a detector to our experiment, we get a different pattern. We will now detect the individual photons as they go through the slit. It turns out that what we get if we look at the photons is not an interference pattern, but a pattern we would expect if photons were going through each slit individually, as they are. Now, if we take the detector away or turn it off and repeat the same experiment, we will observe an interference pattern. It is as if by simply watching the photons, we have changed their motion. This is amazing. Feynman concludes this experiment this way: if you look at the double-slit with a detector, trying to see which hole or slit the photons go through—hole one or hole two—then you can say which one they go through, and you are going to see a noninterference pattern. But when you do not watch which hole the electrons go through, there is nothing to "disturb" them. You cannot see which hole or slit the electrons went through, and you are going to see an interference pattern.[7] Later, this experiment was repeated using electrons with the same results.

This is the heart of quantum mechanics, and it led Heisenberg to state his uncertainty principle. Heisenberg said you cannot design an experiment in such a way to determine momentum and position of a particle at the same time without destroying the interference pattern; therefore, it is impossible to know a particle's position and velocity at the same time.

Feynman writes, "The uncertainty principle 'protects' quantum mechanics. Heisenberg recognized that if it were possible to measure the momentum and position simultaneously with greater accuracy, the quantum mechanics would collapse."[8] Hence, it is impossible to do. To date, no one has figured out a way to measure the position and the momentum of anything simultaneously!

As a result, quantum mechanics is not "classical," or deterministic. It deals only with probabilities, and these probabilities are predicted by Schrödinger's wave equations. The wave function is said to "collapse" when we observe something.[9]

In the quantum world, then, it is when I look at an object like an orange that the wave collapses, or, in essence, reality collapses. Before that, the orange existed in a "super position." I am not saying here that interactions with the world bring reality into existence—a philosophy known as solipsism—but rather, that the rules by which objects evolve are different when we look at them as opposed to when we do not.

It should be emphasized that no one has a clue why photons, or for that matter electrons or any particles, act as they do in the double-slit experiment. The double-slit experiment has now been done with other particles—and in some cases, even atoms themselves—and they all behave the same way. There is no explanation for it; they just do. That is not to say we may figure it out one day, but we certainly have not yet, and it is profoundly mysterious.

There are at least two other properties of quantum mechanics that defy logic: quantum entanglement and quantum tunneling. Quantum entanglement involves two quantum systems that influence one another, though they are very far apart from each other, even light-years! As a result, a change in one system can influence the other. This involves our concept of super-positions again, and randomness, and some have said it requires particles to travel faster than light, but it is randomness that travels faster than light, not the particles themselves. I know this sounds strange and bizarre; nonetheless it seems to be a real phenomenon.

Quantum tunneling is when a particle is able to penetrate

through a barrier that is higher in energy than the particles' kinetic energy. This, too, seems to be an amazing property of microscopic particles, but it has actually led to practical usage.

Quantum mechanics can lead to some very strange interpretations and theoretical consequences. The so-called Copenhagen interpretation is even considered mystical; therefore, it is rejected by many. With this interpretation, objects have pairs of properties that cannot be measured or observed simultaneously; therefore, the act of observing or measuring is irreversible, so that once you look at the object, it has changed forever!

Along these lines, Erwin Schrödinger proposed a thought experiment using a cat in a box, with a flask of poison and a radioactive source. With a monitor, or Geiger counter, also inside to capture radioactivity, when any decay occurs, the flask of poison is shattered, and the cat dies. With the Copenhagen interpretation, the cat can be both dead and alive simultaneously, a sort of quantum superposition. When one finally observes the dead cat, however, the wave collapses!

Erwin Schrödinger

Schrodinger's thought experiment was originally devised to show the absurdity of the Copenhagen interpretation, and yet this thought experiment remains a touchstone for the modern interpretation of quantum mechanics.

My personal belief is that the Copenhagen interpretation is philosophical and not based on reality, and that quantum theory itself is still incomplete. Mitchell Feingenbaum said, "It's an extravagantly good theory, except at some level it doesn't make sense."[10] Nonetheless, it has led to very practical and useful technology, including MRI medical scanners, lasers, electron microscopes, global positioning systems, quantum computers, and even electric toasters, just to mention a few. Clearly quantum mechanics is not simply a theoretical device.

Dark Matter and Dark Energy

This brings us to dark energy and dark matter. Physicists now believe only 5 percent of the universe is made of ordinary matter and energy, with 25 percent being some kind of unseen dark matter, and 70 percent of it being smoothly distributed dark energy. The reason for their conclusions is gravity; there does not seem to be enough mass in the universe to hold galaxies together; therefore, there must be more matter out there. We have yet to identify this matter, but it cannot be the particles described in the current standard model. Let's now look at these phenomena in a bit more detail.

Gravity has been an elusive phenomenon to pin down for physicists who are still trying to understand it and what causes it. Isaac Newton, as we saw, defined the laws of gravity with his famous equation, $F=GM1M2/R^2$, where F is the gravitational force acting between two objects, M1, M2, with M meaning their masses, and R being the distance between the center of these masses, and G is the gravitational constant. In other words, bodies of mass attract each other with a force proportional to their mass and the square of the distance between them. Earth is affected by the gravitational force of the sun, and the moon is affected by the gravitational force of the earth. This phenomenon is, of course, seen throughout the universe, and it is what holds galaxies together. But Newton could not give an answer as to why this is so—it just was.

Einstein came along centuries later, and with his general theory of relativity, he described gravity as a bending, or warping, of space-time, which seems to be a more accurate explanation of what gravity is, but it still does not answer the "why" question. Physicists now think there may be a yet undiscovered particle called the graviton, which may better yet describe gravity. If this is true, such a particle may be described as a quantum of gravity.

What we can say with relative certainty is that there is not enough visible mass in the universe to hold it all together. The extra "stuff" we need to explain the motion of the galaxies is called "dark matter." We do not know what dark matter is made of, but it obviously cannot be emitting or absorbing light. Dark energy, on the other hand, is a kind of energy that exists in empty space and affects the overall curvature of space, as well as the expansion rate of the universe.[11] These effects have been observed, so there is little doubt that dark energy exists, but we don't know what it is. To be sure, theories have been postulated for both dark energy, the most prominent being weakly interacting massive particles (WIMPS) for dark matter, and something called vacuum energy for dark energy, but once again, this is just speculation at this point. The problem for physicists is that calculations of this vacuum energy are absurdly high, and physicists do not know how to solve this dilemma, also referred to as the cosmologic constant problem. Though dark energy and dark matter have not been detected directly, physicists still believe 95 percent of the universe is made up of it, and if that is the case, it would involve the most fine-tuning problem known to physics.

A Unifying Theory

As we have seen in this chapter, two major theories predominate how physicists think the universe works: special relativity and quantum mechanics. Both have some counterintuitive properties—in the case of quantum mechanics, even strange and bizarre properties—yet this, to date, seems to be how it all works.

Science is, by definition, provisional. We know what we know, but we do not know what we don't know! Richard Feynman said it much better: "Each piece or part of the whole of nature is always merely an approximation to the complete truth, or the complete truth so far as we know it. In fact, everything we know is only some kind of approximation, because we do not know all the laws as yet. Therefore, things must be learned only to be unlearned again, or more likely, to be corrected."[12]

At this time we do not have a unifying theory that explains everything, and we may never have one. All the great physicists of the past—Einstein, Planck, Bohr, Schrödinger, Dirac, and yes, even Hawking and Feynman—have gone to their graves never finding the supposed theory of everything.

What I find so amazing is how any branch of science can be so dogmatic when we know science is subject to change. Maybe it is because, as Upton Sinclair said, "It's hard to get people to understand something when their livelihood depends on not understanding it." Intelligent design, for example, is scoffed at and ridiculed and considered "supernatural" and "mystical," yet in many cases, it offers the best plausible explanations for what we see in our universe and world. Dembski has written, "Intellegent design matters because it reveals that nature radiates purpose." Purpose is designed in the universe for those who will open their eyes to it. Even Planck, who did not believe in a personal god, famously said, "All matter originates and exists only by virtue of a force which brings the particle of an atom to vibration and holds this most minute solar system of the atom together. We must assume behind this force the existence of a conscious and intelligent mind. This mind is the matrix of all matter."[13] I believe that mind is God. I end this chapter with the words of Colossians 1:16–17: "For by Him all things were created, both in the heavens and on earth, whether thrones or dominions or rulers or authorities—all things had been created through him and for him. He is before all things, and in him all things hold together." Amen!

Chapter
5

Chaos

"When physics started using mathematics on a large scale, the progress and understanding of the world became so rapid that it cannot be paralleled by the progress in any other field of human activity.
—George Coyne and Michael Hiller

"Somehow the wondrous promise of the earth is that there are things beautiful in it, things wondrous and alluring, and by virtue of your trade, you want to understand them."
—Mitchell Feigenbaum

BEFORE AN ULTIMATE, UNIFYING THEORY OF EVERYTHING CAN BE articulated, scientists will have to incorporate at least one other phenomenon, or possible law. Scientists are all about trying to find order in our universe, and from our previous discussion, it does seem that order is pervasive and allows us to predict how things work, such as relativity and quantum mechanics, as well as the laws of motion and the orbits of planets. But the world is not always predictable. There is a great deal of roughness and randomness seen in the physical universe and in the biological world. Such randomness has been called "chaos." Chaos theory is rather new to the table as a scientific theory, but an obvious phenomenon of randomness and unpredictability is that it is ubiquitous and has been part of our universe since its beginning.

When one thinks of the word *chaos*, it conjures up various ideas such as confusion, disarray, a total lack of organization, mayhem, bedlam, dishevelment, and for those of my generation, even the name of a secret organization in the TV series *Get Smart*. Weather, smoke, turbulence, erratic eye movements, cardiac arrhythmias, and even a dripping faucet are all part of the chaotic world and part of natural law. Such phenomena are hard for scientists to describe from a mathematical standpoint, and therefore, nonlinear equations are incorporated to do just that, though nonlinear equations are "unsolvable." For the most part, scientists try to avoid nonlinear equations, They, as mentioned, are difficult to solve, and they can't be added together, so they are frequently approximated by linear equations.

But it is this "linearization" that makes chaos theory and its phenomenon so interesting, counterintuitive, and unpredictable, but yet not random, either. Chaos theory thus teaches us to expect the unexpected. Edward Lorenz, the so-called father of chaos theory, put it this way: "Chaos is when the present determines the future, but the approximate present does not approximately determine the future."[1] It has been said that where chaos begins, classical science stops. Chaos, therefore, focuses on the deepest or hardest problems of the universe. Author James Gleick writes, "The physics described by Hawking could complete its mission without answering some of the most fundamental questions about nature. How does life begin? What is turbulence? Above all, in a universe ruled by entropy, drawing inexorably toward greater and greater disorder, how does order arise?"[2] Chaos theory was therefore developed to describe better this appearance of randomness in nature and seen in our universe.

Chaos theory is a bit hard to pin down, but in essence, it can be explained as an effort to make order out of disorder. Sometimes this is best explained through "pictures" or "drawings" derived from mathematical equations. In the early 1960s, Lorenz, an MIT meteorologist, attempted to accurately predict long-term weather patterns, and although he could predict accurately weather in the short term, in the long term, it became much more difficult to do because small protuberances can have a very long-range effect, a phenomenon known as the "butterfly effect." Many years before, in 1913, French mathematician Henri Poincaré described what became known as the "butterfly effect" this way: "It may happen that small differences in the initial conditions produce very great ones in the final phenomenon. A small error in the former will produce an enormous error and the latter prediction becomes impossible and we have the fortuitous phenomenon."[3]

Metaphorically, the butterfly effect has been described as a fluttering butterfly, flapping its wings in Texas, causing a tornado in Kansas. "Butterfly events" do, indeed, include weather, and they can have a "point of crisis" that magnifies small changes. It is because we cannot know all the initial conditions of a complex system in perfect detail that we cannot hope to predict the ultimate fate of a complex system. For example, "A tornado is a highly local phenomenon, and trifles of no great extent can determine its exact track," says Norbert Wiener, the late former professor of mathematics at MIT.[4]

This is a very key point in chaos theory. In his masterful work, *Chaos: Making a New Science*, Gleick alludes to an old folklore rhyme to demonstrate:

"For want of a nail, the shoe was lost;
"For want of a shoe, the horse was lost;
"For want of a horse, the rider was lost;
"For want of a rider, the battle was lost;
"For want of a battle, the kingdom was lost."[5]

For some inexplicable reason, I like to watch documentaries on airplane disasters. It turns out that most airplane disasters are either due to pilot error or mechanical failure or a combination of both. Recently, one episode I watched demonstrated a failure that was caused initially by a very trivial event—that is the replacing of a valve with a screw that was the wrong size for the job. This valve was located in the wing near the fuel lines, and as a result, a spark occurred, causing a hole in the fuel line in one of the wings. As a result, the fuel began emptying from the line, and the computer registered such, but the pilot mistook the computer reading as an error and failed to switch off the valve. The entire cache of fuel was lost. Though in a panic, the pilot was fortunately able to glide the plane to a nearby airport located on an island that was just near enough to avoid a huge catastrophe.

I use this as an example of a small, trivial event producing a catastrophic or chaotic event—and we are all aware of such phenomenon. I, for example, would not be surprised if COVID-19 began in the Wuhan virology lab by some trivial event, resulting in the deaths of millions around the global. Of course, we will never know the truth about that, will we?

Lorenz used a water wheel, a "geodynamo," to demonstrate the chaotic behavior of water and water vapor, and he plotted these numbers out on a graph. Then, with the help of an early computer, he generated a figure reminiscent of an owl's eyes or a butterfly, which would later be called the Lorenz Attractor. This, in turn, became an early emblem for chaos theory. An attractor is a pattern produced randomly. Attractors in a chaotic system are known as strange attractors. In Lorenz's figure, the system never intersects and never repeats itself, and Lorenz felt intuitively that this behavior applied to the real world.[6]

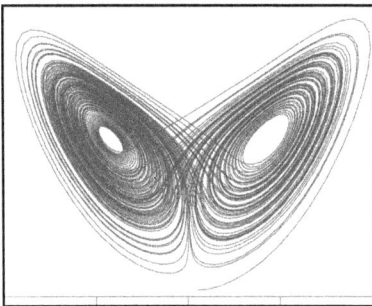

Lorenz Attractor

Within this figure, though, a pattern began to develop, and that is the essence of chaos theory: trying to make patterns, or order, out of chaotic systems. James Yorke, a mathematician, and an early chaos scientist, referring to chaos theory, said this: "The first message is that there is disorder. Physicists and mathematicians want to discover regularities. People say, 'What use is disorder?' But people must know about disorder if they are going to deal with it."[7]

Australian Robert May, a mathematically inclined biologist, began to study how single populations of animals behave over time. He found that with low parameters, populations were stable; with high parameters, populations oscillate; and with very high parameters, they become chaotic or unpredictable. He termed this phenomenon "periodic doubling," which could be represented schematically with doubling occurring until chaos ensues. What May discovered was that this disorder continued until a type of order resumed.

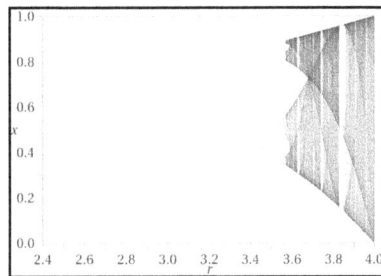

Periodic Doubling

Benoit Mandelbrot, while examining the price of cotton over time of all things, saw the same phenomenon. Deterministic chaos, as it came to be known, could also be seen by studying the records of measles epidemics in New York. Mandelbrot, born of Jewish Lithuanian parents in Warsaw and educated in France, began to see nature as rough, not round; scabrous, not smooth. But in this randomness seen in clouds, mountain ranges, and even lightning strikes, there was a certain amount of order. He believed complexity was not just an accident, and things like the coastline of Great Britain could be viewed as repetitive fractions. The amount of repetitiveness seemed to be measurable and consistent, and Mandelbrot gave this a term, *fractional dimension*, and a constant of 1.2618 could describe this dimension mathematically.[8] Thus, within chaos theory, even with this apparent randomness, there are also underlying patterns, interconnected feedback loops, repetition, self-similarities, fractals, and self-organization.

Helge von Koch, a Swedish mathematician, had already described a similar phenomenon, taking a triangle, then adding a new triangle, one-third the size, to each line of the previous triangle, then repeating this. You could do this "forever," but at various points, you begin to see what resembles a snowflake and then an irregular coastline—in essence, fractals. We see the same phenomenon in nature, such as in the circulatory system with the branching and re-branching of blood vessels until they get to a microscopic level, where arterioles and venules come together. As a result, no cell is ever more than three to four cells away from a blood vessel; this fractal system also applies to the digestive, respiratory, urinary, and nervous systems, as well. The question becomes, how did nature manage to pull this off? Understanding how such patterns were encoded and processed has become a major challenge in biology.[9]

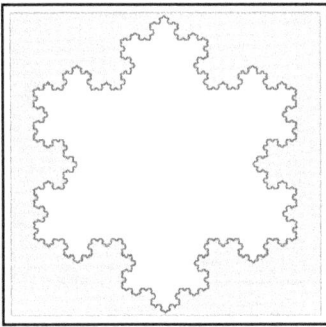

Koch Snowflake

Finally, Mitchell Feigenbaum brought universality to chaos. In working at the Los Alamos National Laboratory starting in 1974, the MIT-educated physicist began to understand how disorder can produce universality. He found that when a system was en route to periodic doubling and splitting into two cycles, then four, then eight, and so on, the splitting made a fascinating pattern—a pattern seen coincidentally by biologist Robert May. In calculating the exact parameter values that produced these splittings, Feigenbaum came up with the ratio of 4.669—that is the ratio of the convergence of periodic doubling converging into chaos, a sort of boundary metaphorically between smooth flow and turbulent flow.[10] With more refinement, this ratio was calculated to 4.6692016090. Feigenbaum had, in essence, created a universal theory, and he believed this theory expressed a natural law about systems at the point of transition between the orderly and the turbulent.[11] Thus, "Chaos explores the transition between order and disorder, which often occurs in surprising ways," writes Christian Oestreicher.[12]

Feigenbaum tried to publish his new theory, but he was rejected repeatedly by the editors of top academic journals because of its novelty. It would seem that science was not ready to accept a new discovery or theory that defied a well-defined discipline. "Science is biased by the customs of their disciplines or by the accidental paths of their own education," writes James Gleick.[13] With this new theory of universality, using Feigenbaum's constant, one could now predict certain biologic systems' behaviors that were measurable and reproducible. You could also help determine when the orderly was becoming disorderly or chaotic. Put simply by Feigenbaum, "It was a very happy and shocking discovery that there were structures in non-linear systems that are always the same if you look at them the right way."[14] With Feigenbaum's functions, scientists began translating them into the complex plane, and "fractals" and fascinating "families of shapes" emerged, a topic we will discuss in more detail when we take a deep dive into the Mandelbrot set.

Chaos is thus far from a complete theory, but it certainly seems to be a real phenomenon of our world and universe. Oestreicher calls it a theory "still in development."[15] Chaos theory helps delineate the noise of truly random events in the universe from the "orderly disorder" that pulls data into visible shapes. "Of all the possible pathways of disorder, nature favors just a few," summarizes Gleick.[16]

Chaos theory is now incorporated by professionals of many disciplines, including climatologists, economists, physicists, and biologists. It is even found in the discipline of medicine, by cardiologists who study cardiac arrhythmias—in particular, ventricular fibrillation—using chaos theory. The big question remains, why? Why does "nature" favor just a few of the possible pathways of disorder? They seem to be there when you look, but who or what put them there?

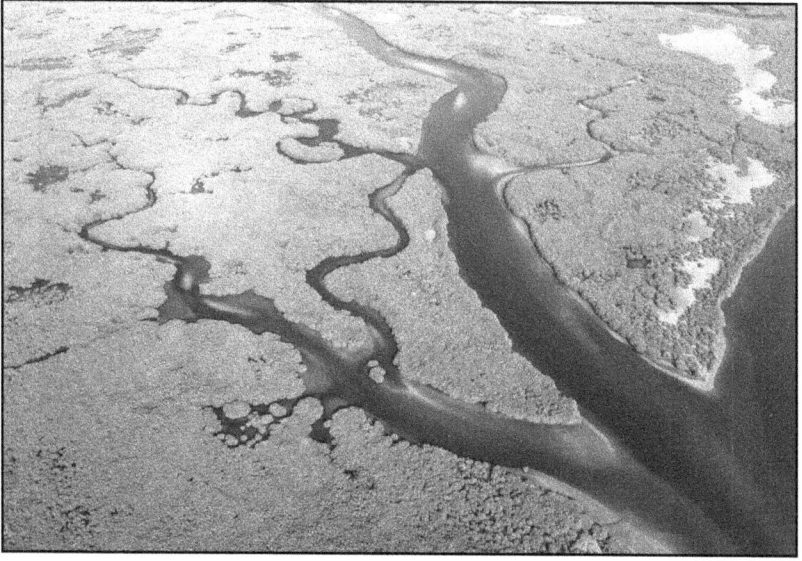

River Delta

Chapter
6

A GREEN WORLD: PHOTOSYNTHESIS AND ATP SYNTHASE

"The machinery of life displays functional coherence on a scale that's presently beyond human comprehension, to say nothing of human imitation."

Douglas Axe

"The conversion of sunlight into chemical energy certainly represents one of the most complex physiological achievements of life."

Günter Bechly

"AND THE GREEN GRASS GREW ALL AROUND, ALL AROUND, AND THE green grass grew all around." So goes the old Appalachian children's nursery rhyme. This poem celebrates life and nature and its symbiotic relationship with trees and birds. We live in a green world with green grass and trees growing abundantly throughout the inhabited planet. This is necessary, as mentioned in chapter 3, as plants produce oxygen essential for life, as well as food for metabolism. This relationship between plant life and animal life is nothing short of extraordinary.

Who doesn't enjoy the smell of green grass, especially in the springtime after a long dormant winter? I remember rolling in the cool green grass during the summertime and how pleasant that felt, and I remember the smell of cut grass during baseball season. Grass conjures up various feelings in us, reminding us of the newness of life and giving us a certain amount of comfort. Remember how the psalmist David begins Psalm 23: "The Lord is my shepherd; I shall not want. He makes me to lie down in green pastures; He leads me beside the still waters. He restores my soul."

Grass is mentioned many times in the Bible; it represents fertility, prosperity, comfort, and abundance, but it also is used to demonstrate the brevity of life. Again, the psalmist, in chapter 10, verse 15, writes, "As for man, his days are like grass; as a flower of the field, so he flourishes. For the wind passes over it and it is gone and its place remembers it no more." In this chapter, we are going to examine two molecules, one responsible for not only the color of grass but also plant life in general, and thus animal life, chlorophyll, and the other adenosine triphosphate synthase (ATP-synthase). Without these two molecules, we simply wouldn't exist, and explaining how they came about, naturalistically, is difficult to say the least.

Chlorophyll resides in the chloroplast of plants, which is an intracellular organelle found primarily on the leaves of grasses and trees. Chlorophyll is light-sensitive, and it reflects green light (hence, plants are green) and absorbs red and blue light. When stimulated by light and in the presence of carbon dioxide (CO_2) and water (H_2O), chlorophyll is able to synthesize carbohydrates (sugars), with the help of ATP for energy, and release oxygen (O_2) into the air. This constitutes photosynthesis, and though we have seen this formula already in chapter 3, I think it bears repeating here: $CO_2 + H_2O \rightarrow CH(\text{carbohydrates}) + O_2$.

The formula is very simple, but the execution is something quite different. It takes two exquisitely formulated molecules to accomplish this task: chlorophyll and ATP synthase. You can never get carbohydrates simply by putting water and carbon dioxide in a bag and exposing them to sunlight—or any other energy

Chloroplast

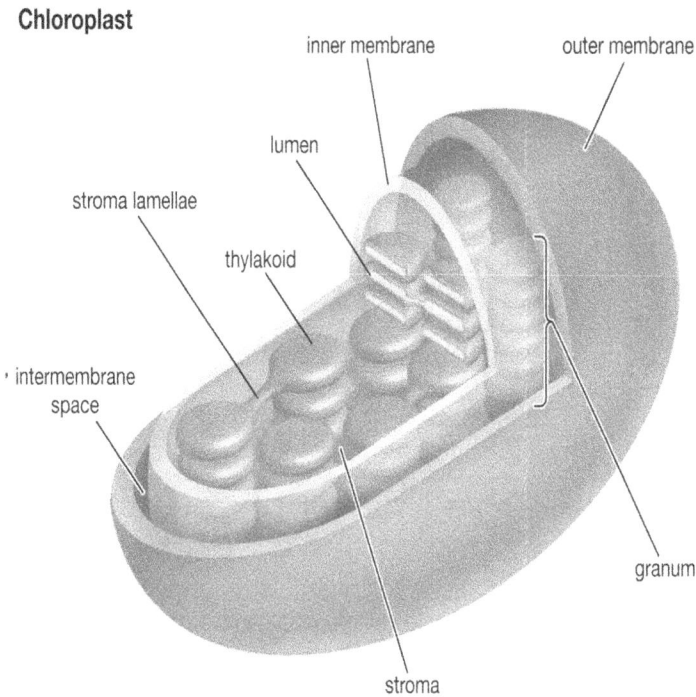

© Encyclopædia Britannica, Inc.

Chloroplast

source for that matter—not that it hasn't been tried with origin-of-life research ongoing. Currently, to make carbohydrates, you need chlorophyll.

Notice, too, that water is a key ingredient. Plants don't grow without water, as water is necessary for the chemical reaction to occur.

As I begin writing this chapter, I am in Navasota, Texas, during the summer of 2023, and here, as well as in other parts of South Texas, we are in a great drought, with no rain seen for fifty-plus days in a row and temperatures consistently running between 105° and 110° Fahrenheit. We have a small horse farm, and we need rain in the worst way, as my mother would say. Pastures are brown, the ground is cracked, the pond is dry, and it's just too hot! As a result, ranchers are resorting to hay to feed the livestock, which is an expensive proposition.

I say this to emphasize the importance of water, plus sunlight, for photosynthesis to occur through the chlorophyll molecule. Sunlight without water produces no growth. I think we take this remarkable conversion of sunlight to life for granted, even sometimes looking at it as a nuisance when mowing the grass and pulling weeds from the garden.

So, exactly how does it work? My goal is not to make biochemists of us all, but a basic—and I do mean *basic*—understanding will help us to appreciate the fine-tuning involved in photosynthesis. It would be impossible to overstate the importance of photosynthesis in the maintenance of life on earth.

Photosynthesis begins with light energizing the chlorophyll molecule. Chlorophyll is a complex molecule whose "job" is to synthesize carbohydrates, which, in turn, are used as energy or food for the plant. The molecular formula looks like this: $C55H72O5N4Mg$. Magnesium is central in its structure, with nitrogen containing porphyrin rings surrounding it, the point here being to demonstrate the complexity of the molecule. What produced this molecule? It certainly is not due to simple chemical reactions. Further, the chlorophyll molecule cannot do its job until it is complete. If any of the atoms in this molecule are missing, it will result in failure to accomplish its task. Evolution, however, demands randomness, chance, for molecules to form with no target function, and that is key. Michael Behe, in his iconic book, *Darwin's Black Box*, calls this phenomenon "irreducible complexity." We will address this again when we look at ATP synthase, which is an even more complex molecule than chlorophyll.

Chlorophyll Molecule

During photosynthesis, energy from visible sunlight (photons) are "captured" and absorbed by photosynthetic pigments in the chlorophyll. This activates electrons in the chlorophyll, raising it to a higher level. Electrons then escape from the chlorophyll, giving it a positive charge, a process known as oxidation. Now the oxidized chlorophyll draws electrons from the water (H_2O), oxidizing them and releasing free oxygen (O_2), as well as photons and electrons.

The energized electrons escape the chlorophyll, find their "way" to electron transport chains, and flow down in steps, releasing energy along the way and pumping protons across a membrane in the chloroplast (the thylakoid membrane) and into the lumen of the chloroplast. These then flow back, through the same membrane, producing energy to synthesize ATP by the enzyme ATP synthase. The ATP synthase "thus accepts one proton from the lumen space into the stroma space to create the energy it needs to synthesize ATP," writes physiologist Jasmine Nirody.[1] In this way, solar energy is converted into chemical energy.

We still have not created carbohydrates yet, and keep in mind, once again, this structure, the chloroplast, just like chlorophyll, must assemble—somehow randomly—before the process can even begin.

In a second electron transport chain, excited electrons flow along to produce protons pumped across the thylakoid membrane to produce more ATP and to generate a compound called NADPH. Now the ATP and the NADPH reduce carbon dioxide from the atmosphere, thus creating carbohydrates. The simplified formula looks like this: CO_2+ATP+NADPH→CH(carbohydrates)+ADP+NAPP. All of the above is occurring in two stages, the light dependent and the light independent (the Calvin cycle).

Simply put, "the energy captured from the light energizes the transfer of matter from water in the form of electrons and protons to carbon dioxide. These form reduced carbon compounds, carbohydrates, and release free oxygen (our O_2) as a byproduct—thus transducing light energy into chemical energy and stored in the reduced carbohydrates upon which we feed to obtain metabolic energies," writes Dr. Michael Denton in his book *Children of Light*.[2]

Dr. Denton, physician and biochemist, calls the chlorophyll molecule the most important light-harvesting pigment on earth. It makes us all "light eaters," and without it, we would not exist. It is the only mechanism on earth capable of oxidizing water and releasing oxygen, and the only mechanism for producing the vast quantities needed in our atmosphere for aerobic life.

Biochemist Douglas Axe summarizes photosynthesis this way: "More than any human invention, photosynthesis is an ingenious exploitation of the natural regularities of the universe, radically different from anything those regularities produce on their own. To grasp this, think of photosynthesis as the reverse of burning fuel, because that's what it amounts to."[3] This "boggles the mind," writes Axe.[4] To emphasize again, it is inconceivable to believe that this remarkable molecule, chlorophyll, could have come about by purely random, undirected, naturalistic means. For that matter, why would it? The total effects of photosynthesis on a global scale are immense, fixing three hundred trillion kilograms of CO_2 per year and liberating two trillion kilograms of oxygen per year.[5]

Douglas Axe

As we mentioned in chapter 3, the sun produces predominantly visible light, and it is visible light that is necessary for photosynthesis. Another illustration is warranted to show how vast the electromagnetic wave spectrum is. Per Dr. Denton, the wavelengths vary by an unimaginably large factor of 10 to the 25th power.[6] Visible light makes up only a very minuscule portion of the spectrum, and thus we are very fortunate. To imagine how large 10^{25} is, Dr. Denton represents it as a stack of playing cards reaching the Andromeda galaxy.[7] We on earth thus live in a "Goldilocks" region of the electromagnetic spectrum, with enough energy of the sun to raise electrons to a higher level, but not too much energy to squelch organic matter.

This Goldilocks effect also applies to the heat generated by the sun. It may seem we have a high range of temperatures on earth, between -20 Celsius to 120° Celsius, but this is really a very narrow range. The world could be both much hotter and much colder, but if it was, life would not exist as we know it. This narrow range of temperatures that comes from the sun results in a very small amount of ionizing radiation, as well as very little infrared or microwave regions, which helps life thrive.

As mentioned, water is essential for life, because it is essential for the photosynthetic reaction to take place, as you recall from our formula. The chemical reaction simply won't happen without H_2O. Much has been written about the properties of the water molecule and how it is fit for life, but for brevity's sake, I would simply say that water has just the right properties to facilitate life on earth. When scientists probe other planets, what are they always looking for? Water—because life is tied to water.

The hydraulic cycle, which is the fact that water exists in three forms, solid, liquid, and gas—its ability for erosion, its low viscosity, and the fact that water can travel through the root system of a plant to the leaf (as a result of water's high surface tension, its counterintuitive tensile strength, and its hydrogen-bonded network)—all are critical for life, and once again speaks to the fine-tuning we see in the universe.

ATP Synthase

The energy currency of life is a molecule known as adenosine triphosphate. All life is made up of cells, and cells need energy to function, whatever that function is, be it plant or animal life. The dephosphorylation of ATP to ADP creates this energy.

Dephosptorylation is the removal of phosphate group by hydrolysis. It is this simple chemical reaction that creates energy.

Animals, and humans, cannot just "eat" ATP to obtain this molecule and thus produce this energy. Animals must eat foodstuffs, such as carbohydrates, proteins, and fats, then digest them and eventually synthesize ATP from ADP; this occurs in the chloroplast of plants, but in the cells of animals, it takes place in the mitochondria by ATP synthase. "ATP synthase is one of the wonders of the molecular world," writes chemist David Goodsell in a periodical called *Molecule of the Month*.[8] Goodsell goes on to write of ATP synthase, "It is an enzyme, a molecular motor, an ion pump and another molecular motor all wrapped up in one amazing nanoscale machine!"[9] Some have even said this molecule looks much like a turbine.

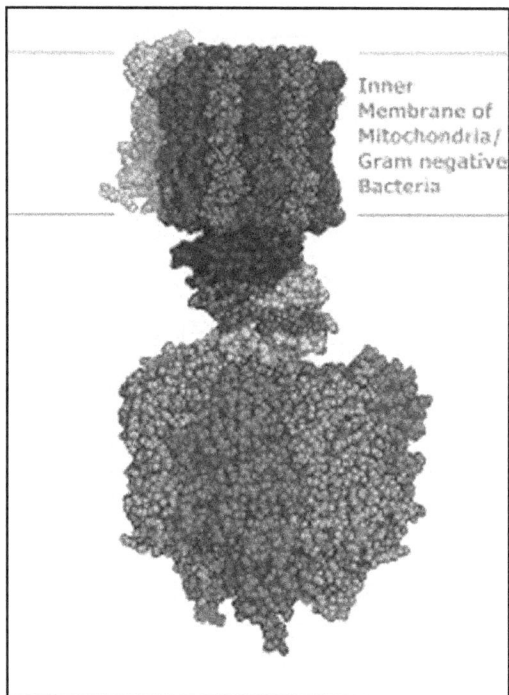

Inner Membrane of Mitochondria / Gram negative Bacteria

ATP Synthase

In my college physiology class, I remember reading Guyton's textbook on physiology about ATP and ATP synthase. That was in 1974, and at the time, how all this worked was "poorly understood," a term used frequently by Guyton. We know much more now, but there are many parts of the process that are still a mystery, and furthermore it is somewhat difficult for scientists to precisely define "energy." Probably the best we can say is that energy provides power for work, and energy is released by this dephosphorylation.

I don't want to get too "chemical" here, but ATP is produced in the Krebs Cycle, or the tricarboxylic acid cycle, the memorization of which is the bane of all medical students. In brief, when carbohydrates are ingested, they go through an oxidation process that produces chemicals, which then, in turn, go through reduction processes to produce ATP. Oxygen is required for this to occur, which, fortunately for us, the atmosphere has plenty of, thanks to . . . you guessed it, photosynthesis! The end product is carbon dioxide (CO_2), which, of course, is released into the atmosphere through the respiratory system by exhalation. The CO_2 thus released is now, of course, used to produce more carbohydrates by the plant life. This has been referred to ingeniously as the carbon cycle.

Clearly, this Krebs Cycle is much more detailed, but suffice it to say, this symbiotic relationship between plant life and animal life is difficult to ascribe to random, purely by chance, naturalistic processes.

To be clear, ATP does not get synthesized without ATP synthase. ATP synthase, as we have seen, is a nano-machine and very complex. How did ATP synthase come into existence by naturalistic mechanisms? It is a valid question to ask the naturalist. This machine, from an evolutionary point of view, must be manufactured one step at a time with no target, per the evolutionist. This boggles my mind!

This takes us back to "irreducible complexity." Behe described irreducible complexity as "a single system composed of several well-matched, interacting parts, that contribute to the basic function, wherein the removal of any one of the parts causes the system to effectively cease functioning."[10] Behe goes on to write, "Natural selection can only choose systems that are already working, then if a biological system cannot be produced gradually it would have to arise as an integrated unit, in one fell swoop, for natural selection to have anything to act on."[11]

Once ATP is dephosphorylated and releases energy, it turns back into ADP once again, to have the whole process repeated over and over and over, with ATP synthase able to work in both directions, both catalyzing ATP and creating it. Once again, it is impossible to overstate just how important this is. It is estimated we use between 100 to 150 mol-L of ATP daily, which means ATP is recycled 1,000 to 1,500 times per day. This means the body basically turns over its weight in ATP daily, as the ATP used for energy must be resynthesized.

If you have paid attention, you have noticed that it takes ATP to produce ATP, requiring ATP synthase. Let that sink in! It creates a chicken-and-egg scenario, now, doesn't it?

In summary, the ultimate source of energy on earth is the sun. Plants get energy from the sun, then produce carbohydrates through photosynthesis. Animals, including people, eat carbohydrates produced by plants to derive energy and to sustain life and growth. The grand processes are dependent on two remarkable molecules: chlorophyll and ATP synthase.

God had a purpose in mind during His creation—that is, to create human life and to sustain it. It is no coincidence, I believe, that light was created on the first day, with water already present, and after the atmosphere was created on the second day, plant life followed on the third. After plant life was established, animal life was created. Since that time, life has continued with this wonderful mechanism, photosynthesis, creating food essential for us all.

As a side note, it is interesting that evolution has a hard time saying which came first: animals or plants. They would admit that photosynthesis came later; therefore, it would seem life had to begin with animals.

Evolutionists say life first appeared as a simple cell and then developed into multicellular organisms. Then plants developed the ability for photosynthesis. Wow, just like that, they just developed this ability! Evolutionists also say that multi-celled organisms, such as animals and plants, only appeared when there was enough atmosphere in the oxygen. Where did the oxygen come from? The first such organisms were very simple—a loose network of cells held together by a protein-rich cellular matrix, the cell wall—but where did that come from? You see, a cell cannot exist without a cell wall. This above scenario, without the questions, was taken from the internet from Edward Draper, professor at the University College London. Sounds like a typical "just so" story frequently told by evolutionists with not a scintilla of evidence. Oh, well!

Chapter
7

THE CARDIOVASCULAR AND RESPIRATORY SYSTEMS

"The human body is an engineering wonder, and in no small part because of its many masterfully navigated engineering trade-offs, which afforded a remarkable resilience across a long span of life, a life that includes a rich variety of activities, the ability to thrive in a wide range of diverse environments and the capacity to reproduce itself.
—Steve Laufmann and Howard Glicksman

"We cannot find any organ or system of significance, in all of life, that could have been created gradually, one small step at a time."
—Steve Laufmann and Howard Glicksman

IN THE PRECEDING CHAPTER, WE SAW HOW FOOD IS PRODUCED using photosynthesis, and how energy is derived from this food in the form of ATP, which occurs inside of the mitochondria of the cell. We further showed how the Krebs Cycle, from which this ATP is made, is dependent on oxygen. The dilemma for an organism is how to get oxygen to the cell and how to get rid of the by-products of cellular respirations, primarily CO_2 and water. We certainly cannot absorb oxygen from the air.

It is key to remember that the cell is the primary mover of life. We all began first as one cell, then, quickly after fertilization, we became many cells, and by the time we were born, we were composed of trillions of cells. Each one of these cells depends on oxidative cellular respiration to get whatever job it has to do done, and there are many, many different types of cells, with unique functions necessary for our survival. To get oxygen to the cells depends on two very important "organs," or better yet, systems: those being the respiratory system and the cardiovascular system, and the primary organs of these systems being the lungs and the heart. Clearly, the lungs breathe in air through the mouth or nose into the large airways of the lungs, and this air obviously contains oxygen. Through an exchange with the lungs, and via an immense capillary system, oxygen is transported by way of red blood cells and hemoglobin to the cells throughout the body, where it is then taken in to accommodate cellular respiration, after which the primary by-product of CO_2 is taken from the cell back to the lungs, where it is released back into the atmosphere by expiration.

This is a very simplistic explanation, which is dependent on other systems to function properly, such as the brain, the musculoskeletal system, and various regulatory receptor cells that regulate how much oxygen is taken in and how much CO_2 is expelled, which is critical for life. Keep in mind, from an evolutionary standpoint, all this would have had to have occurred simultaneously and by pure chance without any direction. The respiratory system is of no use if oxygen cannot be transported to the cells, and the circulatory system is of little use if it has no oxygen to deliver to the cells. Yes, the circulatory system also takes other nutrients, absorbed from the gastrointestinal tract, to the cells, but this is of little benefit to the cell if oxygen is not there to start the process of cellular respiration.

From a macroscopic point of view, both systems very much resemble fractals. Why is this? The simple answer is that it cannot be any other way. In order for oxygen to cross into the circulatory system, it must be done at the cell membrane level, requiring the alveoli in the lungs to get smaller and smaller and smaller. This also applies where the capillaries exchange oxygen for CO_2; they have to get smaller and smaller and smaller, and all this takes on the form of fractals. I don't know about you, but I find this whole process absolutely amazing. Clearly, purpose seems to be present here. So, very briefly, let's examine each of these systems in more detail.

The Respiratory System

It is safe to say, I think, that there is no physiological process more vital for life than breathing. When we are at rest, we inhale and exhale some five hundred milliliters of air every five seconds, and in an average lifetime, we will take nearly five hundred million breaths.[1] We extract 250 milliliters of pure oxygen every minute, which, as we have seen, is then carried to the mitochondria inside our cells by the red blood cells via the circulatory system, where it will oxidize food, generating energy.

Michael Denton points out how fortunate it is that air is of low density, or it would be difficult for breathing to occur. Were air denser, our respiratory systems would not be able to do the work; it would simply be too strenuous for our systems to accomplish. It is also helpful that air has a low viscosity, some fifty times less than water. "A gas substantially more viscous than air would pose a serious challenge," writes Denton in his marvelous book, *The Miracle of Man*.[2]

We also see that air has a rapid diffusion rate, and this is critical, as well. For example, the diffusion rate of the gases in air is eighteen times faster than it would be in water.[3]

In essence, the properties for our breathing with lungs is ideal, thus fit "for both ventilation in the conductivity zone and for transport via diffusion in the respiratory zone, where ventilation is inefficient."[4]

As we have seen, air exchange occurs at the alveolar membrane in the lungs. These alveoli resemble little grapelike sacs microscopically, and they number some five hundred million in the average human body. The membrane where oxygen exchange occurs is extraordinarily thin, as you might imagine, some 0.2 microns across. This thinness is about the thickness of a soap bubble film.[5] This must be the case for oxygen to diffuse into the blood while CO_2 goes in the opposite direction.

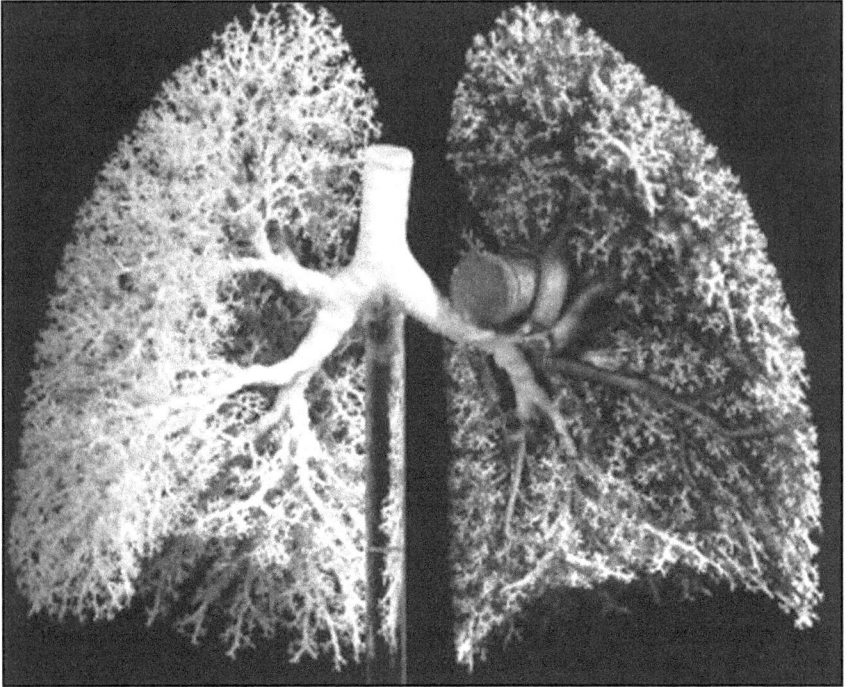

Lung

The total surface area of these five hundred million alveoli is 130 square feet, or about three-quarters of a tennis court. Denton calls this an extraordinary feat of bioengineering, and Ewald Weibel of the *Swiss Medical Weekly* writes that it is "impressive" and amounts to "bioengineering optimization."[6]

The "urge" to breathe, fortunately something we do not have to think about, comes from the medulla of the brainstem via the spinal cord. The sensors, which reside in the arterial system, detect levels of oxygen and carbon dioxide in the blood, and this information is then "sent" to the brainstem. Thus, respiration is controlled automatically without a conscious thought.

The actual work of breathing involves the musculoskeletal system by way of the diaphragm and the muscles of the rib cage. Thus, the brainstem will send messages to these muscles, causing us to breathe faster or slower, depending on the amount of O^2 needed or the amount of CO^2 to be rid of. Finally, inside the large airways of the lungs are smaller, fingerlike projections called cilia. Cilia are vitally important to help move secretions in and out of the lungs. Beating together in a wavelike fashion, these cilia, which are like very tiny hairs, move mucus, bacteria, and foreign materials out of the lungs., to be expelled by cough or sneeze.

Admittedly, this has been a very brief, superficial rendering of the respiratory system, but I believe it suffices in demonstrating how sophisticated and marvelous it is. Trying to explain how it came into existence by evolutionary processes is just "storytelling," as Steve Laufmann and Howard Glicksman put it in their book, *Your Designed Body*. As they say, "How would any unintentional evolutionary process build this system?"[7] Where did the parts for the control mechanisms come from? And how would any creature survive while waiting for these systems to come into being? No one can answer this so far by evolutionary, naturalistic means.

The Cardiovascular System

The heart is one of the earliest organs to form in the developing baby, beginning to take form in the third week after fertilization. It won't develop all four chambers until the tenth week, which is about when a Doppler can reliably detect a heartbeat. Unlike the lungs, the heart becomes functional early, as the baby needs nutrition for its other developing organs, nutrition supplied maternally via the placenta. by way of the umbilical cord. If an individual lives to be eighty years old, his or her heart will have beat about two billion times. The heart itself contains billions of muscle cells, specifically designed to resist fatigue and contract automatically, a feature for which you and I are surely most grateful!

The heart pumps blood to our cells through an amazing, complicated, beautifully arranged series of arteries, which ends in arterioles. The blood will be brought back to the heart by the venules and veins, to be oxygenated yet again and pumped back out to the cells, delivering 250 milliliters of oxygen each minute.

Of course, this all requires perfect timing, timing coordinated by the heart with its own intrinsic pacemaker, located in the right atrium called the sinoatrial node. The sinus node, as it is also called, sends electrical signals through a series of nerves that branch off to the left and right sides of the heart, telling it when to contract. Dr. Michael Denton calls this a "paragon" of bioengineering, "fine-tuned to satisfy the need to derive metabolic energy from oxidating to complex organisms like ourselves."[8]

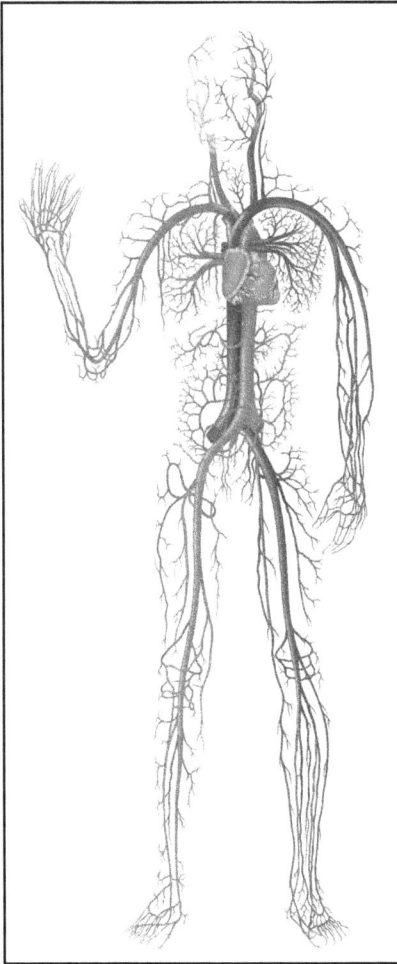

Circulatory System

The heart, as I am sure you know, is a muscle with four chambers—the right atrium and ventricle, and the left atrium and ventricle—separated individually by valves that allow forward flow but prevent backward flow. Blood from the superior and inferior vena cava enter the right atrium, where it is pumped into the right ventricle to then be pumped through the pulmonary valve into the pulmonary artery to the lungs. As we have seen, in the lungs, the blood rids itself of CO_2 via the small arterioles, then picks up a fresh

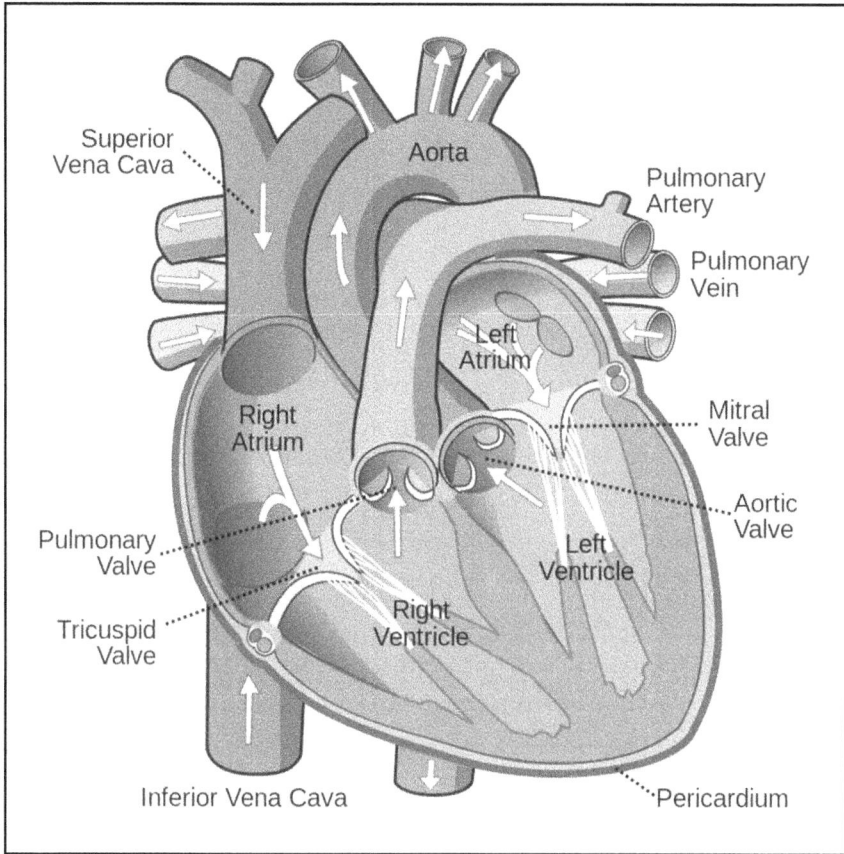

Heart

supply of oxygen. Blood from the lungs then is transported back to the heart through the pulmonary vein into the left atrium, where it is then pumped into the left ventricle. From the left ventricle, blood goes through the aortic valve to be pumped into the aorta and then to the systemic arteries. It is estimated that our bodies have some sixty thousand *miles* of blood vessels![9]

All this pumping takes a lot of energy—energy supplied to the heart through its own arterial system or blood supply, the coronary arteries. Blocking one of these arteries acutely causes a portion of the heart muscle to die, a process referred to as a myocardial infarction, or colloquially, a heart attack.

For blood to reach the organs of the body, blood pressure must be maintained through the muscles of the arteries themselves. Too high and a stroke or end-organ damage can occur. Too low and blood cannot make it to the organs where it is needed. If that organ happens to be the brain, the individual will experience syncope, which results in blacking out.

It is at the capillary level where the magic of diffusion occurs. The arteriole intermingles, if you will, with the venule, intermixed with cellular tissue, and oxygen is exchanged for CO_2, again, a by-product of cellular respiration.

Veins, unlike arteries, do not have muscular walls; therefore, they require contractions of the skeletal muscles to push blood back toward the heart. Inside the veins are parachute valves that do not allow blood to flow backward. If these valves become damaged, edema or swelling can result, most typically seen in the lower extremities, a condition referred to as venous insufficiency. Keep in mind, to be functional, the arteries and veins must be present together. Evolution necessitates they develop simultaneously, by chance which is problematic.

As can be imagined, all this requires significant feedback-and-control mechanisms, primarily all conducted through the autonomic nervous system. This system will tell the heart when to beat faster or slower and when to raise or lower blood pressure through sensors located throughout the body. All this "information" must be processed very quickly, and fortunately for us, signals from the automatic system travel at about one-third the speed of sound.[10]

Various chemicals and hormones are involved, as well, including acetylcholine, which tends to slow the heart rate, and epinephrine, which tends to speed it up. These chemicals, in coordination with the sinoatrial node, control cardiac output. These hormones dictate the shunting of blood to organs that are needed most, especially to muscles the flight or fight response.

To summarize, the heart is a pump that moves blood to and from all the organs and cells of our bodies. It has its own circulatory system and unidirectional valves to prevent backflow. It uses multiple control systems to direct flow where needed at the pressures required to do so. Finally, it is able to react to the body's changing needs for oxygen at a very rapid rate.

The cardiovascular system is a wonder; it is extraordinarily complex and exquisitely orchestrated to do its job. Humans have tried to replicate parts of it—including through the invention of the artificial heart—but this has not been very successful. To date, the longest living recipient of an artificial heart transplant was Peter Houghton of the United Kingdom, who lived seven years with it, though his quality of life was not robust.

Hemoglobin

To carry oxygen to the fetal cells during development after fertilization, blood must be produced. Blood is made up primarily of red blood cells, which contain molecules of hemoglobin, designed to transport oxygen. It is estimated there are twenty trillion red blood cells in our bodies at any one time, and they last about four months; we lose two hundred billion red blood cells each day. Red blood cell production is controlled by the kidneys, through a hormone known as erythropoietin (EPO). EPO travels to the bone marrow, where stem cells are located and where red cell production occurs.

One liter of blood holds about three milliliters of oxygen. Oxygen, then, is transported by the hemoglobin molecule, which contains four atoms of iron. It is onto the iron atoms that oxygen "sticks." Without iron, the hemoglobin molecule is useless, and iron-deficiency anemia occurs when the organism either cannot or does not ingest enough iron or loses iron somehow. Too much free iron in the system is toxic, so fortunately, the liver manufactures a transport protein called transferrin to get iron from the gastrointestinal tract to the bone marrow, where blood is made. All this, once again, demonstrates a feedback mechanism that is controlled mostly by the liver. This control "is yet another exquisite system for staying in yet another crucial Goldilocks zone," says Steve Laufmann and Howard Glicksman.

One more thing about the red blood cells should be noted—that is their size, shape, and malleability. The red blood cell is relatively small. It is the only cell line in our bodies without a nucleus, losing it once it gets into the circulatory system. The red blood cell can also bend and change shape very easily, a critical characteristic at the capillary level that allows the cell to get into the very small spaces needed for diffusion to take place, and this points to a highly specialized design and purpose.

Cytochrome C

Finally, I would be remiss if I did not discuss at least one more molecule needed for cellular respiration, that being cytochrome C oxidase. It performs the last critical step in oxidative metabolism, and Earl Frieden identifies it as probably the most vital enzyme to all aerobic life.[11]

This enzyme, which requires iron, zinc, copper, and magnesium, binds oxygen, reduces it with electrons, and converts reduced oxygen to water with the help of other cytochromes. This is absolutely vital for life, and it is found in all aerobic—that is, oxygen-requiring—organisms, including you and me.

My purpose in these last two chapters has been to demonstrate just how remarkable our bodies are, and how much "apparent" design it contains. We could discuss so much more, including our vision, hearing, the central nervous system, the musculoskeletal system, the renal system, the endocrine system, the gastrointestinal system, and so on, but for our purposes we will leave it here.[12]

For me, it is inconceivable how all this could have come about by random, blind chance, which is what evolution requires us to believe. As Denton has said, there is "indeed a profound fitness in nature for beings of our biology—that we do indeed occupy a central teleological (purpose) in the natural order."[13]

I would like to end this discussion with a quote from Abour H. Cherif, found in Denton's book, *The Miracle of Man*: "To keep us alive and living, the human body performs millions of complex functions throughout our lifetime. For example, in just 60 seconds, the human body takes 15 breaths, its heart beats 70 times, its tear ducts moisten the eyes 25 times, its brain conducts six million chemical reactions, its bone marrow produces 180 million blood cells, its skin sheds 10,000 particles of skin, and about 300 million of its cells die and/or are replaced. Furthermore, the human body manages to 'extract the complex resources needed to survive, despite sharply varying conditions, while at the same time, filtering out a multiplicity of toxins.' . . . The human body is a remarkable biological machine that is supported and maintained by well-structured and interdependent body systems and their unique organs. . . . It has about 100 trillion cells, 60 miles of blood vessels, a 3-pound brain with 50 to 100 billion nerve cells and amazing thinking capacity, and 2.5 billion heartbeats in a lifetime of 75 years, to name a few of its unique characteristics."[14]

There is a reason this has the appearance of design and purpose—and that is because there is!

Chapter
8

ADAPTATION, INSTINCT, AND JUST-SO STORIES

"To make even the simplest creature, the master-designer must have intended for life to exist, planned the deepest foundations of the universe to make this possible, and acted to make it so.
—Steve Laufmann and Howard Glicksman

"Despite the excited and optimistic claims that have been made by some paleontologists, no fossil hominid species can be established as our direct ancestor."
—Richard Lewontin

Adaptation is a universal characteristic of life. By *adaptation*, I mean change or evolution in order to survive. We see this in the simplest of organisms, such as bacteria, to the most complex, including even human beings. Adaptation is not a conscious effort, nor does it occur in just one generation. As a crude example, a black bear migrating to the north does not consciously decide to change into a white bear in order to blend in with the surroundings for the better ability to catch prey for food. We all agree adaptations such as that would take some time to occur. In smaller animals, that time can be shortened, such as in bacteria, which adapt much faster than mammals. Bacteria can become immune or resistant to antibiotics very quickly, primarily because of their ability to reproduce rapidly and in large numbers.

The obvious question is, why would an organism or animal "wish to adapt"? This is where natural selection, or survival of the fittest, comes in. Animals have no direct will to propagate the species, but natural selection is the process by which this happens. In our crude example, if a rarely born white bear is able to survive longer in the Arctic, more and more white bears will survive and be able to pass along their genetic material until there are virtually no black bears left to be found. Once again, this crude example of adaptation is not the result of a conscious effort by the bear; it happens naturally, though nature does not really "select" anything. Sometimes this adaptation is aided by mutations. A mutation is a change in the genetic makeup of the organism. In other words, there is a change at the chromosomal level. If that change results in some benefit to the organism—which, by the way, it almost always never does—that change will be passed along to subsequent progeny.

What I have just described is basically Darwin's explanation for how evolution works, found in his monumental work, *On the Origin of Species*, except Darwin knew nothing about genetics or chromosomes, as his book was published in 1859, almost one hundred years before James Watson and Francis Crick would discover the structure of DNA. Very shortly after its discovery in 1953, Crick realized the significance in the structure and proposed what he called the "Sequence Hypothesis," that is that genetic code for producing proteins is found in the DNA itself, based upon the arrangements of the nucleic bases, adenine, thymine, guanine, and cytosine. Neo-Darwinists later extrapolated from this that a random mutation, or change, in the DNA sequence could explain how evolution works, and if enough changes occurred, new species could develop.

Charles Darwin

On the surface, this may seem plausible, but it has a major problem. For a change to occur that produces a new species or kind, new information must happen that can be handed down to the next generation. The problem with Neo-Darwinism is that mutations invariably result in *less* information, not *new* information. Michael Behe, in his extraordinary book, *Darwin Devolves*, shows that the best way for an organism to adapt is to break something—that is, to break some portion of the DNA—and this actually produces less information, not more. This point is extremely important. Behe refers to this as the "first rule of adaptive evolution, that is break or blunt any functional gene whose loss would increase the number of the species' organism."[1]

Natural selection by random mutation thus becomes "devolutionary," or as Behe writes, "fiercely devolutionary."[2] "Strangely, in the space of a century and a half, Darwinism has gone from the chief candidate for the explanation of life to a known threat for life's long-term integrity," says Behe.[3]

This devolution is self-limiting, and it prevents changes at the level of families or above. Kinds, in other words, do not change into other kinds, and this is abundantly clear when one examines the fossil record, where no transitional forms—that is transitions from one kind to another—are to be found. They are just not there. So, no matter how much time is available, there is no evidence that kinds can change into other kinds, and it just is not going to happen.

"Purposeful design extends very deeply into life," writes Behe.[4] Darwin's theory, on the other hand, requires random chance and relies on the presumption that repeated rounds of random variation and natural selection can build elegant, integrative biological systems, thus changing species. In fact, at best, Darwin's theory is restricted to modifying a few preexisting features of an organism, but it cannot result in dramatic change. "No serious evidence is ever presented that selection acting on random variation can, say, convert lungs into swine bladders or produce feathers (or pork bellies), let alone such sophisticated systems," says Behe.[5]

Darwin's Galapagos finches are often cited as evidence for evolution. In actuality, Darwin said nothing of the finches found at Galapagos Island in his book *On the Origin of Species*, but others would raise this bird to an iconic level, citing how the finches on various islands in the Galapagos developed characteristics, such as changes in their beaks, that would allow them to survive better, depending on what insects were available for food on the various islands. But it is important to understand that chromosomal studies show no differences in the Galapagos finches.[6] Natural selection in this instance clearly did not result in a new kind—the finches always remained finches.

Notice, I am not arguing that minor variations in DNA cannot be beneficial or helpful, but they are severely limited in scope. For significant change to occur to produce another kind, additional information is necessary, and that is beyond the ability of a mindless process to perpetuate it.

One group of animals Darwin did speak of in *Origins* was domestic animals, such as cats and dogs. Through selective breeding, all types of dogs have been produced from the original canine kind. You have very short or very large dogs, very hairy or not-so-hairy dogs, slow dogs, fast dogs, white dogs, black dogs, red dogs, gray dogs—all kinds of dogs exist. We now know these changes, through mutations, result in loss of information, thus damaging the species or kind. Most domestic dogs, for example, would not last long in the wild; they are damaged goods.

Behe writes, "The effects of a mind can be recognized by the purposeful arrangement of parts, even when the possessor of the mind that arranged them is nowhere to be found."[7] Design is evident to anybody who looks. But, of course, materialists such as Richard Dawkins would say it is just an illusion of design we are seeing.

God is the only intelligence capable of creating life. Mankind never has created life, and, in my opinion, never will be able to, from scratch, in spite of untold efforts that have been and continue to be tried. James Tour, renowned chemist from Rice University, speaking on origin-of-life experiments, says that such experiments have never come close to producing anything remotely like life.[8] Dr. Tour, probably the world's greatest nano-scientist and synthetic chemist and someone who as much as anyone knows how to create molecules, has said, "We not only have not drawn closer to creating life, we have actually moved further away."[9] Dr. Tour explains the problem: Even if somehow molecules could come together, randomly, to form a simple carbohydrate (which so far has not happened in origin of life research), they have no capacity to "learn." Says Tour, "Say it took 400 million years to get a certain point in synthesis, but now you have to go back and make more. But how do you go back and make more? Nature never kept a laboratory notebook. So even if it could make more, it doesn't know how to, so it's got to start all over again. But it doesn't know how to. It doesn't know why to start over again because it doesn't know what it's going toward."[10] And keep this in mind: Tour was just talking about a simple carbohydrate. Evolution requires thousands of other molecules, such as proteins, to randomly assemble; thus the problem is exacerbated exponentially. Simply put, there, as of yet, has not been an experiment devised that can show proteins can assemble randomly to produce anything remotely resembling life.

This brings us to a couple of tactics used by evolutionists against the design argument, tactics that are fallacious in nature. One is commonly referred to as the bait-and-switch argument, and the other is the strawman fallacy.

The bait-and-switch argument is used very frequently, and it confuses *microevolution*, a term many evolutionists despise, with *macroevolution*. *Microevolution* is adaptation, and no one denies this takes place. This is primarily what Darwin showed in his studies of the Galapagos. *Macroevolution* is change from one kind to another kind, for which there is precious little, if any, evidence. Origin of life, or so-called molecules-to-man evolution, is evolution on a grand scale, for which there is zero evidence, yet it prevails among materialists, as it is really all they have. Evolutionists will lump all these together and thus claim those of the design argument do not believe in any form of evolution, which, of course, is a fallacy.

Very similar to the bait-and-switch is the strawman fallacy. This fallacy involves representing an opponent's position and proceeding to refute the misrepresentation rather than what the opponent really claims. You might say the bait-and-switch is a specific type of the strawman argument, but the strawman fallacy is often used in misrepresenting those with the design argument, especially those of the intelligent design community as a whole.

Another argument the evolutionists and materialists will use is directed at the designer Himself. It goes something like this: If I were designing an animal, I would not have designed it just that way. It is a very presumptive argument and makes erroneous assumptions, primarily of which no one in the design community argues that the design of each animal is perfect, so we are back to the strawman. But also it is an arrogant assumption that all facets of design are entirely understood because they are not. Scientist are learning more and more about design and function as time progresses so what may seem a poor design in fact isn't, though, most importantly, most of the so-called design flaws are no such things!

The classic so-called design flaw in humans is the design of the oropharynx and the trachea (windpipe) and the esophagus. Evolutionists tell us this design puts humans at undue risk for choking, and if there were a God, He would not have designed our bodies this way.

Eating requires food to go from the mouth to the back of the pharynx, or throat, then down the esophagus, which lies just behind the trachea. To prevent choking, the epiglottis must close to keep food from entering the windpipe or trachea. Abby Hafer, in her book, *The Not-So-Intelligent Designer: Why Evolution Explains the Human Body and Intelligent Design Does Not*, writes, "A better design system would keep the tubes for air and food separate to avoid unnecessary fatalities."[11]

In rebuttal, let's first understand that swallowing is an automatic process that every human being in the world does thousands of times a day, and mostly subconsciously, without incident. Choking is, in reality, a rare occurrence. As Laufmann and Glicksmann point out, three separate actions protect the airway while we are swallowing. First, muscles close to the larynx contract, then other muscles move the larynx up and forward and hide it under the tongue, and finally,

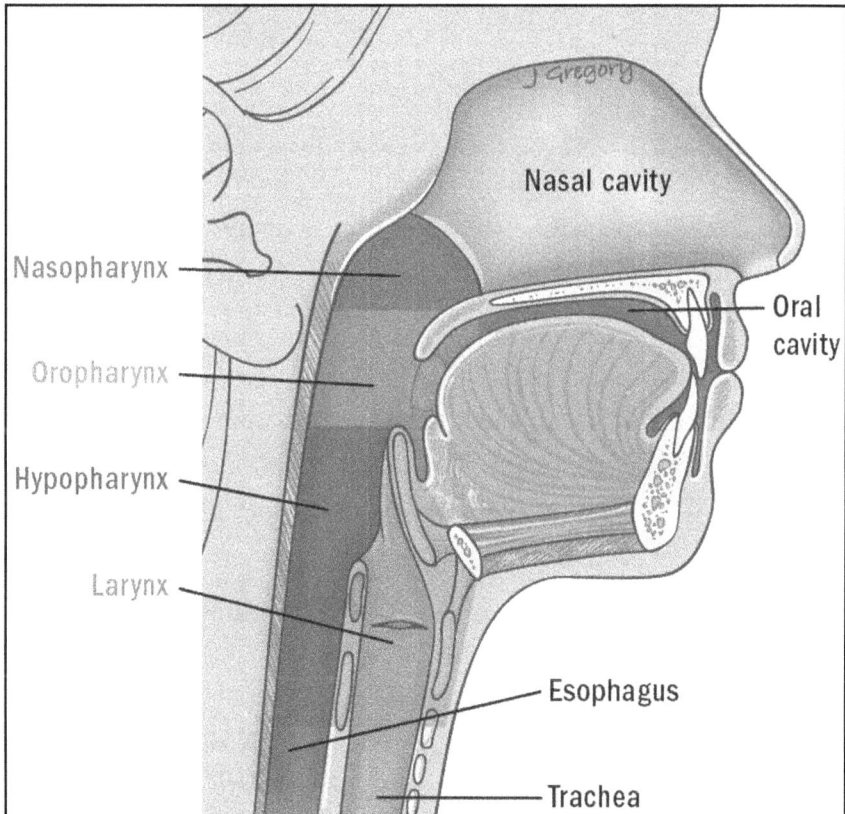

Oropharynx

this action, combined with other muscles, actively opens the upper esophagus to allow food to enter. "The timing and coordination are remarkable," say Laufmann and Glicksmann, "and demonstrates exquisite design."[12] Thus, the pharynx lets us breathe and eat, as well as speak. The question not answered by critics is, how would you design this system? As we have seen in the previous chapter, the body requires vast amounts of oxygen, and this system affords that. A change anatomically would require a complete reconstruction of the head and neck, as well as the lungs and stomach, and who's to say which system would be better? Yes, choking is a risk. Nonetheless, this system is well-designed to prevent such an event.

Many, if not most, episodes of choking are the result of degradation of the system by disease or injury. Strokes, Parkinson's disease, dementia, and multiple sclerosis are just a few disease processes that increase the risk of choking. Of course, sometimes choking occurs when a person tries to swallow something that is too big or doesn't chew their food sufficiently. Other times, people, especially children, put things in their mouths that they shouldn't. Finally, drugs, especially alcohol and illicit drugs, put a person at risk for both choking and aspiration, due to their effects on the nervous system.

There is another issue, too, and that is the evolutionists' assumption that if the airway and esophagus were separated, more choking would not happen—but this is an erroneous conclusion. No matter where the airway is placed, blockage could occur, and therefore choking could always happen.

Nathan Lents, an evolutionist, writes, "The human throat is simply too complex for a random mutation—the basic mechanism of evolution—to undo its fundamental details."[13] But wait, is he telling us that mutations produced this so-called defect but cannot undo it? Let us point out, once again, that humans thrive with this so-called defect! These arguments amount to no more than legal rubbish.[14] Engineers know there are always going to be trade-offs with design, and this is the case with the swallowing mechanism. It does not in any way negate the design argument. Once again, Laufmann and Glicksmann write, "The human pharynx is more accurately viewed as a clever, elegant solution to a complicated set of competing design objectives, with justifiable choices requiring trade-offs, within rigid constraints."[15]

We could discuss other so-called flawed designs in the human body, but they all become "question begging" and circular. They assume a premise and then set out to prove it, and for the evolutionist faithful, this may sound good, but it's really no more than the just-so stories they love telling.

Instinct

It has been over sixty-five years, but the memory of the event is still very clear, almost like a video running in my mind. I was four or five years old at the time and still riding a tricycle, not yet possessing the abilities to ride a bike. My older brother and a friend of his began to ride their bicycles around the block, late in the afternoon, with darkness approaching. I, like a little puppy dog, decided to follow them on my tricycle, but try as I might, I could not keep up. Before long, it was totally dark, except for the streetlights, and I was lost. Even now, I remember the sense of abandonment and anxiety this situation produced. I could simply not figure out how to get back home.

At that point, some kind neighbor found me in the street, asked me my name, and eventually called the police. The police came and were able to call my parents, who showed up shortly thereafter, none too pleased with either me or my brother. They were embarrassed, as was I, and this experience is etched indelibly on my consciousness. What is really sad is that I was only a few blocks from home!

Now, I begin this section with this story to point out that if I were a homing pigeon, this would have not happened. Pigeons have an innate ability to find their way home, and it is not a learned behavior; they are born with it. They can find their way home back to the roost from extremely long distances away, and in very bad weather conditions. This attribute of pigeons has been used for centuries for communication purposes, and it has even been used in wartimes in the past, and not so far back. The question is, where do pigeons get this unique ability? As we have said, this behavior is not learned, and it is instinctive, or innate, within the neurosensory apparatus of the pigeon.

As you might expect, explaining instinct by an evolutionary model is at best difficult. Research about instinctive behavior, also referred as complexed program behavior to avoid design implications, is vast, and thousands of papers are published regarding this. Birds, turtles, ants, termites, bees, moths, and many more animals have been and continue to be studied, and we know a lot more about these innate behaviors than we did, but what we know little about, from an evolutionary biology point of view, is how these behaviors came to be.

What I want to make very clear is that I am not falling back on a God-of-the-Gaps explanation. You do not prove there is a god by simply pleading ignorance. In other words, just because we cannot explain all the behaviors of instinctive animals does not prove they were necessarily designed by God. We have come a long way in discovering how certain innate phenomena function, and no doubt we will learn even more. But once again, it is not how they work, but how they got that way to begin with, and this does have design connotations because of the explanation that fits the evidence, or inference, to the best explanation.

Unlike the Galapagos finches, Darwin devoted a full chapter to instinct in *On the Origin of Species*. Darwin certainly offered no evolutionary mechanism for instincts, but he nonetheless believed instincts could occur over a large period of time, undirected and randomly by natural selection or survival of the fittest. Note this passage from his book: "No complex instinct can possibly be produced through natural selection, except by the slow and gradual accumulation of numerous, slight, yet profitable, variations."[16]

Before proceeding further, we need to define *instinct*. John Alcock has defined *instinct* as "a behavior that appears in fully functional form the first time it is performed, even though the animal may have had no previous experience with the cues that elicit the behavior."[17] *Innate behavior*, which I will use interchangeably with *instinctive behavior*, is defined by James and Carol Gould as inborn natural circuits responsible for "data-processing, decision-making, and orchestrating responses in the absence of previous experience," quoted in Eric Cassell's exquisitely researched book, *Animal Algorithms; Evolution and the Mysterious Origin of Ingenious Instincts*. Cassell notes that animal behavior scientists, and especially animal behavioral psychologists, reject some of the implications of instinctive behavior, and as mentioned, prefer the term *complex program behavior*, thereby avoiding any bias associated with those of the design persuasion, or teleologists, which implies purpose.

But a rose by any other name is still a rose, so I will use the less cumbersome word, *instinct*. Instinct does, in fact, describe complex behavior that is purposeful and programmed, meaning unlearned. It is also contingent, meaning necessary, and it is heritable, that is, able to be passed on to subsequent generations.

Knowledge of instinctive behavior goes back millennia and is even written about in the Bible: "Go to the ant you sluggard," writes the author of Proverbs 6:6. "Consider her ways and be wise, which, having no captain, overseer or ruler, provides her supplies in the summer, and gathers her food in the harvest." Is this not speaking of instinctive behavior?

Aristotle, in the fourth century BC, studied animal behavior in his book *Movement of Animals* and wrote, "We must take for granted principles of this universal character which appear in all nature's work. Of these is that nature creates nothing without purpose."

As noted before, Darwin was keenly aware and even awed by certain instinctive animal behavior, but keep in mind, Darwin also believed animals could inherit learned behavior, a belief held by his predecessor, Jean-Baptiste Lamarck. For example, if I perfected my golf swing (a work still in progress) before their birth, my sons or daughters would be born with an inherited ability to hit a golf ball perfectly. Today we know such nonsense is not true, yet in Darwin's time, this notion was accepted. As we have said, instincts are not learned, and study after study with naïve animals proves this. To be fair, Darwin would not extend this to all "long-continued and compulsory habits," especially those found in domestic animals.[18] Darwin did his own research, observing the instincts of bees and other animals, and he was struck by how magnificent it all was, but he "saw no difficulty, under changing conditions of life, in natural selection accumulating slight modifications of instinct to any extent, in any useful directions. In some cases, habit or use and disuse have probably come into play. I do not pretend that the facts given (in this chapter) strengthen in any degree my theory; but none of the cases of difficulty to the best of my judgment annihilate it."[19]

I would like to look at just a few examples of instinctive behavior and see what fits the evidence best: evolution or intelligent design. Einstein once wrote, "The most incomprehensible thing about the universe is that it is comprehensible."[20] After researching this subject, I can almost say the same thing about instinct—that what makes it so fascinating is, at least to some extent, its comprehensibility!

Take, for example, migrating birds. "There are feats of migration in the animal kingdom so awe-inspiring and mysterious that researchers have yet to unveil all their secrets, much less explain how these abilities evolved in the first place," writes Eric Cassell in his chapter, "Navigation and Migration." Marcos Eberlin, in his book, *Foresight*, writes, "Migrating birds have out-of-this-world capabilities."[21] They use methods for navigation similar to ones humans had to invent, like the global positioning systems we use today, as we have no innate sense of direction.

There are many migrating birds, with the Arctic tern completing the longest migration. Over several months, the terns begin their journey in the northern Arctic and travel all the way to the South Pole, spend the summer there, then fly back, a round-trip journey of twenty-five thousand to thirty thousand miles.[22] As it turns out, the Arctic tern as well as other migrating birds, such as the common swift (*Apus apus*), use the earth's magnetic field to navigate.

Arctic tern

How is this done? First, we know they have magnetic sensors in the retina, nose, beaks, and inner ear. Though the exact mechanism is still poorly understood, two primary candidates for these sensors are magnetite, a highly magnetic oxide mineral (Fe_3O_4), and cryptochrome, a photoreceptor protein also found in many plants and animals. Magnetite-based sensors somehow detect the magnetic field and "extract relevant information."[23] Cryptochrome, designated Cry4, when energized by light, secretes an electron from one of its electron pairs, forming a radical pair. A radical pair thus is formed "when it has two unpaired electrons that are connected by what is known as quantum entanglement," a phenomenon discussed earlier in this book.[24] As we have noted, then, this "strange" behavior involves the actions of one particle affecting the actions of another particle, such as position, spin, etc., instantaneously, no matter how far away they are from each other. Theoretically, at least, such entangled pairs could produce a picture in the bird's eye so they could see magnetic fields and navigate. Researchers have shown this entanglement lasts 100 microseconds, which exceeds any comparable man-made molecular system.

"The question is this, how can a living system have evolved to protect a quantum state, as well as—no, better—than we can do in the lab with these exotic molecules?" writes physicist Simon Benjamin.[25] It seems implausible, doesn't it, to believe a bird can navigate through the earth's magnetic fields using radical pairs and quantum entanglement, and such process has come about by random chance through some evolutionary processes? To have any functionality, this system would have needed to have been implemented all at once.

Once the information concerning the magnetic field reaches the brain of a bird, that information then must be processed. Pigeons, for example, can detect direction, intensity, and polarity of magnetic fields.[26] The neurons, then, respond to the magnetic vectors and help the bird navigate to its destiny.

Some birds also use the sun as a compass to aid their navigation. This is an extremely complex process, as the sun is constantly moving relative to the earth. By determining the angle between due north and the sun's vector on the horizontal plane, an angle known as the azimuth angle, the birds are able to navigate. Other tools of navigation include polarized light compasses and celestial navigation compasses; these require complex geometry, yet even birds and ants use these techniques.

Regardless of which navigational tool is used, birds have somehow developed programmed algorithms to compute their routes. The origin of these algorithms is the issue, isn't it? Although some learning does occur and pigeons do improve their ability to navigate with experience, most of their behavior is clearly innate, as shown by juvenile, naïve, birds.[27]

Interestingly, pigeons, who fly mostly during the day using the sun compass, have the ability to switch to a magnetic compass to navigate on cloudy days. There are many examples of outstanding feats performed by migrating birds that could be cited, but I like this quote from Cassell's book from Kenneth Able: "We still cannot explain in a detailed, mechanistic way how birds do what we know with certainty that they do; return with incredible precision of timing to pin-point locations on the earth after traveling thousands of miles in the interim."[28] It remains "a riddle wrapped in a mystery inside an enigma."[29]

Ants

Let's now go to the ant. Ants are social insects that exhibit many instinctive behaviors associated with social group lifestyles, including agriculture, division of labor, caste systems, consensus building, symbolic language, and even territorial wars.[30] Eusocial species are those, usually with a single female, or caste females, who are productive, while others care for the young, gather food, and provide protection. This, per insect social researcher Karen Kapheim, is "one of the most complex social behaviors known to animals."[31] Keep in mind, ants have a very, very small brain, so all these traits must be innate.

On our farm in Texas, we have several species of ants, including fire ants and leafcutter ants. The fire ants are a great annoyance, but the leafcutter ants exhibit very interesting behavior. They can be seen going two directions, some carrying bits of leaves one way and others going the opposite direction to gather more leaves. In referring to this species of ants, of the genus *Atta*, Edward O. Wilson and his colleague, Bert Hölldobler, pioneers in instinctive social behavior, write, "If a congress of naturalists were to gather to choose the seven wonders of the animal world, they would be compelled to include the bizarre and mighty civilizations of the Attine leafcutters."[32] These ants farm and fertilize a fungus for food, and they cut leaves from trees to provide the fungus with mulch. They must cut the leaves to a size suitable for them to carry, which they do. Frequently, they work in tandem to cut twigs, like two people sawing a log. The ants will follow tracks back to their nests, like I have seen on our farm, and these tracks can go a long way, as much as 150 meters or more. Sometimes the transfer can occur like a bucket brigade, passing leaves from one ant to another. During this endeavor, they prepare the leaves by stripping away the outer waxy layer.

The *Atta* colonies usually have only one queen, with up to several million workers. By estimates, the ants can harvest thousands of pounds of plants per year and up to fifty thousand square feet of leaf area.[33] They are choosy about their leaves and selective about their fungus. The ants also produce growth hormones and even secrete antibiotics to depress competing fungi and microorganisms.[34] Hölldobler and Wilson refer to the ants as a superorganism, with its symbiotic relationship with the fungi, and it is thus "more than the sum of its parts."[35]

Finally, these leafcutters "have a positive effect on the ecosystem, producing large amounts of organic matter in the soil," per Eric Cassell.[36] The nutrients left behind in the soil are rich in chemicals

Leafcutter Ant

such as calcium and potassium, and they help tree growth through increased root production. What an amazing animal is the leafcutter ant. I will forever view them a little differently now when I see these ants, which are everywhere!

There are many, many examples of other animals that are social in nature, some of which build enormous nests whose architecture rivals the best of mankind. Termites build nests both underground and aboveground, and some of those above the ground have reached heights as much as twenty-three feet. This, by comparison, would be six thousand feet in human construction relative to the termite size.

One last example will suffice, and that is the honeybee. Darwin was enamored by the honeybee. In *On the Origin of Species*, he wrote, "He must be a dull man who can examine the exquisite structure of the comb, so beautifully adapted to its end, without enthusiastic admiration."[37] Further, he wrote, "Granting whatever instincts you please, it seems quite inconceivable how they can make all the necessary angles and planes, or even perceive when they are correctly made."[38]

Honeycomb construction involves individual behavior with vast amounts of coordination, from selecting a tree site, selecting materials for construction, maintaining temperatures, and thus constructing an impressive three-dimensional shape. It is hard to believe honeycomb construction could just evolve, no matter how much time you would allow for such. "The origin of individual behaviors, the algorithms that control the behaviors, and the complexity of the social colony and coordination among the bees," all require explanation for origin from an evolutionary point of view.[39]

Bees also have their own navigational system using visual landmarks, the sun as compass, and polarized light as compass to cover as much as 150 square meters around a nest.[40] A scout bee will locate food, navigate back to the hive, and communicate the location of the food by a "waggle dance," called by experts the second-most information-rich exchange in the animal kingdom—second only to human language.[41] As you might expect, the details of this dance are not completely understood, but somehow the honeybee "knows," or learns, how to interpret this dance. It seems the direction of the dance and its verticality represents the angle of the vector to the food source relative to the sun.[42] This is extraordinary, to say the least. Apparently, the duration of the dance conveys the distance to the food source, and exactly how this is accomplished is still to be determined. Even more impressive, this dance compensates for the movement of the sun per time. How can Darwinian evolution explain all of this? "The origin of individual behaviors algorithms that control the behaviors and the complexity of the social colony and coordination among the bees,"[43] all require an explanation for their origins from an evolutionary viewpoint.

Beehive

Before leaving the topic of instinctive behavior, I would like to say something about the maternal instinct. Not as much is written about maternal instinct, I think because it is simply taken for granted. We raise horses on our farm and witness the birth of new foals during the spring. Once the foal is born, it begins to walk almost immediately. It also begins to feed by nursing immediately, and it seems no matter how ornery the mare might have been before the birth, suddenly she becomes protective of this new foal, which becomes her primary interest. It is truly an amazing thing to see.

The question is, why? Why should a mother horse, or for that matter, any mother, care whether or not their offspring survive? The easy answer is to propagate the species, but why? Do any of my mares care a lick about the equine species surviving? I think not. The best and really only explanation is that this maternal behavior is, indeed, instinctive, but from where did it arise?

Erwin Schrödinger, of quantum theory fame, once wrote that "life is something that goes on doing something longer than you would expect it to do." Physicists such as Sean Carroll try to explain that the purpose of life is to increase entropy. I think not! Tell that to the mother of a newborn. As an intern on my OB rotations, I was privileged to witness many births. The joy of these mothers, no matter how difficult the labor was, was a beautiful thing to see, and tears were frequently shed. Life replicates life because that is what life does—as part of God's purpose. There is no other explanation needed.

Just-So Stories

Recently, I visited the National Museum of Natural Sciences, a Smithsonian museum along the National Mall in Washington, D.C. It should more properly be called the "National Museum of Fantasy and Lies," as it is a memorial to Charles Darwin, almost elevating him to godlike status.

Upon entering the facility, one is inundated with evolutionary theory presented as evolutionary fact. Just-so stories abound—from how whales left dry land to live in the ocean, to the evolution of flight, to the ascent of man from apelike creatures with likenesses of their faces smiling, dark-skinned, and hairy.

I was especially amazed by the depiction of the evolution of the whale. Hanging from the ceiling of this museum was a massive blue whale, followed by smaller and smaller creatures, culminating in a land animal called *Pakicetus* that was smaller than a large dog, walking on all fours! Herman Melville would've been shocked! In his classic, *Moby Dick*, Melville spent a whole chapter called "Cetology" discussing the various types of cetaceans and their many characteristics, from porpoises to whales, but nothing that I saw hanging from the ceiling could have been remotely placed in this category.[44]

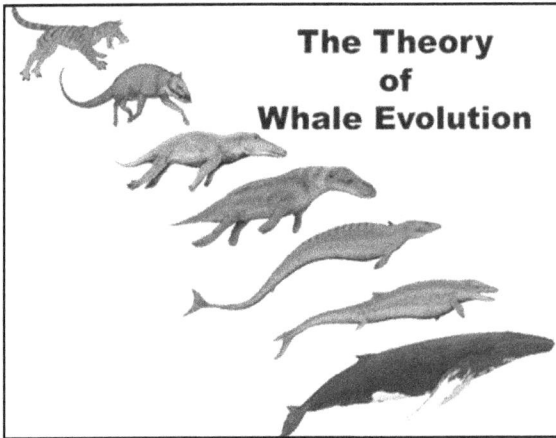

The Theory
of
Whale Evolution

Whale Evolution

For many years, evolutionists were in love with the evolution of the horse. *Eohippus* was for them the best example found in the fossil record of evolution and its transitional forms, and it was depicted in every high school textbook, with drawings showing the propagation of the horse. In my book *The Evolution Delusion*, I detail the several flaws in the *Eohippus* record, including the problem found in the so-called geologic column. Specifically, the primitive horse supposedly began with multiple toes, evolving into a hoofed animal like we see today. But the geologic record shows three-toed *Eohippus* living at the same time as one-toed *Eohippus*. This, from an evolutionary standpoint, should not be.[45]

The new darling of evolutionary theory is the whale. For many years, whales were thought to have originated from the ocean, eventually making their way to land. Not so anymore. Newer evolutionary theory, based on the fact that ancient whale fossils are found with land fossils, holds that whales began as land animals and evolved into ocean-dwelling animals. Why? That is not entirely clear, but just as evolution has gotten it wrong with *Eohippus*, so have they with the whale.

In the 1990s, a fossil was found by evolutionists that allowed them to string up a story, and now whales have become a new icon of evolution, hence their prominence in the Museum of Natural History. This story was based on one-bone similarity between a land-dwelling creature called *Pakicetus* (a Pakistani whale, since it was discovered in Pakistan) and that of a whale, even though the rest of the animal apparently looked nothing like a whale. This small bone was the involucrum, a bone found in the middle ear of both animals. A year later, another fossil was found older than ancient whale fossils, but younger than *Pakicetus*. This fossil had four legs and a long tail, could swim and walk, and was thus labeled *Ambulocetus natans*, or "swimming walking whale" by its discoverers.[46]

A few months later, an even younger fossil was found in Pakistan that was a supposed intermediate called *Rodheocetus*. At the time, the late evolutionist Stephen Jay Gould wrote, "The embarrassment of the past absence has been replaced by a bounty of new evidence and by the sweetest series of transitional fossils an evolutionist could ever hope to find."[47] These discoveries were, therefore, labeled by Gould as "picture-perfect" intermediaries and a "triumph in the history of paleontology."[48]

There are problems, though. First, the fossil found of *Pakicetus* was only the skull, so the body was not found and, it must be assumed, filled in by paleontologists. Second, it cannot be shown that any of the animals in the typical evolutionary drawing of the whale series were ancestors or descendants from one another. These pictures are, therefore, misleading at best. In fact, none of the so-called ancestors to modern or even ancient whales were whales at all. Third, *Pakicetus*, our first "walking whale," was classified solely on the basis of the one ear bone, an involucrum, but other animals that are non-whales also have this bone. "In other words, the involucrum is diagnostic of cetaceans, except when it isn't," writes Jonathan Wells in his book, *Zombie Science*.[49]

Think about this: How much evolution do you suppose it takes for a land animal to become a sea animal that spends its entire life in the ocean? Supposedly, whales accomplished this in eight million years, which is preposterous!

The *cetacean*, or whale, must develop a tail or fluke for propagation that contains no bones. The fluke is extremely important; it can be flexed up and down relative to the body, enabling the whale to move quite effectively through the water. The whale also needs a dorsal fin for stability as it moves along.

The whale's breathing apparatus would need a massive change as well. All cetaceans breathe through a "blowhole" on top of the head, necessitating a significant relocation from their land animal predecessors. This would be no small feat, evolutionary-wise.

Because whales can make very deep dives, some as much as nine thousand feet below the surface of the ocean, they would also need to evolve structures that could stand an immense increase in pressure at nine thousand feet, some two hundred times the pressure at the surface. To survive, the whale has collapsible lungs and rib cages, and many of their ribs are unattached. This collapsing of the lung keeps the whale from taking in too much nitrogen, thus preventing decompression sickness (something human divers call "the bends"), which is potentially fatal.

Then there is the problem of reproduction. The male cetacean's testicles are inside their body, unlike that of other mammals. As a result, they must have a countercurrent heat-exchange mechanism to keep the testicles "cool" in order for sperm to survive. "If this engineering arrangement were due to evolution, the relocation of cetacean testicles to the inside, could not have preceded the counter-current heat exchange system. Otherwise, the whale would have been sterile, an evolutionary dead end," writes Wells.[50] Further, what would be the adaptive advantage of this countercurrent heat-exchange system developing before the testicles were inside? The answer is none!

Also, cetaceans nurse their calves, clearly underwater, but you guessed it, this would take a significant evolutionary change, as well. The nipples of the whale are recessed in slits near its genitalia. When the calf feeds, milk is ejected by the mother, and the milk is three to four times more condensed than that of cow's milk, more like yogurt; thus the calf gets more nutrition in a shorter period of time.

It seems extremely unlikely that all these changes, plus many more, could have evolved in eight million years—or, for that matter, at all. Wells calls this a "tall order." Further research, as we have noted, now shows that DNA mutations do not produce beneficial anatomical features.[51] We are back to just another "just so" story. The evidence for the evolution of the whale is no better than that of *Eohippus*, and the failure of the fossil record to demonstrate transitional forms was and is still one of the biggest problems in evolutionary theory, the lack of which remains an embarrassment. You see, "with enough imagination, anyone can invent a story about how land animals evolved into whales. But an imaginative story is not empirical science."[52]

Morganucodon ochleri

Back to the museum, there is the Hall of Mammals with a sign saying, "Welcome to the Mammal Family Reunion! Come meet your relatives," which contains probably the most egregious bit of propaganda I saw there: the "Evolution Theatre," a theater for children primarily. In front of the theater is a glass box that houses a curious-looking animal, what Casey Luskin calls, "the idol of the museum," whose scientific name is *Morganucodon oehleri*. As I entered the theater, there were families with children eating their popcorn and sipping on their Kool-Aid, ready to enjoy the show. It begins with the film projected on the screen, which depicts a "time far away when dinosaurs roamed the earth." Initially, we see the landscape with many dinosaurs in the background, then, emerging on the surface of the earth, is our hero and the star of the show, Morgie, a rat-like creature that looks a lot like the animal encased in the glass box in front of the theater. Morgie, in fact, represents this creature, and the point of the film is to show how mammals survived the great asteroid that killed off the dinosaurs. We see the asteroid hitting the earth, and catastrophe abounding, with Morgie at this point determining to go subterranean. By going subterranean, Morgie is able to escape this catastrophe, and after millions of years of evolution, Morgie became an ape-like creature that then would eventually become us—or human. If it wasn't so pathetic, it would be funny. But this is presented as fact, not fiction, and sadly, it is witnessed by millions of people each year. The Smithsonian Museum of Natural History had 4.3 million visitors the year prior to COVID. Worst of all, this is supported by our tax dollars! It is enough to make you almost sick.

What is not found in the museum is a display telling just how highly unlikely it is for life to have begun purely by random combinations of chemicals. Nothing is said about how life begets life, and we have never witnessed life coming from non-life, the so-called law of biogenesis. Nor do we find any mention of the lack of fossil evidence for evolution and its failure to demonstrate transitional forms. There was a display about the Cambrian Explosion, but it dismissed its real significance, that being the fact that twenty-three phyla of animals appear abruptly in the fossil record without precursors.

You see, anyone can make up a story and construct it to sound true, but that doesn't make it so! It seems to me that the purpose of the Museum of Natural History is the indoctrination of visitors, especially the young, with evolutionary theory using fairy tales and just-so stories.

MATHEMATICS—THE LANGUAGE OF GOD

Geometry is unique and eternal and it shines in the mind of God. The share of it has been granted to Man is one of the reasons why he is in the image of God.

—*Johannes Kepler*

"Why should we be able to develop formal mathematical models that capture material reality? None of this has anything to do with survival."
—*J.W. Richards*

TWO PLUS TWO EQUALS FOUR. THE SQUARE ROOT OF FOUR IS TWO. C squared equals A squared plus B squared in a right-angle triangle (the Pythagorean Theorem). A—the area of a circle—equals pi R squared. What do all these have in common? Obviously, they are all mathematical equations, but where do they come from? We tend to take mathematics for granted. Secularists would argue that math was invented by man, but I would argue it was not *invented* by mankind but rather *discovered*. Certainly, the notation system was invented by man, but the *essence* of the equations are already baked into creation.

One could also say most of these equations are axiomatic—universally accepted by all. Two plus two equals four everywhere in the world, and for that matter, everywhere in the universe. We live in an age of relativism, where truth is relative, and there are some who might deny this truth. After all, we live in a society where some individuals cannot even define what a woman or a man is. But, of course, that is a different discussion for a later time.

It would, therefore, be safe to say that sane, reasonable, logical people are going to accept that two plus two equals four. It is the fabric of reality—but what is mathematics, and how did it get here in our physical universe?

Mathematics, and hence numbers, are a concept of quantity and are abstract, meaning they exist in the mind only. Yes, we have the Arabic 2 and the Roman *II*, but these are merely physical representations of an idea or concept. They are not the concepts themselves. The numbers cannot be physically touched or seen, but they exist in the mind. You cannot bump your toe on the number two, for example. "Humans discovered numbers and the relationships between them," says astrophysicist Jason Lisle.[1] But the numbers existed before man and in the mind of God, and it is God who was responsible for their existence. "It has been the privilege of human beings to discover these rules by the gift of logical reasoning that the Lord has so graciously given," writes Lisle.[2]

Mathematics can even predict things long before they are observed. The Higgs Field Theory was predicted mathematically fifty years before the Hadron Collider in Switzerland confirmed the Higgs Boson in 2012, thus validating the Higgs Field Theory.

St.Augustine, fourth- and fifth-century philosopher and theologian, wrote: "Coming now to the science of numbers, it is clear to the dullest apprehension that it was not created by man, but was discovered by investigation. . . Having fixed laws which were not made by man, but which the acuteness of ingenious men brought to light."[3] Because we are made in His image, we are aware of God's "natural" revelation, a concept alluded to by the apostle Paul in his letter to the Romans.[4] Numbers, then, are universal, are invariant, and have always been what they are. The universe "obeys" mathematical laws without violation. Johannes Kepler, the great seventeenth-century astronomer and mathematician, once wrote that to do math is to "think God's thoughts after him." The sixteenth-century astronomer Galileo Galilei held that "the laws of nature are written by the hand of God in the language of mathematics" and that the "human mind is a work of God and we are one of the most excellent."[5]

Isaac Newton believed it was the mathematical nature of the universe, thus its intelligibility, that was remarkable.[6] More currently, the late John Polkinghorne wrote: "Science does not explain the mathematically intelligibility of the physical world, for it is part of science's founding faith that it is so."[7] Philosopher Keith Ward puts it this way: "The continuing conformity of physical particles to precise mathematical relationships is something that is much more likely to exist if there is an ordering cosmic mathematician who sets up the correlation in the requisite way. The existence of laws of physics . . . strongly implies there is a God who formulates such laws and ensures that the physical realm conforms to them."[8]

Even atheists understand that the universe has obeyed fundamental mathematical laws from its inception. Stephen Hawking admitted, "It is difficult to discuss the beginning of the universe without mentioning the concept of God."[9] These laws demonstrate a very logical, reasonable mind. This creates a dilemma for the secularist, that is, Why would the universe obey laws at all, if it is not controlled by any rational mind?

Stephen Hawking

Eugene Wigner, Hungarian physicist and winner of the 1960 Nobel Prize in physics, in his paper "The Unreasonable Effectiveness of Mathematics in the Natural World," wrote, "The great mathematician fully, almost ruthlessly, exploits the domain of permissible reasoning and skirts the impermissible. That his recklessness does not lead him into a morass of contradictions is a miracle in itself: Certainly, it is hard to believe that our reasoning power was brought, by Darwin's process of natural selection, to the perfection which it seems to possess." Wigner, a secularist, further wrote, "It is difficult to avoid the impression that a miracle confronts here, quite comparable in its striking nature to the miracle that the human mind can string a thousand arguments together without getting itself into contradictions, or to the two miracles of the existence of laws of nature and of the human mind's capacity to divine them."[10]

The problem for the atheist is the inability to distinguish mechanism from agency. John Lennox writes, "In philosophical terms they make a very elementary category mistake when they argue that, because we understand a mechanism that accounts for a particular phenomenon, there is no agent that designed that mechanism."[11] For example, Kepler would not argue that because he discovered how planets orbit the sun, it required no agent—Kepler, of course, being a believer in God. "The miracle of the appropriateness of the language of mathematics for the formulation of the laws of physics is a wonderful gift, which we neither understand nor deserve," wrote Wigner.[12]

Without a mind, mathematics does not exist, and since our universe is governed by these laws, it is reasonable to conclude that our universe is controlled by a rational mind. The writer of the book of Hebrews, in chapter 1, says, "God upholds all creation by the expression of his power."

Stephen C. Meyer is the author of the popular book *Return of the God Hypothesis*, in which he gives three proofs for God: one, that the universe had a beginning; two, that the universe is fine-tuned; and three, that the biological world is based upon the information found in DNA. In a recent lecture, he reported a discussion of his book with an eminent mathematician who was quite accepting of the book, but critical nonetheless. His critique: Meyer had omitted mathematics as a fourth proof of God!

Many of the great thinkers of the so-called Enlightenment were mathematicians and also theists. Nicholas Kusa, Blaise Pascal, Gottfried Wilhelm Leibniz, Johann Bernoulli, Colin MacLaurin, Leonhard Euler, Maria Agnesi, Augustin-Louis Cauchy, Georg Cantor, Nicolaus Copernicus, Tycho Brahe, John Napier, and Galileo Galilei were all believers in God.

As mentioned earlier, Kepler was also a believer, and he makes for an interesting study. Johannes Kepler, born in 1571 and contemporary with Galileo, was, in fact, a devout Lutheran Christian and a brilliant scientist and astronomer, as well as a mathematician. Kepler believed God had a mathematically rational plan for the universe from the beginning of creation, which, in essence, existed from eternity in God's mind.[13] Kepler viewed his entire life's work as a

Johannes Kepler

long, intensive effort to bring glory to God, who, Kepler believed, was the Creator of all things. Melissa Cain Travis, in her book *Thinking God's Thoughts*, writes, "The mathematically rational plan for Creation—the archetype—existed from eternity in the mind of God; the material manifestation of the archetype is the copy that natural philosophers investigate, and the image of God and human beings includes the higher rationality that enables us to study nature using observation, mathematics, and innate preferences for beauty and simplicity." These were the three fundamental principles Kepler held as part of a cosmic harmony that enabled mankind to unlock the secrets of nature.[14] Kepler would thus reject that mathematics is an invention of man to describe the natural world.

Melissa Cain Travis

147

In our example, two plus two equals four, and the Pythagorean Theorem is true—independently of the human mind.

Kepler and virtually all those mentioned above predated Darwin, thus Darwinian evolution. There are, however, many mathematicians who postdate Darwin who are very skeptical, including polymath David Berlinski. Berlinski, in his book *Science after Bible*, writes that other mathematicians are doubters of the Darwinian theory of evolution, as he himself is. He notes that a number of his friends and colleagues, such as Daniel Gallin, M.P. Schützenberger, René Thom, Gian-Carlo Rota, Lipman Bers, Paul Halmos, and Irving Segal, had serious issues with Darwinism and neo-Darwinism.[15]

What is the issue? First, most mathematicians are a bit distrustful of biologists in general, and they consider the science of biology "primitive and dishonest."[16] Berlinski, for example, calls biology a derivative science. Why? you might ask. Likely it's the fact that mathematics is probably the purest of all sciences. It tends to be less speculative and deals only with hard logic. A mathematician is, therefore, more likely to see through the absurdity of evolution, not from a philosophical viewpoint, but from a mathematical, computational viewpoint.

A pure mathematician in the 1940s and 1950s, like John von Neumann, considered evolution simply a placeholder, awaiting a more real, fully defined theory. Many mathematicians see problems associated with Darwinism. For example, the mathematician can understand the lack of evidence seen in the fossil record, something paleontologist David Kitts, writing in the *Journal of Evolution*, alluded to. Kitts states, "It has presented some nasty difficulties for evolutionists, the most notorious of which is the presence of 'gaps' in the fossil record. Evolution requires intermediate forms between species and paleontology does not provide them."[17] Pure, hard scientists, such as mathematicians and physicists, understand this more fully than biologists or Darwinians, who have already decided on its merits. The facts that virtually no multicellular fossils are found in the pre-Cambrian rock strata, and that beginning with the Cambrian geologic formation there is an explosive proliferation of animal life, are problems for evolutionists, and they are certainly major problems for the hard scientists.

Berlinski points to three other things that contributed to von Neumann's skepticism regarding Darwinism. First, evolution seems to have required "a miracle." Berlinski quotes Kurt Gödel in how unlikely evolution would be, starting from a random distribution of elementary particles, and compared the likelihood of molecules-to-man evolution occurring to the chance of the atmosphere spontaneously separating into its components entirely by chance.[18] Second, von Neumann thought Darwin's theory was inadequate, because, in reality, it wasn't a theory at all; it failed to meet the scientific definition of a theory. Third, von Neumann was unsure whether evolution could ever explain how animals and plants just assembled themselves by chance. Berlinski speaks of an instance, late in von Neumann's life, when he looked at a house in the distance, and realized how absurd it would be to think that such a house could just assemble itself. Berlinski notes that von Neumann was not necessarily accepting intelligent design, but nonetheless, in a letter to colleague George Gamow, von Neumann wrote, "I still somewhat shudder at the thought that highly purposive organizational elements, like proteins, should originate in a random process."[19]

Nonetheless, Darwin's evolution remains scientific dogma, though it shouldn't be. There are mathematicians, such as Berlinski, William Dembski, and others, who denounce it, and I suspect there are many silent mathematicians of the day who have serious misgivings regarding molecules-to-man evolution, but in the milieu of academia, it has become, as Berlinski puts it, "totemic," and to speak against it—that is, evolution—can result in serious repercussions to one's academic career. This genetic problem extends to other sciences as well, unfortunately, but more and more, we are beginning to see a shift, and if you will allow me, a "swerve."

We are beginning to see a kink in the armor of neo-Darwinism, and I believe there is a beacon of hope for the intelligent design movement. In a 2016 nationwide survey, 93 percent of American adults agreed that teachers should have the freedom to objectively discuss both the scientific strengths and weaknesses of evolutionary theory. Furthermore, in the same survey, 87 percent think people can disagree about what science says on a particular subject without being anti-science, and 94 percent think it is important for scientists to have different views.

It should be noted, the survey cited above was taken from both liberals and conservatives, with both more or less agreeing to those same questions with the same frequency. Jonathan Wells concludes that as a theory, Darwinism is in crisis. He bases this on the fact that a growing number of biologists now acknowledge there are serious problems with the modern evolutionary theory.

This does not come from a rejection of scientism, but rather a realization that the theory of evolution is seriously flawed. In 2010, a group of non–intelligent design scientists met in Vienna to challenge evolutionary dogma; that being that organisms could evolve solely by the gradual accumulation of small variations preserved by natural selection and that DNA was the sole agent of variation and unit of inheritance. In 2015, the journal *Nature* published an exchange of scientists who felt the need to rethink the notion of molecules-to-man evolution, writing that there needs to be a "conceptual change in evolutionary biology." In a 2009 journal, *Trends and Genetics*, breakdowns in tenets like the "tree of life" and "natural selection" as a main driving force indicates "the modern synthesis has crumbled, apparently beyond repair." Other groups of scientists also doubt that evolution can cause new anatomical structures to evolve. Casey Luskin writes, "Twenty-first-century science seems to be taking biology beyond universal common ancestry and rejecting the neo-Darwinian 'Tree of Life'." In 2019, a Yale University computer scientist named David Gerlentler announced he would no longer "accept Darwinism for the major innovations in the history of life." Gerlentler is especially perplexed by the evolutionist's inability to explain the origin of life.

Since then, more than one thousand doctoral scientists have signed a document called a "scientific descent from Darwinism." Dissenters were from all over the world, including such prestigious universities as Princeton, MIT, Dartmouth, and the University of Michigan. There are likely many more scientists who question Darwinism, and journals are full of criticism of many aspects of the theory, but most scientists are reluctant to speak out publicly in fear of opening a door to religion or intelligent design. Jonathan Wells writes that this results in "a kind of groupthink," in which one fears intimidation, discrimination, demotion, and a possible loss of job, which is a very real concern.

Evolution is becoming more and more a less-tenable idea. John West notes, "The growing number of scientists who are publicly skeptical of neo-Darwinism has made it harder to deny the existence of real scientific controversies over Darwinian theory." We can only hope these scientists will not continue to close their minds to the idea of an intelligent designer and thus rid us of neo-Darwinism, which has been called a "universal acid" that "dissolves traditional ideas about morality, human responsibility, and God."

Thus, neo-Darwinism may be on its way out. As Winston Churchill once said, "This is not the end. This is not even the beginning of the end. But maybe it is the end of the beginning."[20]

When one of the biggest proponents of Darwinian evolution today is a fellow who goes by the moniker "Professor Dave" on YouTube, who is neither a professor nor a PhD-credentialed scientist, you know the theory is in trouble. His foul-mouthed invectives and ad-hominem arguments are a disgrace to true science. He is a bombastic, bumptious, bloviating blowhard. It would appear that Darwin apologists are getting scarcer and scarcer! Also, resorting to the multiverse theory is a desperate move to avoid any acknowledgment of design, as we discussed earlier. It's even more desperate to believe we live in a computer simulation!

Why not acknowledge there is an intelligent mind responsible for the universe, and His created mathematics and physical laws are responsible for its workings. The psalmist wrote many years ago, "Be still, and know that I am God; I will be exalted among the nations, I will be exalted in the earth."[21] Furthermore, the prophet Isaiah wrote of God: "My plan will be realized, I will accomplish what I desire" (Isaiah 46:10).[22]

"Mathematical truths are universal, invariant, abstract entities without exception, precisely because God is an omnipresent, unchanging, sovereign being who thinks," says Jason Lisle.[23] And it's because we are made in His image (Genesis 1:27) that we are able to discover some of these mathematical truths. A secularist worldview cannot make sense of this. Because mathematical laws are conceptual, they, therefore, require a mind. The fool says, "There is no God" (Psalm 14:1; 53:2), as do the secularists, and yet the universe obeys mathematical laws invariably. The worldview of the atheist is, therefore, inherently contradictory.

This is not to say that mathematics is complete, as it certainly isn't. Berlinski has written, "If the twentieth century has demonstrated anything, it is that there are limits to what we can know. What we might wish and what we can have are not necessarily the same."[24] I would add it is safe to say we don't even know what we don't know!

Even in this, there can be witnessed design for purpose, as mathematics is a language—a vehicle for thought which makes comprehensible things that can only be felt or sensed in the physical world. It is a tool to accomplish one of the designed purposes for man – to bring glory to God in the stewardship of His creation.

Chapter
10

MATHEMATICS IN THE NATURAL WORLD

The continuing conformity of physical particles to precise mathematical relationships is something that is much more likely to exist if there is an ordering cosmic mathematician who sets up the correlation in the requisite way.

—Keith Ward

The graceful curve of the nautilus seashell occurs in nature more than any other shape. Its lines trace out an exponential spiral. Each of the spiral's successive swirls is wider by seemingly arbitrary but fixed factors.

—Gerald Schroeder

ACCORDING TO DAVID BERLINSKI, IN HIS SOMEWHAT RAMBLING, but nonetheless superlative book, *Science After Babel*, Albert Einstein wrote that mathematical objects were the free creations of the human mind.[1] That mathematics exists is really not in doubt, but if Einstein is correct, then it follows, per Berlinski, that without a human mind, there would be no numbers. If this proposition is true, though, we have a problem, because that would make numbers nonexistent before man. That would also hold true for the laws of physics, and if the laws of physics were once false, "of what use is any physical retrodiction—any claim at all about the distant past," says Berlinski.[2] As stated in the previous chapter, numbers transcend time and space, and they point to a Being that also transcends time and space. This is not a new concept drummed up by intelligent-design fanatics. In fact, the concept of the eternity of numbers goes all the way back to the ancient Greeks.

Aristotle, in his work *Metaphysics*, wrote that the Pythagoreans (the first mathematicians) "regarded numbers as fundamental to physical reality—the substance of all things and the principle of all things."[3] Claudius Ptolemy, writing between 100 and 170 AD, wrote that mathematics serves "as a type of intellectual bridge that enables the natural philosopher to make inquiries into the beautiful and well-ordered disposition of nature."[4]

For the Greek philosophers, mathematics included arithmetic, geometry, astronomy, and harmonics (music), later to become known as the Quadrivium.

Even pagan writers understood this. Proclus Diadochus (between 412 and 485 AD) said of mathematics, "It reveals the orderliness of the ratios according to which the universe is constructed and the proportion that binds things together in the cosmos."[5]

Eventually, we get to Johannes Kepler, scientist of the sixteenth century, who thought that mathematics and its understanding was a way to gain a glimpse into the mind of God. Philip Melanchthon, instructor to Kepler, believed "the human mind may be said to be numbered in its capacity to seek order and regularity, and . . . in this it reflects the mind of God, and in this way human observation of the heavens is able to offer a route to better knowledge of God," says historian Charlotte Methuen.[6] Melanchthon based his belief chiefly on Romans 1:20, which says, "For since the creation of the world His invisible attributes are clearly seen, being understood by the things that are made, even His eternal power and Godhead, so that they are without excuse."[7]

It was because of the numerical laws that Kepler was able to formulate his great laws of planetary motion. Well before Isaac Newton, Kepler described the motions of the planets as elliptical around the sun, that the line between a planet and the sun (the radius vector) sweeps out equal areas in equal time, and the square of a planet's period is directly proportional to the cube of its mean distance from the sun. These planetary laws have now been verified, some three hundred years–plus since Kepler.

It is impossible to improve on Berlinski, so I will quote him yet again: "To the extent that mathematical physics is mathematical, it represents a form of knowledge that is not causally evoked. To the extent that the mathematical physics is not causally evoked, it represents a form of knowledge that is not empirical. To the extent that mathematical physics represents a form of knowledge that is not empirical, it follows that the ultimate objects of experience are not physical either."[8]

So, when we say Pythagoras *invented* the Pythagorean Theorem, we are really meaning Pythagoras *discovered* what was already there in nature—that is, the square of the area of a triangle, whose side is the hypotenuse, is equal to the sum of the areas of the squares of the other two sides, $C^2 = A^2 + B^2$. The same can be said for calculus, which was discovered independently by Isaac Newton and Gottfried Liebniz, German mathematician, scientist, and philosopher in the late seventeenth century, a discovery unlikely if calculus was not part of the reality of our universe.

I believe this same thought of discovery also applies to relativity and quantum mechanics, the former elucidated by Albert Einstein in the beginning of the twentieth century, and the latter first put forth by Max Planck and then developed by Niels Bohr, Werner Heisenberg, Erwin Schrödinger, Richard Feynman, and others. These theories have so far stood the test of time, have been validated, and seem to be how our universe functions, and if so, they were there from the beginning and are part of the reality we experience. Even the advent of the computer age and the algorithm are results of mathematics. The algorithm has been called the second greatest scientific idea of the West, with there not being a third.[9] Berlinski has called the algorithm the "beauty that governs the mathematician's soul."[10] As a result, we have telecommunications with satellite triangulation with a massive global network of computers, with information moving at the speed of light. We have data from everywhere and on every topic imaginable traversing the world in nanoseconds because of the algorithm.

We are living in an algorithmic world, with the algorithm making decisions about every transaction you can think of, from carrying out massive computer computations, to putting dinosaurs on the silver screen, to predicting the future, and to even arming and aiming cruise missiles. It would be hard to overstate the importance of the algorithm, which had its birth from brilliant mathematicians sixty years ago, including Kurt Gödel, Alonzo Church, Emil Post, and A.M. Turing.

Mathematics, as expressed in the natural world, is mysterious, elegant, beautiful, rational, and defiant of explanation, other than that there has to be a rational, logical mind behind it. Take, for example, the so-called Golden Ratio. Mathematically speaking, two qualities are in the Golden Ratio if their ratio is the same as the ratio of their sum to the larger of the two qualities, expressed 1 + square root of √5)/2, which equals 1.618033. Knowledge of this ratio goes as far back as 300 BC—found in Euclid's *Elements*—though Greek mathematicians Euclid and Pythagoras did not refer to it as the "Golden Ratio." Many years later, Italian mathematician Luca Pacioli, in his book *De Divina Proportione*, with illustrations by Leonardo daVinci, felt this ratio was divinely inspired in its simplicity and orderliness.

Closely associated with the Golden Ratio is the Fibonacci sequence. The Fibonacci sequence is a set of steadily increasing numbers where each number is equal to the sum of the preceding two numbers. Credited to thirteenth-century Italian mathematician Leonardo Pica (whose nickname was "Fibonacci"), this sequence can actually be traced back as far as 200 BCE in Indian literature, and even possibly further back than that, into 1200 BCE, as seen in ancient Sanskrit. The sequence then looks like this, 0, 1, 1, 2, 3, 5, 8, 13, 21, 34, 55, 89, 144, 233, etc., etc.

The Fibonacci sequence is not the same as the Golden Ratio, but a closer look at the sequence shows a very close similarity of the ratios, with the two preceding numbers, except for the 0, 1, 1, 2, beginning, being approximately two-thirds.

Using Binet's formula, the ratio of two consecutive Fibonacci numbers tends to the Golden Ratio as it increases. Fibonacci numbers appear unexpectedly in mathematics, and the sequence has multiple applications, even in computer algorithms.

Geometrically, the Fibonacci sequence looks like this:

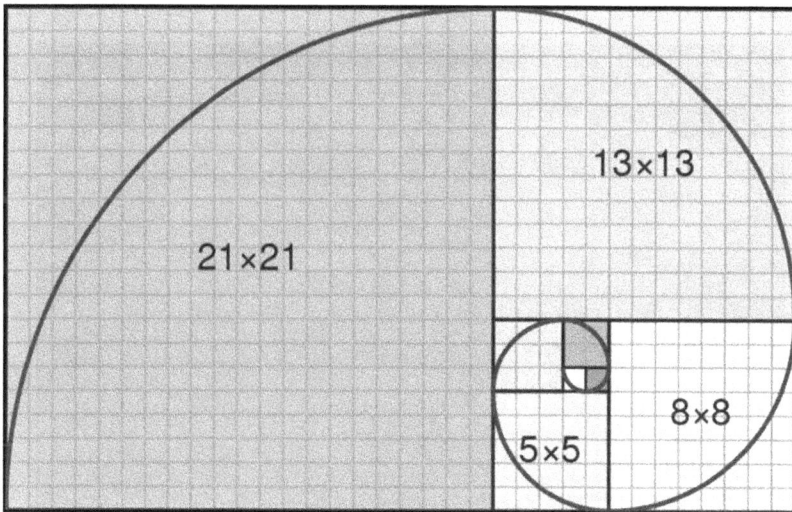

Fibonacci Sequenca

Pineapple

The significance of the Golden Ratio in the Fibonacci sequence is how often they appear in nature. Biologically, they are seen in many areas, including branching trees, the arrangement of leaves, the fruit sprouts of a pineapple, the arrangement of pine-cone bracts, and the flowering of the artichoke.

This ratio, 1.618, referred to as Phi, is seen in various spiral formations. Using the Golden Rectangle, the ratio of the sides A/B is equal

Nautilus

to the Golden Mean (Phi) and results in a "nesting process" that can be repeated into infinity—and this takes this spiral shape. This spiral shape is seen in biology in snails and in the nautilus, but it is also seen in the spiral galaxies and hurricanes, as well as other natural phenomena.

Spiral Galaxy

Hurricane

We also see this unique ratio in various animal body plans, including the human face, and even in the DNA molecule itself. The DNA molecule measures thirty-four angstroms long and twenty-one angstroms wide, with a ratio of 1.690476, closely approximating Phi. This Golden Ratio, which is seen virtually everywhere, has a very pleasing quality to it. As a result, artists and architects have used the Fibonacci spiral as an expression of an aesthetically pleasing principle, a rule

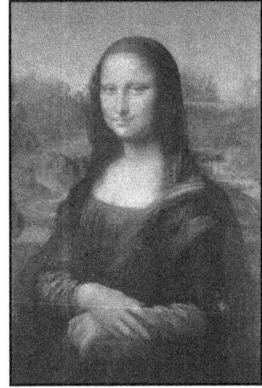

Mona Lisa

of thirds, if you will. In the composition of a picture, rather than strictly centering, the rule of thirds allows for a more pleasing flow. The *Mona Lisa*, painted by Leonardo daVinci, and the ceiling of the Sistine Chapel, painted by Michelangelo, are examples of this. Many buildings of the Renaissance period were constructed using this rule of thirds, and even before the Renaissance, the Parthenon, the Egyptian pyramids, and the Taj Mahal used this rule.

Sistine Chapel

This brings us now to the concept of Pi. Anyone who has taken beginning geometry knows that the area of a circle is equal to Pi (π) R², where R is the radius of the circle and Pi is equal to the number 3.1459 . . . The question is, Where does Pi come from? Pi was first calculated by Archimedes of Syracuse in the 200s BC, although it was known two thousand years earlier by the Babylonians, the Babylonians using three times the square of the radius, which equals three. In 1650 BC, the Egyptians calculated Pi to the value of 3.165. Archimedes, then, using the Pythagorean Theorem to find the area of a circle, and using two regular polygons, calculated Pi to be between 3 1/7 and 3 10/71. Pi has been further refined throughout the ages; most recently, it has been calculated to the one hundred trillionth digit, the ability to do so thanks to the speed of computers made possible by a computer engine of Google Cloud. The point is, Pi is an infinite number and will continue to be expanded. These observations concerning the Golden Ratio, the Fibonacci sequence, and Pi are just more evidence of how numbers reflect a supreme consciousness and show the regularity and orderliness of nature. In essence, they have a purpose!

Kurt Gödel, one of the most brilliant and influential mathematicians of the twentieth century, in his ontological proof of God, reasoned, "If the world is rationally constructed and has meaning, then there must be such a thing as an afterlife. For what sense would there be in creating a being (man) which has such a wide realm of possibilities for its own development and for relationships to others, and then not allowing it to realize even a thousandth of those possibilities." Gödel's "Ontological Proof"—that is, the metaphysical proof of our being—used mathematical logic to show the existence of God as a "necessary truth."[11]

In an interview with Kirk Cameron of TBN, John Lennox once said the reason he was a believer was "because mathematics works." Furthermore, in an interview with Eric Metaxas, Lennox said, "One of the most powerful evidences, to my mind, that there is an eternal mind behind the universe is first of all that we can do science, that we can do it in the language of mathematics, that we have language we can use. We can use abstract concepts that are not material to describe things that are physical. All of those point in one direction, and one direction only, and it's this: 'In the beginning was the Word,' not particles."[12]

John Lennox

160

We will never absolutely prove the existence of God either mathematically or otherwise, but I believe mathematics gives us an insight to an all-powerful, omniscient Being who thinks logically and reasonably, in whose image we are created.

Chapter
11

MANDELBROT

Philosophy is written in this all-encompassing book that is constantly open before our eyes, that is the universe, but it cannot be understood unless one first learns to understand the language and knows the characters in which it is written. It is written in mathematical language and its characters are triangles, circles and other geometrical figures; without these, it is humanly impossible to understand a word of it, and one wanders around pointlessly in a dark labyrinth.

Johannes Kepler

Applicable mathematics was worked out in an abstract exercise by pure mathematicians, long before it was applied to the real world. The original investigations were entirely unconnected with the eventual application.

John Lennox

IN THE CHAPTER ON CHAOS THEORY, YOU MAY RECALL THAT mathematicians have discovered that equations can sometimes result in certain shapes when grafted on an x- and y-axis. We saw this with the bifurcation diagram of Robert May, and it was further delineated and described by Mitchell Feigenbaum. Michael Barnsley and John Hubbord started incorporating complex numbers with certain equations, and when they were plugged into a computer, amazing shapes occurred, with especially strange things occurring around the boundaries of these images, boundaries with infinite complexity.[1]

Previously, during World War I and long before the advent of sophisticated computers, French mathematicians Gaston Julia and Pierre Fatou, using various iterations, developed what came to be known as the Julia sets. These images came in various guises and shapes, some in circular arrangements, some in spirals, and some even disconnected, almost snowflake-like shapes, all originally created by hand drawings. Then, in the late twentieth century, Benoit Mandelbrot, a character we have already seen, began "experimenting" and generalizing with the Julia sets, expanding on the work of Robert Brooks and Peter Matelski, and he discovered the granddaddy of all sets, the Mandelbrot. What he discovered was a phenomenon so beautiful, fascinating, and intriguing that it would not have been possible to have been found without the advent of the computer—and fortuitously, Mandelbrot worked at IBM. By the late 1970s and early 1980s, computers had become fast enough to analyze certain sets of numbers as defined by their iterative functions. Before this time, computers were simply too slow to allow it.

So, in 1978, Brooks and Matelski defined a particular mathematical set using complex numbers. A set of numbers is simply a group of numbers that have something in common. Sets can both include and exclude. For example, a set of even numbers includes even numbers and excludes odd numbers. A set of negative numbers—such as -2, -7, -8, -1/2—excludes one, three, nine, etc. Many sets, such as those mentioned, are easy to recognize, even when the numbers are large. The number 25,789 is an odd number, and this is instantly obvious. Other sets are not so easily recognized, however. Consider prime numbers, which are natural numbers that cannot be formed by the product of two natural numbers other than themselves and one. Or put another way, a prime number is a whole number greater than one that cannot be exactly divided by any whole number other than itself and one, such as 2, 3, 5, 7, 11, etc. In his beautiful and excellent book *Fractals*, Jason Lisle asked: "Is 14,351 in the aforementioned set" of prime numbers? You cannot tell just by looking; it takes some work to learn the answer, and it turns out that the number is the product of 113 and 127, so it does not belong in the prime number set; therefore, it is not a prime number (14,351 divided by 113 = 127)[2].

Working at IBM and using the most sophisticated computers of the time, Mandelbrot took the set defined by Brooks and Matelski and began working to see what this set would look like two-dimensionally when generated by a computer. As a result of his work, this set took on Mandelbrot's name.

Mandelbrot had already been working on what became known as "chaos theory," and as we have seen, he developed a way of measuring roughness, or the irregularity of an object. In 1975, Mandelbrot coined the term *fractal* to describe these irregularities, which are really repeating patterns. Mandelbrot viewed fractals as "a way of seeing into infinity."[3]

The Mandelbrot set involves the iteration Z squared + C $\rightarrow$ Z, where Z is initially zero.[4] This probably means nothing to you, the reader, so let's explain it. Per Dr. Lisle, the value of the number Z is squared, then added to a different number, C, to become the new value of C, which is plugged back into the formula, and so on. More conventionally, this formula looks like this: $Z^n + C = Z^n + one$. It turns out that this number, represented by C, is the number we are looking at to see if it belongs in the Mandelbrot set.

Jason Lisle

The symbol Z^n represents numbers that are unbounded because they get larger and larger, looking like this: 0, 1, 2, 5, 26, 677, et cetera, et cetera. For the Mandelbrot set, we are seeking the bound numbers. For example, does the number -1 belong to the Mandelbrot? With C equaling -1, putting this in the formula, $Z^n -1 = Z^n + 1$. By convention, the first value of Z will always be zero. Square this number (still zero) and subtract one, and you get a -1. We take this and plug it back into the formula, -1 sequence (+1) - 1 is zero. Plugging it back into the formula, we get the sequence of 0, -1, 0, -1, 0, -1, et cetera, et cetera. The absolute magnitude never gets above one. This is a bound number, hence a part of the Mandelbrot set.

Using natural numbers, this remains a difficult task to calculate manually without a computer, that is, to define whether a number belongs in the Mandelbrot set or not, but add to the picture of complex numbers, it becomes almost impossible.

Complex numbers are not numbers most of us use in our day-to-day lives, but nonetheless they exist and are part of the Mandelbrot set. Complex numbers include so-called imaginary numbers, which are negative numbers that, when squared, produce a negative number. In real numbers, when a negative number is squared, it results in a positive number, but not so with imaginary numbers. But how can this be? For this, we need a grid or a plane, known as the Argand plane, with imaginary numbers being on a different axis directly above or below zero. They are neither right nor left, are not positive and not negative, and yet they are not zero either. These are imaginary numbers.

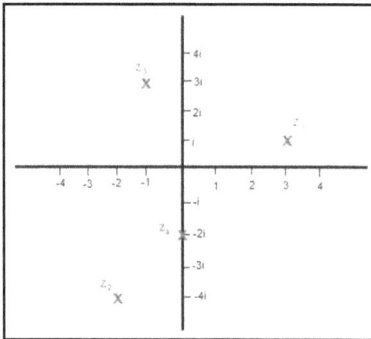

Argand Plane

Numbers that are not on either axis are called complex numbers, a hybrid of real and imaginary numbers.

Going back to the Mandelbrot set, using complex numbers and plugging them into the formula, if a sequence gets larger without limit, it is not part of the set. On the other hand, if a number and its sequence does not get larger and larger, it is bound and part of the Mandelbrot set. As mentioned, computers can perform these calculations rapidly with many numbers, including real and complex ones, and when mapped out on the Argand plane, a remarkable pattern emerges.

The computer can systematically check each spot on the Argand plane and see if a sequence of the two remains bound or unbound after a series of iterations. The computer assigns a color to the point of whether it does or does not belong in the set. Originally, black was the color of the numbers in the set, and so the other colors were red or yellow if the numbers are not in the set. What you get looks like the image on the inside cover of this book.

By convention, brighter colors are used around the edges that represent numbers that are very close to belonging inside the set, but yet are not, and that makes all the difference! In other words, these numbers cannot "make up their mind" as to whether they belong in the Mandelbrot set or not. In the picture above, black represents the numbers in the Mandelbrot, yellow regions that are very close to it, and dark red for those numbers that are not close at all. By using this map, you can easily check if a number belongs to the Mandelbrot set or not.

What is really amazing about this is not that we have a map, but rather its shape and the nuances of this shape. This shape is totally unpredictable. The shape first discovered by Brooks and Matelski, in 1978, and further defined by Mandelbrot, was not what they expected nor imagined.

The largest part of the shape is called the cardioid, or heart-shaped structure.

But it's the edges of the cardioid that are so amazing. Around the edges, we see circular bubbles, along with what are called dendrites, or branches that are rooted to the bubbles and extend outward. These dendrites are

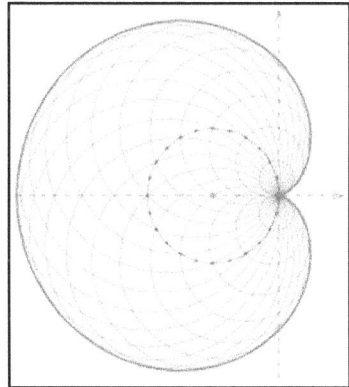

Cardioid

very "wiggly," except for the antenna that extends to the left of the cardioid on the real-number line axis, which is perfectly straight and ends exactly to C equal minus two.

What boggles the mind is that when we zoom into these bubbles, we find *more* shapes that look like the mother shape, and this represents a set of an infinite number of smaller versions of itself built into itself.

Furthermore, when we zoom into the dendrites, we find another interesting phenomenon. The branches follow a precise geometric formula, with the branches growing by odd numbers in perfect sequence—to infinity! To the right of the largest bubble, or circle, the branch is split to an even number to infinity. The further you zoom into Mandelbrot, the more mini and mini and mini Mandelbrots you find, and every time you find one of these Mandelbrots, you start the whole process over, diving into more Mandelbrots into infinity! I would encourage you to go to YouTube to find some of these computer-generated programs that go deeper and deeper into the Mandelbrot and witness these incredible shapes and designs that are really indescribable on paper. These types of structures represent what we have defined as *fractals*.

As we have stated, a fractal is a geometric shape whose parts resemble the whole. In this case, every mini Mandelbrot is very similar, though not exactly, to the entire Mandelbrot set. No matter how much we zoom in, the basic shape remains the same, and fractals are property known as scale in variance. As it turns out, the Mandelbrot set has many sections that exhibit this phenomenon.

The Mandelbrot has been studied extensively, as you might imagine. As a result, various names have been given to the areas of the Mandelbrot where discoveries of recurrent shapes have occurred. It is not our purpose here to discuss all these areas, but I would recommend Jason Lisle's book, *Fractals*, or any of the number of YouTube videos that have been produced regarding the Mandelbrot, to witness these. To mention just a few areas, we have the Seahorse Valley, the Double Spiral Valley, and the Elephant Valley, as seen on the inside covers of this book. At these areas, which are primarily around the edges of the Mandelbrot, we see images that resemble seahorses, elephants, and double spirals.

Each time you dive into these various shapes, what do you find? More Mandelbrots. What is very curious is that, if you turn the Mandelbrot on its side and observe the x-axis going to infinity, you will find a bifurcation pattern exactly as described by Feigenbaum!

German mathematician Heinz-Otto Peitgen and German physicist Peter H. Richter, a team of scientists working at the University of Bremen, essentially turned their careers over to the Mandelbrot set. They began studying the Mandelbrot set extensively, especially paying attention at the boundaries, or edges, of the Mandelbrot set. It is at the boundary where a Mandelbrot set program spends most of its time and makes "all of its compromises." Here at the boundaries, as mentioned, a program cannot absolutely, of certainty, decide whether it falls inside the set or not, which brings us the fascinating shapes that we find. James Gleick, in his book, *Chaos*, puts it this way: "It is as if they are balanced between competing attractors, one at zero and the other, in effect, ringing the set at a distance of infinity."

Peitgen and Richter then began looking at boundaries of magnetization and non-magnetization of materials. Much like the Mandelbrot set, these boundaries displayed particularly beautiful complexity, with shapes becoming progressively more tangled with knobs and furrows. "As they varied the parameters and increased their magnification of details, one picture seemed more and more random, until suddenly, unexpectedly, deep in the heart of a bewildering region, appeared a familiar oblate form, studded with buds: the Mandelbrot set, every tendril and every atom in place. It was another signpost of universality. Perhaps we should believe in magic," they wrote. This was evidence of the Mandelbrot appearing in a natural phenomenon.

So, it is important to understand that, much like calculus and the Pythagorean Theorem, the Mandelbrot was a discovered phenomenon—not an invented phenomenon—and this is key! All these regions of the Mandelbrot set are mathematically true. Computers simply followed the math and had no creative power. Now, it's true that humans defined the set, and humans added various colors to the computer to define the Mandelbrot shape, but the shapes are a result of the math, and they followed the rules of the mathematics. It is very clear the computer is not creating the exquisite beauty we see; it's embedded in the math, and mathematics is embedded into the fabric of our reality. As Jason Lisle writes, "The beauty of fractals comes not from people or computers, but from the numbers and the law of mathematics."[5] "What must also be understood is there is no randomness in the Mandelbrot set. It obeys an extraordinary precise scheme leaving nothing to chance whatsoever," wrote John Hubbard.[6]

Consider infinity. We live in a finite world. We are born, and we die. The sun rises; the sun sets. Seasons come; seasons go. There's a beginning to a movie, and there's an end to a movie. Even our universe itself is considered finite. It had a beginning, and it will have an end.

God, on the other hand, is infinite. There was no beginning to God. This is implied at the "burning bush," when God revealed His name to Moses in Exodus 3:14 as the "I Am." God, therefore, transcends time and space; He has always been and will always be. Admittedly, this is a very difficult concept for humankind to grasp. We attend a sporting event, such as a baseball game, and expect there to eventually be an end to that game. We are just programmed this way—nothing goes on forever, and everything has a start. But we are built in the image of God, and maybe, just maybe, something like the Mandelbrot set can at least give us a glimpse into infinity. We delve into the Mandelbrot and see all these mini-Mandelbrots, and we quickly understand that each of these mini-Mandelbrots contains an infinite number of more Mandelbrots. "As a result, we are not merely exploring infinity, but an infinite number of infinities," says Dr. Lisle.[7]

The Mandelbrot "existed" long before Benoit Mandelbrot discovered it. "It existed as soon as science created a context—a framework of complex numbers and a notion of iterated functions. Then it waited to be unveiled. Or perhaps it existed earlier, as soon as nature began organizing itself by means of simple physical laws, repeated with infinite patience and everywhere the same," Gleick has written.[8] Or maybe it existed even "in the beginning."

Thus, by using the laws of logic and mathematics, we get to learn more about infinity, and this is just with the Mandelbrot set. If we change the formula for other iterations, we get more extraordinary sets and designs, though my preference is still for the Mandelbrot, from an aesthetic point of view.

So, possibly, the Mandelbrot set exists in part to help us to fathom infinity or perhaps even proof of intelligent order and design. Maybe Kepler was right—God does think mathematically!

Besides helping us contemplate infinity, and thus God, are there any other practical uses of the Mandelbrot set? It turns out there are. As we have seen, the Mandelbrot represents fractals to us. I dare say, before the movie *Frozen*, most people had never heard the word *fractal*. In the movie, Idina Menzel sings the iconic, Academy Award–winning song, "Let It Go," which references "frozen fractals all around," clearly referring to snowflakes, which are, of course, indeed fractals. Because of Benoit Mandelbrot, who referred to himself as a "fractalist," we now have a concept of fractals, and we can notice that, in nature, fractals *are* all around us.

Mandelbrot further developed his theory of roughness and self-similarity in nature from his studies. Again, we have noted that things typically considered "rough," or chaotic, such as clouds and shorelines, actually have a degree of order. As we saw with the Golden Ratio, this order is also seen in the branches of trees and the tree leaves themselves, which are also fractals; in the animal world and the human world, the circulatory system, the respiratory system, the renal system, all are fractals. We also see fractals in very widely unrelated physical phenomenon, such as mountain ranges and river deltas, and even in lightning. As a result of Mandelbrot's research, fractals have had applications in a wide variety of fields, such as statistical physics, anatomy, neurology, information technology, computer graphics, chaos theory, and many, many more. Mandelbrot won many awards and professional honors, and he was called by one mathematician, one of the greatest mathematicians of the late twentieth century. Because of this, he became a fixture of the scientific lecture circuit, compared with such luminaries as Albert Einstein and James Watson.[9]

Fern

It would seem the physical universe bears a striking resemblance to the abstract world of mathematics. The question, once again, is "Why?" One might say it's because the physical world "obeys" mathematical laws and the forces of nature, such as gravity and electromagnetism, and it acts in such a way as to demonstrate this. We know that snowflakes look like they do microscopically, with six sides, because the shape of the water molecule is determined by the forces between the atoms. But even this is only so because the universe is so structured that the physical laws demand obedience. If you do not think so, drop the book you're holding in your hand now and see if it floats in the air!

Fractals point to a common, single creator or source designer. The ubiquity of fractals is seen in randomly unrelated phenomena which "time and chance" cannot explain.

Of course, many don't care *why* the universe obeys mathematical laws, and we alluded to this in the introduction to this book. But there has to be a reason why, and I profoundly believe that answer is God. As we have

Mountain Rrange

seen previously, mathematics is in the mind; it is abstract. David Berlinski has written, "The truth of mathematics makes reference to a domain of abstract objects: they are not within space and they are timeless. Objects that are beyond space and time can have no causal powers."[10] Yet, physical laws obey this abstraction. This brings us back to the great dilemma, doesn't it? Without a mind, there can be no mathematics, and only a Christian worldview has a good explanation for whom that mind belongs to. It is God, who is sovereign over the entire universe, and it is He, as we have seen, who holds all things together by His power.[11] "Fractals exist in the abstract world of mathematical thought and also in physical reality because God's mind controls both," says Lisle.[12] The Mandelbrot set, with all its grandeur and beauty, helps us at least, just a bit, to understand this character of God and, hence, it helps us understand His purpose.

Chapter
12

THE GREAT DESIGNER AND HIS ETERNAL PURPOSE

Stephen Hawking, "Heaven is a fairy story for people afraid of the dark." John Lennox's reply, "Atheism is a fairy story for people afraid of the light."

"For atheists, facing arguments for God's existence is one thing. Facing God Himself is another."

—*Douglas Axe*

IN THE PREVIOUS CHAPTERS, I HAVE LAID OUT THE CASE FOR A Great Designer, or Creator, of the universe. In this chapter, I will unequivocally, undeniably, and unapologetically identify precisely who this Designer is. The evidence for a Designer is "absolutely overwhelming," and it "points toward an intelligence behind life's creation," says Walter Bradley, former professor at Texas A&M University.[1] Stephen Meyer says, "Science supports a theistic belief," for which there is "robust evidence."[2] In fact, theism provides the best explanation for the ensemble of the scientific evidence.

This evidence comes from cosmology in the form of the Kalam Argument—that is, what has a beginning has a cause; from physics, from the exquisite fine-tuning of the universe; from astronomy, from the earth's unique place in the universe; from biochemistry, evidence from irreducible complexity; from biology, as seen in the DNA molecule and its unique ability to carry and transfer vast amounts of information; and from consciousness and the evidence of true will, a topic upon which we will expand.

By contrast, materialism, or naturalism, requires believing that nothing produces everything, non-life produces life, randomness produces fine-tuning, chaos produces information, unconsciousness produces consciousness, and non-reason produces reason.[3]

British physicist Edmond Whitaker wrote, "There is no ground for supposing that matter and energy existed before and was suddenly galvanized into action. For what would distinguish that moment from all other moments in eternity? It is simple to postulate creation *ex nihilo*—divine will constituting nature from nothingness."[4] Further, William Lane Craig believes "it is indisputable that there has never been a time in history when the hard evidence of science was more confirming a belief in God than today."[5]

So, the question becomes, if there is a God, who is He, and what characteristics would we expect Him to possess? There are, after all, many religions in the world that believe in a higher being, and it makes sense that they cannot all be right. So, who is God—in this case, our Designer, or Creator?

William Lane Craig

We would definitely expect God to transcend time and space and exist from eternity. Even Stephen Hawking acknowledged that if there was a beginning, you would expect a creature with these attributes.[6] We would also expect God to be omnipresent, omnipotent, and omniscient, and be of a supreme intelligence, the likes of which we cannot begin to comprehend. He would be fully able to create the universe by His very word. The Creator also would be personal, explaining things by agent and volition and free will.[7] Craig says, "He can create a new effect without antecedent determining conditions. He would decide to say, 'Let there be light,' and the universe would spring into existence."[8]

This eliminates deism, the belief that God created the world but has since left it to run on its own. Per Meyer, "The deistic God never intervenes in nature, yet we are seeing evidence of intelligent design in the history of life."[9] A pantheistic view doesn't work, either, for the same reasons. The god of the universe is not "everything and in everything," and pantheism cannot explain how the universe began. Finally, we would expect the Creator to be spiritual rather than physical.

Lee Strobel has written, "The creator that emerges from the scientific data is uncannily consistent with the description of the God whose identity is spelled out in the pages of the Bible."[10] In his book *A Case for the Creator*, he goes on to quote thirteen passages that illustrate his point. Psalm 102:25 alludes to His creative capacity: "In the beginning you laid the foundations of the earth, and the heavens are the work of your hands." Deuteronomy 4:35 speaks to His uniqueness: "To you it has been shown, that you might know that the Lord himself is God; there is none other besides Him." Psalm 90:2 reads, "Before the mountains were born, you brought forth the earth and the world, from everlasting to everlasting," alluding to God's being uncaused and timeless. His Spirit nature is indicated in John 4:24: "God is a spirit." Genesis 17:1 states, "I am God almighty," the One whom Millard J. Erickson indicates: "God is personal, an individual being with self-consciousness and capable of feeling, choosing, and having a reciprocal relationship with personal and social beings."[11]

Lee Strobel

God shows His freedom of will in Genesis 1:3: "Let there be light." His intelligence and rationality are seen in Psalm 104:24: "Oh Lord, how manifold are your works! In wisdom you have made them all. The earth is full of your possessions." Nahum 1:3 speaks to His immense power, stating, "The Lord is great in power." God's creativity is indicated in Psalm 139:13–14: "For you created my innermost being: you knit me together in my mother's womb, I praise you because I am fearfully and wonderfully made, your works are wonderful, I know that full well." His caring nature is noted in Psalm 33:5: "The earth is full of his unfailing love." First Kings 8:27 points to His omnipresence: "The heavens even the highest heaven cannot contain you." Colossians 1:16, which states, "For everything, absolutely everything, above and below, visible and invisible, everything got started in Him and find its purpose in Him," indicates He has given humankind purpose. Finally, as Strobel writes, Isaiah 25:8 says that God "will swallow up death forever."[12]

With these Scriptures in mind, and based upon both internal and external evidence, it is time to identify the Creator of the universe. John 1:1–5 states, "In the beginning was the word, and the word was with God and the word was God. He was in the beginning with God. All things were made through Him, and without Him nothing was made that was made. In Him was life, and the life was the light of men. And the light shines in darkness and men did not comprehend." This passage is, of course, speaking of Jesus Christ.

So, when Genesis 1:1 says, "In the beginning God created the heavens and the earth," the apostle John identifies that Person as Jesus Christ, one of the Godhead, which also includes God the Father and the Holy Spirit.

Where is the proof of such a bold statement? Are we to blindly believe John's gospel? He further writes in verse 18 of the same chapter: "No one has seen God. The only begotten Son who was in the bosom of His father, has declared Him."

First understand that God is not hidden from us. The apostle Paul, in speaking to the Athenians in Acts 17, stated, "He [God] is not far from any of us for in Him we live and have our being." Second, it is not a blind faith that requires one to believe what I have stated here. Sir John Templeton wrote, "Faith does not imply a closed but open mind. Quite the opposite of blindness, faith appreciates the vast spiritual realities that materialists overlook by getting trapped in the purely physical."[13]

The proof that Christ is the Creator rests in Christ Himself. Christ claimed deity and equality with God, and to deny this is to deny Scripture. Jesus said, "I and the Father are one," found in the gospel of John, 10:30. Also, in answering Philip in John 14:9, Jesus said, "Anyone who has seen me has seen the Father." Finally, in Philippians 2:6, Paul wrote, speaking of Jesus, "Who, being in the form of God, did not consider it robbery to be equal with God, but made himself of no reputation, taking on the form of a bond servant and coming in the likeness of man."

Jesus came to the earth, born through a woman, with one sole purpose in mind, and that was to redeem mankind. Sin separates us from God, and Romans 13:22 states, "For all have sinned and come short of the glory of God." We cannot be right before God if we have sinned; therefore, there had to be a way for those sins to be forgiven—and that way was through Jesus Christ. John 3:16–17 reads, "For God so loved the world that he gave his only begotten son, that whoever believes on him should not perish but have everlasting life. God did not send his son into the world to condemn the world, but that the world might be saved."

But once again, where is the proof? Today, there are deranged people, and maybe some not-so-deranged people, who claim deity. We scoff at these people, understanding that such statements and claims are ludicrous. Jesus claimed deity, yet many believed Him. Why? Jesus understood how incredible His claim was; therefore, He backed it up with miracles. Once again, I turn to the gospel of John, where in chapter 10:7–38, Jesus said, "If I do not do the works of my Father, do not believe me; but if I do, though you do not believe me, believe the works, that you may know and believe that the Father is in Me, and I in Him."

Jesus performed many, many miracles during His short, three-year ministry on earth, including healing the blind, the lame, and the sick; raising the dead; walking on water; and turning water into wine. These miracles were witnessed by thousands, including, of course, His apostles. Peter, along with James and John, even witnessed the Transfiguration of Christ, where he heard the voice say, "This is my beloved Son, in Him I am well pleased."[14] In ending His gospel, John wrote, "This is the disciple who testifies of these things, and wrote these things; and we know that his testimony is true. And there were also many other things that Jesus did, which if they were written one by one, I suppose that even the world itself could not contain the books that would be written." George Stokes, a great physicist of his time and one of the pioneers in spectroscopy, as well as a Lucasian professor of mathematics, wrote, "Admit the existence of God of a personal God, the possibility of miracles flows at once."[15]

The ultimate proof of Christ's deity came with His resurrection. There are multitude of evidences that the resurrection was a real event in history and witnessed by many. First, it was witnessed by Mary Magdalene; Joanna; Mary, the mother of James; and other women who came to His gravesite. Second, it was witnessed by His disciples, including Thomas, who saw and possibly touched His wounds. The resurrected Jesus was also seen by two disciples on the road to Emmaus, and Paul wrote that He was seen by over five hundred people at once, most of which were still alive when Paul wrote his letter to the Corinthians. Furthermore, Christ's ascension into heaven was witnessed, as well. The physician Luke confirmed this in Luke 24, as did Mark in his gospel, chapter 16.

The importance of the resurrection cannot be overemphasized, because it is the basis of Christianity, and without it, Christianity falls. Paul, who also saw the risen Savior, said to the Corinthians in his first letter to them, in chapter 15, verse 13: "And if Christ is not risen, then our preaching is empty and your faith is also empty." Then, in verse 17, he wrote, "And if Christ is not risen, your faith is futile; you are still in your sins! Then also those who have fallen asleep in Christ have perished. If in this life only we have hope in Christ, we are of all men most pitiable."

I realize many people, if not most of the people, in the world are skeptical of these things, doubting the resurrection was a real event. This is not surprising, for many did not believe the apostles as well, even though the apostles confirmed their testimony with various miracles and wonders imparted to them by the Holy Spirit. In Paul's preaching to the Athenians, there were three responses: 1) those who believed; 2) those who mocked; and 3) those who would hear more. Their responses are similar to what we see today, as well.

But keep this in mind: History tells us that all the apostles except John were put to death in the most gruesome of ways for what they believed. Let that sink in! The apostles went to their deaths willingly; they were with Jesus before His death, and as we have seen, they witnessed His resurrection and ascension. John Warwick Montgomery writes, "It passes the bounds of creditability that the early Christians could manufacture such a tale and then preach it among those who might easily have refuted it simply by producing the body of Jesus."[16]

Further, it is highly unlikely that Jesus' disciples would have just made up the story of His resurrection. Paul Little asks, "Are these men, who helped transform the moral structure of society, consummate liars or deluded madmen? These alternatives are harder to believe than the fact of the resurrection and there is no shred of evidence to support them."[17]

Jesus' disciples spent the rest of their lives after His resurrection preaching the gospel, in spite of severe persecution, and not one of them ever recanted or denied their belief. How extraordinary! Paul Little further writes, "Men will die for what they believe to be true, though it be in actuality false: they do not however die for what they know to be a lie."[18] Josh McDowell, in his monumental work, *The New Evidence That Demands a Verdict*, put it this way: "Hypocrites and martyrs are not made of the same stuff."[19] This one fact alone, that Jesus' disciples were willing to suffer persecution, beatings, imprisonment, and even martyrdom for the cause of Christ, is enough to convince me and many others that Christ was the Son of God and was resurrected on the third day after His death. What is very obvious is that, in spite of these persecutions, Christianity flourished, with the Roman Empire "surrendering" to it by the fourth century. Historian Norman Davies writes that this "surrender to Christianity, was irrigated by the blood of martyrs."[20]

Josh McDowell

The resurrection of Jesus Christ becomes the most important event in human history. Please note, no other religion or religious leaders make such a claim—that is, of resurrection—not Muhammed, not Buddha, not Confucius, not Zoroaster, and not Joseph Smith. The resurrection is thus unique to Jesus Christ. Certainly, many will deny it and ask for more evidence or proof. But proof will never be good enough for these individuals if they are of a closed mind and any amount of evidence will be ignored. Hebrews defines *faith* as the "assurance of things hoped for, the conviction of things not seen."[21] Paul told the Roman Christians, "So then faith comes by hearing, and hearing by the word of God."[22] Ultimately, one decides for him or herself, but Jesus said, "Blessed are those who have not seen, and have believed." He was talking to you and me.

Let me emphasize this: this plan for Christ's coming was there from the very beginning. This plan, this purpose, was put into place in eternity past; so indicates Paul to the Ephesians in chapter 4 of his epistle. It was even foretold in Genesis 3:15: "And I shall put enmity between your seed and her seed (Christ); he shall bruise your head (Satan) and you shall bruise his heel."

God's Plan for Humankind

So, the question remains: Is there a purpose God has given to you and me? I think there is. Materialists think there is nothing special about humans. To give a flavor for this, notice this quote from Bill Nye, the so called Science Guy, to the American Humanist Association in 2010: "I'm insignificant . . . I'm just another speck of sand. And the earth really, in the cosmic scheme of things, is another speck. And the sun, an unremarkable star . . . And the galaxy is a speck. I'm a speck on a speck orbiting a speck among other specks among still other specks in the middle of specklessness. I suck!" But Genesis 1:26 disagrees: "Then God said, 'Let us make man in our own image, according to our own likeness, let them have dominion over the fish of the sea, of the birds of the air, and over cattle and over all the earth, and over every creeping thing that creeps on the earth.' So God created man in his own image, in the image of God he created him; male and female he created them." This image does not refer to the physical attributes of man, as those are not dissimilar to animals. We have eyes, ears, brains, arms, legs, hearts, lungs, etc., much like any other animal. So, Genesis must be alluding to something else that makes us unique. But what?

Once again, the materialist says humans are just a part of the animal kingdom and there is nothing special about us. We are made up of molecules, just like the rest of the animal world. The implications for this are obvious, but setting that aside, I would have to vociferously disagree with the materialist. Humans are quite different from other animals. First, they are different in their intellectual capacity. Much has been said about the similarities of humans to apes or chimpanzees and how we share a great deal of DNA with primates. How much DNA we share can be debated, especially when you look at the expression of that DNA in the form of protein production, but only a fool would say that apes and chimpanzees are intellectually equal or even close to being intellectually equal to humans. There is a vast, *vast* difference between us, and not even millions of years of evolution can account for this. Humans can read, write, and as we have seen, compute elaborate mathematical equations.

Humans also possess the ability for discovery. Humans are aware of the universe and the surrounding planets and galaxies. As we have noted, mankind has discovered many of the various laws that govern our universe. The animal kingdom certainly does not possess these capacities. Melissa Cain Travis wrote that it is this "higher rationality that enables us to study nature using observation, mathematics and innate preferences for beauty and simplicity that makes us the image of God."[23]

What animal ever wrote a symphony like Beethoven's Ninth, crafted a sculpture of King David like Michelangelo did, or painted a picture of the sky such as Van Gogh's *Starry Night*? Animals do not send themselves to the moon and back or develop computers or higher technology. To be sure, the song of a mockingbird, the graceful flight of a falcon, the beautiful design of the honeycomb—these are all wonderful traits to see and admire and enjoy, but they fall far short of what mankind is capable of. Further, humankind has a moral code, something animals do not possess. There are certain things we know—right from wrong, such as murder, rape, thievery—that animals do not possess. Maybe this is also a way in which we are made in the image of God.

Mankind is also endowed with free will, though materialists would deny this. If you think about it, denying free will is self-refuting, because for someone to convince you to deny free will, he or she is using their free will to do so! So, from the very beginning, God indicated we have a free will. Eve and Adam were told not to eat of the Tree of Knowledge Good and Evil, and that if they did, they would die.[24] Before this action, sin did not exist, or at least it had not happened yet in the human realm. Adam and Eve had the free will to eat or not to eat, and they chose to disobey God; thus sin and death entered the world. What happened after this? Genesis 3:7 says, "The eyes of both of them were opened, and they knew they were naked." Were they sinning by being naked before they ate of the fruit? Were they sinning by being naked after they ate the fruit? In verse 11, God asked two questions: "Who told you that you were naked?" and "Have you eaten from the tree of which I commanded you that you shall not eat?" Notice that Adam does not answer the first question. They had apparently decided on their own to sew fig leaves to cover themselves. This may represent the first act of a social contract between these two. God, at this point, had not ordered them to clothe themselves. But now Adam and Eve had "become like one of Us, to know good and evil." This admittedly is hard for us to grasp, but clearly, they had free will and could have chosen not to sin, yet they did so by eating of the forbidden fruit. They died spiritually immediately, and physically much later on, with death entering the world for all mankind.

Afterward, Cain freely chose to commit murder, killing his brother Abel, and he was condemned for it. The Old Testament is full of examples of people exercising their free will. We see Joshua telling his kindred that he and his house would choose to serve the Lord (Joshua 14), obviously indicating that he could also have chosen not to.

This concept is covered over and over in the New Testament, as well, with many examples. Ananias and Sapphira, who kept back a portion of the sale of their property, suffered severe consequences for their lying when they claimed to have given all of the proceeds to the church, but did not. Peter told Ananias, "While it remained was it not your own? And after it was sold, was it not in your own control? Why have you conceived this in your heart? You have not lied to men but to God."[25] Clearly, they had the free will to do as they wished, and they did so—but with severe consequences. It should seem that free will is axiomatic, that is self-evident, but still there are those who would continue to argue otherwise. They have to, if they are materialists, because it is a logical conclusion of their philosophy. For the materialists, humans have no control over their behavior any more so than they have control over a physical-chemical reaction, since we are but an accumulation of chemicals.

But even science itself refutes such dogma. Dr. Michael Egnor, a neurosurgeon, points to several experiments that confirm free will. Wilder Penfield, in his book, *The Mystery of the Mind*, wrote about his experiments with conscious individuals. With brain stimulators in place, he could "cause" a person to move their arm or leg. He could also ask that individual to move their appendages voluntarily. In all cases, the individual could tell the difference between the involuntary and voluntary movement.

Furthermore, Penfield could not invoke abstract thought using electrical stimulation. "Penfield found no abstract thought or any experience evoked by surgery or seizure, i.e., he couldn't evoke calculus or philosophy," writes Dr. Egnor.[26]

Physiologist Benjamin Libet, using brainwave technology, studied the response time between brain activity and the resultant musculoskeletal activity of individuals. Libet would ask the volunteers to push a button while monitoring brainwave activity. He found the brain activity would spike 300 milliseconds before the volunteer consciously decided to push the button. Initially, this was interpreted as evidence against free will, but occasionally, Libet would ask the volunteer to veto their decision to push the button. When this occurred, there was *no* brain activity. This veto power was not from the brain! Libet called this "free won't," but in essence, he was demonstrating free will.[27]

Other experiments in observation show that even severely brain-damaged patients maintain will and abstract thought, and then a multitude of documented near-death experiences show that, even in the absence of heartbeat and brain activity, such individuals still experienced awareness and mental experience. The point here is that even though you and I know there is free will, neuroscience also supports it strongly, as well.

As we have alluded to, denying free will has serious ramifications. Without free will, there is no right or wrong, no moral or immoral behavior, no sin. Criminals are thus no different from a mad dog. We do not impart criminality, for example, to President Joe Biden's dog Commander, who was finally removed from the White House for biting some twelve or more people. We don't say this dog has "sinned." But I hope, as we have shown, humans are not animals, and we *do* have the ability to choose right from wrong. If not, it would not be entirely absurd to suggest incarcerating criminals before they acted. That, of course, would be crazy, but our criminal justice system seems to act as if criminals don't have a choice, as we have seen recently with No Cash Bail, etc. There is thus no moral agency, no right, no wrong, no innocence or guilt!

In this scenario, things like euthanasia become more palatable. Dr. Egnor refers to philosopher Hannah Arendt, who points out that totalitarian systems are unconcerned with actual moral guilt or innocence. The Holocaust was just "human livestock management," and Stalin did not starve millions of Ukrainians because of any laws they broke. "The cornerstone of totalitarian rule is the denial of free will—the denial of moral guilt and

Dr. Michael Egnor

innocence," writes Dr. Egnor.[28] Further, he writes, "Denial of free will is a metaphysical error, a scientific misunderstanding, a reputation of human dignity, and an existential threat to humanity."[29]

The soul who sins will die. "The son shall not bear the inequity of the father, neither shall the father bear the inequity of the son, the righteous of the righteous shall be upon him, and the wickedness of the wicked shall be upon him," wrote Ezekiel.[30] We do not inherit sin, so this passage states. We are all born with free moral agency, and hence we have the ability to decide right from wrong, and our entire judicial system is based on this notion. This is a clear distinction between humans and the animal kingdom. So, maybe it is this free will that distinguishes humans from animals, and in this way, we are made in the image of God.

My contention, however, is that the primary way we differ from animals is our soul. Human beings are given a soul—and not just the breath-of-life soul—and this is important. The soul I'm talking about will persist after death and into eternity. Dr. Gerald L. Schroeder, in his excellent book, *Genesis and the Big Bang*, notes that the word in Hebrew *nefesh* is the life-giving spirit or soul that all animals possess. However, mankind was additionally imparted the *neshamah*, which is quite different. This is seen in Genesis 2:7. The writer of the book of Hebrews wrote, "But we are not of those who shrink back to destruction, but of those who have faith in the preserving of the soul." In Matthew 10:28, Jesus said, "Do not be afraid of those who kill the body but cannot kill the soul. Rather be afraid of the one who can destroy both soul and body in hell." In addition to the other attributes, then, humankind has a soul that makes us most like God, and that soul will answer to God, as it is the soul that will endure long after this body has vanished from the earth.

Strangers in a Strange Land

This brings us to the central theme of this book: God's purpose and His purpose for mankind. I do not propose to know the mind of God, but He has not left us totally ignorant, for in His Word He has revealed to us at least a portion of His thoughts. First Corinthians 2 provides a good commentary on this subject. It reads, beginning in verse 12, "For what man knows the things of a man which is in him? Even so, no one knows the things of God except the spirit of God." Further, Isaiah wrote in chapter 59:8–9, "For my thoughts are not your thoughts, nor are your ways my ways, says the Lord. For as the heavens are higher than earth, so are my ways higher than your ways and my thoughts than your thoughts." Isaiah also wrote in 43:6 that "God created His people for His glory."

Thus, from Scripture it would seem that God created the world and mankind for His own glory. John 1:3 says, "Through Him all things were made; without him nothing was made." The psalmist wrote in 19:1, "The heavens declare the glory of God, the skies proclaim the work of His hands." Paul wrote to the Romans in 1:20, "For since the creation of the world, God's invisible qualities—His eternal power and divine nature—have been clearly seen, being understood from what has been made, so that people are without excuse." To what does that refer? Clearly, from this passage Paul is referring to an excuse for not believing in God! Earlier, in verse 16, he proclaimed he was not ashamed of the Gospel of Christ: "For it is the power, the salvation to everyone who believes." Then, in verse 22, Paul wrote, "Because, although they knew God, they did not glorify him as God, nor were they thankful, but futile in their thoughts, and their foolish hearts are darkened." As a result, these people, professing to be wise, change the glory of God the incorruptible into an image made like corruptible man.

From these verses, it is evident that God expects to be glorified and that mankind was made to do just that. Animals do not worship

God, only humans. We have been placed on this earth, given an immortal soul, in order to glorify God. Sadly, few there are who seem to know this.

When Jesus was asked what the greatest commandment was, what did He say? "You shall love the Lord, your God, with all your heart and with all your soul and with all your mind."[31] That just about says it all, doesn't it? Yet, Jesus went on to say, "You shall love your neighbor as yourself."[32] It would seem that our purpose on earth is twofold: love God, and love your neighbor. This passage encompasses all other passages and commands, because Christ said, "If you love me, you will keep my commandments."[33] But who is my neighbor?

A lawyer asked Jesus this very question, just as Jesus had told him about the two greatest commandments. Jesus answered the man with a story that has come to be called the Parable of the Good Samaritan. In it, Jesus pointed out that the one who helped the poor victim in this story was the one who would have seemed most unlikely to do so—that was the Samaritan. You see, the Samaritans were despised by the Jews, even considered worse than dogs. Yet it was the Samaritan, not a Levite and not a priest, who came to the aid of this poor man. And he—that is, the Good Samaritan—went above and beyond to help his fellow man, even willing to pay the innkeeper where he took the man more money if necessary.

The clear teaching of this passage is that our responsibility—yes, even our purpose—is to do good to all men, no matter who they are. It is easy to help a relative or a friend, not so much a random stranger, yet it is necessary. In Matthew 5:43-44, Jesus said, "But I say unto you, love your enemies, bless them that curse you, do good to them that hate you, and pray for them who despitefully use you and persecute you." This is, admittedly, not easy, yet it is something we must do. Paul told the Galatian Christians, "As we have opportunity, let us do good unto all men, especially unto them who are of the household of faith."[34] But what does "good" look like? First John 3:17 reads, "But whoever has this world's goods, and sees his brother in need, and shuts up his heart from them, how does the love of God abide in him? My little children, let us not love in word or in tongue but in deed and in truth." We are to be doers of the Word, therefore, doers of good, so writes James in his letter (1:22). James further says we are to fulfill the royal law when we love our neighbor as ourselves.[35]

Who can deny that our purpose on earth is doing good toward all men when we have the opportunity to do so? Thus, we are to be lights in a dark world: "Let your light so shine before men, then they may see your good works and glorify your father in heaven," said Jesus in His mountain sermon.[36] This then leads us to the final purpose, one most of us don't think about, which is that our journey on earth is preparatory. Paul says our citizenship is in heaven.[37] James says, "Our life is like a vapor, that appears for a little time and then vanishes away."[38] We, therefore, are to redeem the time we have on this earth.[39]

We are, in essence, waiting for a life hereafter, and our life here is to be lived in expectation of that life, which is preparing us for it. We have not seen that new realm, but Paul may very well have, and if so, he is the only one in history to report about it. Look what he says in 2 Corinthians 12. He seems to be talking about himself here, but whoever it was, was caught up in a third heaven, whether literally or spiritually, Paul did not know. That person—again, mostly likely Paul himself—was "caught up" in paradise and heard inexpressible words that he was not permitted to utter. What we do know, whether from this experience or not, Paul was not afraid of death, and he looked on the afterlife as not only better, but "far better."[40]

We are thus strangers in a strange land. Just as Abraham was a stranger in the land of Canaan, so are we here on the earth. Peter refers to Christians as "sojourners and pilgrims."[41] The writer of the book of Hebrews, in chapter 11, refers to those faithful who were now dead to have been "strangers and pilgrims" on the earth. We then are preparing for eternity.

This is difficult, if not impossible, for us to grasp, but I liken it to this. Before I was married, I had had only an idea of what being married would be like. I could imagine or guess, but I could not really know until I was actually wed. Now, after fifty years of marriage, it is hard to remember what it was like when I *wasn't* married. This is how I perceive it will be in eternity. Life on earth here is just a blip in time, after that comes eternity—and, like the song says, once we are there ten thousand years, "we have only just begun." I like the way Daniel King ends his wonderful book, *Does God Exist?* There he writes, "The life we live while on earth, from a Christian perspective, is a proving ground of sorts, the stage for a superior realm, the likes of which we have not hither foreordained imagined. We believe this because we believe God exists. We are convinced that the weight of the evidence is on the side of the believer. God has spoken in his own defense in a whole host of ways. If we decide to deafen ourselves to the sound of his voice, we ignore it to our own hurt. Here, we must see to it that we do not refuse to hear Him who has spoken (Hebrews 12:25). See that you refuse not Him who is speaking."

Chapter
13

The Dark Side

A Darwinian understanding of morality makes it very difficult to condemn as evil any human behavior that has persisted because every trait that continues to exist even among a subpopulation has an equal right to claim nature's sanction. Presumably even antisocial behavior such as fraud, pedophilia, and rape must continue to exist among human beings because they were favored at some point by natural selection and therefore have some sort of biological basis.

—*John G West*

Darwin's lasting importance was precisely his banishment of purpose in life.

—*Michael Behe*

RUDOLPH HÖSS WAS A FAMILY MAN WITH A WIFE AND FIVE CHILDREN. He lived in a nice house with a beautiful garden and pool, and for all appearances he was a perfect dad, reading bedtime stories to his children at night and providing every need for his family. His subordinates at work revered him, and his superiors praised him. If you were one of his friends, you would find him engaging and cordial and pleasant to be around. He loved his pet dog and had a magnificent black horse, which he enjoyed riding, and he loved to fish in the stream that was near his house.

For all intents and purposes, Höss and his family lived an idyllic life, and they adored their home so much that when Höss was promoted in his job and had to move, his wife elected to stay behind with the children while he took an apartment at his new location, coming home for holidays and weekends whenever he could.

But there was a dark side to Rudolph. You see, Rudolph Höss was the commandant of Auschwitz Concentration Camp, which housed thousands of Jews who were incarcerated there for no reason other than their ethnicity. Worse than being incarcerated, the Jews were being systematically murdered by the use of Zyklon B gas, then incinerated in ovens built at Auschwitz. The black smoke of their incinerated bodies would rise up daily, and since the Höss house was immediately adjacent to the camp, separated only by a large gray wall topped off by barbed wire, his wife and children would see this smoke daily and hear the sounds of gunfire and torture going on in Auschwitz as they played and tended to the garden. The garden was even fertilized with ash from the crematory ovens.

Höss not only was a commandant, but he was actively involved with the mass murders, even designing the rooms and ovens where men and women and children would be herded into "showers," where the Zyklon would be released, asphyxiating them, then carted off to ovens to be cremated. He was proud of his work, and he had no remorse; he had been taught that Jews were not really human, and further, that they were directly responsible for all of Germany's prewar woes and thus must be exterminated. Of course, Höss was not alone in this ideology of hatred, as it was perpetuated throughout Hitler's Germany.

How could such ostensibly civil people have sunk to such depths of degradation, where evil had become so routine? This is a question historians have been asking for decades. Hannah Arendt, a young Jewish reporter who herself narrowly escaped the concentration camps, when covering the trial of Adolf Hitler, referred to the "banality of evil." By dehumanizing the Jews, Eichmann and Hitler's minions were able to dupe an entire society into participating either tacitly or overtly in committing such horrible atrocities. Unfortunately, as we shall see, that mindset of hatred persists in various places in our world today, allowing for barbaric activity with not only no remorse, but even glee.

There is a darkness in the world, a darkness of pure evil that will do unspeakable things, things unimaginable, to normal people. It is real, and if you doubt that, you have not paid much attention to recent events. In the United States, we see murder, rape, and all types of carnage portrayed daily in our major cities. Look at New York, Chicago, Los Angeles, Houston, and virtually any other major city, where every week, people are being shot, robbed, beaten, hijacked, etc. This especially seems to be worse on the weekends. Things are not getting better, but are getting worse, and no one seems to have an answer on how to curtail it.

As I write this chapter, Israel was just attacked by the terrorist group Hamas, who killed indiscriminately Jewish women, children, and the elderly, with some reports even describing the decapitation of infants. The stories coming out of Israel are nothing short of horrific. There are stories of families being tied up with their hands behind their backs and burned while still alive. There are stories of indiscriminate shooting and torture that are unimaginable. There are even verified reports of women being raped multiple times by multiple individuals, breaking femurs and pelvic bones in the process. The women often begged to be shot before which they ultimately were. It is hard to think that human beings can do this to their fellow man; nonetheless, it is occurring. The stated aim of Hamas is to rid the world of as many Jews as possible and to destroy the State of Israel. On the first day of the invasion, Hamas killed over 1,400 Israelis, and at least at the time of this writing, thirty-one Americans, with hundreds more taken captive to be used as human shields and/or held for ransom. If this is not evil, what is?

What is particularly perplexing is that here in the United States, thousands are protesting *in favor of* the Palestinians, as if the Israelis were responsible for the atrocities of Hamas. These protesters are not coming from the right, nor are they Nazi skinheads. On the contrary, these protests are coming from the far left; they chant "from the river to the sea," which means to push the Israelis from the Jordan to the Mediterranean—out of their country. Jewish students on college campuses are being harassed, threatened, and in some cases, even beaten. Such antisemitism has not been seen since the late 1930s in Adolf Hitler's Third Reich.

Hamas, which is nothing more than a puppet of Iran, has somehow created a scenario in which it, the aggressor, has become the victim. And who is suffering now? The Palestinians, just as I suppose Hamas had intended, to sway the world's opinion against the Jews.

In 2022, the Russians under Vladimir Putin invaded the sovereign state of Ukraine in their lust for power and land, resulting in tens of thousands of deaths to this point, with estimates ranging anywhere from fifteen to twenty thousand, no one knowing for sure.[1] The fighting there continues, with no end in sight at the time of this writing.

Now there are rumors of an imminent invasion of Taiwan by the communist Chinese, and who knows where that will lead. It seems to me we are closer to a third world war than we have been at any time in the past seventy-five years. Also currently in China, the Uyghurs and other Turkic Muslims are held in camps on a scale not seen since World War II. In 2020, the BBC reported that over five hundred thousand Uyghurs were being detained in what they called "concentration camps," forced to do hard labor, with many put to death. It has been reported that Communist Party leaders in China murder healthy Uyghur Muslims to sell their organs to wealthy Saudis in need, who are fussy about accepting organs from non-

Muslims and will pay a high premium, up to one million dollars per murder. Of course, the Chinese government denies all these claims—but who are you to believe?

We also see gruesome carnage from time to time coming out of Africa. For example, in Rwanda, in 1994, during a hundred-day period, estimates are that about eight hundred thousand people were slaughtered like cattle. Then, in 2003, in Darfur, Sudan, over four hundred thousand were killed. And of course, in times past we have seen the genocide that occurred in Cambodia in the 1970s, with estimates as high as 25 percent of the population being put to death by Pol Pot. Finally in Bosnia-Herzegovina, estimates of over two hundred thousand people were murdered in the name of genocide. We could go on and on, but the point is that evil does exist, and this is nothing new. Mankind seems to have a penchant for violence, with Paul in Ephesians 2:3 stating that "we are by nature children of wrath," yet recall from chapter 2, that mankind is "supposedly" more noble and less violent than we were centuries ago. Seems unlikely!

In Genesis 1:31, God observed His creation and proclaimed, "It is very good." It did not take long for things to change, did it? By the end of Genesis 3, man has fallen and has been kicked out of the Garden of Eden for disobeying God and eating of the Tree of the Knowledge of Good and Evil. Then, in Genesis 4, the first murder occurs, with a jealous Cain killing his brother Abel. By the time we get to Genesis 6, God is completely fed up with man because the hearts of men were continually turned toward evil and involved in wickedness. As we know from Genesis 6:6, God was even sorry that He had made man and it grieved Him. Genesis describes the world at this time as corrupt and violent, and as we know, the earth was destroyed by a flood—except for eight souls, including Noah and just a few animals. Since the times of Noah, there have always been wars and rumors of wars, and in most of them, it is difficult to even determine who's in the right and who's in the wrong. Certainly, the type of brutality we've seen in the Ukraine and Israel would be hard to justify on any level, and I am certain God is not being glorified in those states.

In America, we have seen the influx of drugs and human trafficking, primarily at the southern border. The drug cartels are brutal, savage, unmerciful, and willing to kill with no regard to human life whatsoever. These atrocities go on daily, and although you and I may never be witness to them, they nonetheless occur and defy contemplation. Of course, with the influx of all the illicit drugs in our country, plus the insatiable desire for these drugs, tens of thousands of people are dying yearly in America due to overdoses, especially due to the very potent drug fentanyl.[2]

How is this evil and violence explained? Materialists and secularists have a hard time defining it, and they even prefer to avoid the word *evil*. After all, according to them, we are just a product of atoms and molecules, and hence, we really possess no moral compass. Yet there is evil, and there has been since the Garden of Eden, when Satan, in the form of a serpent, tempted Eve to do what had been expressly forbidden by God to do.

Satan was more crafty than any other creatures God had made, thus he tempted her with a lie, saying that she surely would not die if she ate.[3] There appears to have already been an alien on the earth at that time, Satan, who had the capacity to disobey God and had actually done so; he now was encouraging the first humans to do so, as well. When Eve saw that the fruit was good for food, pleasant to the eye, and desirable to make one wise, she ate and gave her husband, Adam, to do so as well. When asked why she ate, Eve responded that the serpent (Satan) had deceived her, and she ate. As we know, death then entered the world. Though Adam and Eve did not die immediately, death resulted as a consequence to all mankind.

Some have asked why a loving God would allow evil to enter the world. If Satan is a created being, then does that not make God ultimately responsible for evil? This is a somewhat emotionally charged question, but the answer comes in the form of a subject we have already discussed, and that is free will. Mankind was created with free will, and it would appear that Satan, along with his minions, were also created beings who had a free will. Admittedly, we are not given a lot of insight into this, but from what we can discern, Satan appears to have been a fallen angel. In Isaiah 4:12–15, Satan is referenced as *Lucifer*, which means "the son of the morning." This passage seems to indicate that Satan attempted to exalt himself to be equal to or even above God, for which he was brought down and thrown out of heaven. Ezekiel 28, no doubt literally referring to the king of Tyre, nonetheless, metaphorically refers to one who was once wise and beautiful, in Eden and the anointed cherub, who became filled with violence and who sinned, being full of iniquity.[4] In Luke 10:18, Jesus told the seventy disciples who rebuked demons that he "saw Satan fall like lightning in heaven." Here Jesus seems to be indicating that Satan will be defeated, and so will sin and death.

Satan is described in various other ways as well: as the tempter (Matthew 4:3); ruler of demons (Matthew 12:20); god of this age (1 Corinthians 4:4); the evil one (2 John 5:18); a roaring lion (1 Peter 5:8); and the father of lies (John 8:44). Satan tempts us to sin through the lust of the flesh, the pride of life, and the lust of the eyes, just as he tempted Eve and just as he tempted Christ in the desert, though certainly, as the Son of God, Christ was tempted in ways above and beyond what we as mere mortals have ever been tempted to do.

The book of Revelation describes a war in which we are currently engaged. The outcome of this war is predetermined and not in doubt; nevertheless, it rages on. It is not a physical battle per se, with guns and bombs and rockets, but it is a spiritual battle between good and evil, between Satan and his angels, against Christ and His Church. Much of the book of Revelation deals with the judgment of Babylon, a representation of Rome, for its persecution of the Church, but

Revelation 20 indicates that Satan is the "dragon," the old devil, and that he will be bound for a thousand years—a figurative time period, I believe—after which he will be released from his prison to deceive the nations, eventually to be defeated and cast into the lake of fire with his false prophets and demons, to be tormented day and night "forever and ever."[5] The book of Revelation is certainly not one of the easiest books of the New Testament to understand, and there are different views regarding its interpretation, but I believe there are certain things that are indisputable. First, the dragon will be defeated, and second, the Lamb, Christ, will be victorious. This should give us some comfort when we see the evil perpetrated in the world today. God once destroyed the world with water, but He promised to never destroy the earth that way again. But the third certainty from Revelation is that the whole world, including the universe, will ultimately be destroyed with fire, and a new heaven and earth will appear.[6]

The apostle Peter gives us more detail in the third chapter of his second epistle. Beginning in verse 7, he writes, "But the heavens and the earth which are now preserved by the same word, are reserved for fire until the day of judgment and perdition of ungodly men." In verse 10, he writes, "But the day of the Lord will come as a thief in the night, in which the heavens will pass away with a great noise and the elements will melt with fervent heat; both the earth and the works that are in it will be burned up." Then finally, in verse 13, Peter writes, "Nevertheless, we [meaning Christians], according to His promise look for new heavens and a new earth in which righteousness dwells." Peter goes on to warn his readers in verse 17 to beware lest they fall, "being led away with the error of the wicked."

One question agnostics and skeptics grapple with, as do some Christians, is why is there evil and wickedness in the world? And furthermore, why do terrible things sometimes happen to good people? J. Warner Wallace states in his book, *Cold-Case Christianity*, that "the problem of evil is perhaps the most difficult issue to address because it is emotionally loaded." First, let's acknowledge that all death is tragic, no matter the age of the person or the circumstances. At its peak in 2004, AIDS had killed over two million people. The total number of deaths from AIDS has been estimated at thirty-six million to date, and in third-world countries, especially where therapeutics are not as readily available, people are still dying of this disease. Since its inception in 2019, the World Health Organization estimates that close to seven million people have died from COVID. There are those who say these diseases represent some type of punishment God has dealt to mankind. I for one do not buy this, any more than the Black Plague or the Great Influenza epidemic of 1919 was a punishment delivered by God.

The truth is that tragedy occurs to all men, both the just and the unjust. Jesus Himself even says as much. In Luke's gospel, Jesus referred to the collapse of the Tower of Siloam and the Galileans who died by the hand of Pilate. Jesus said, "Do you suppose that these Galileans were worse sinners than all the other Galileans because they suffered these things? I tell you, no . . ." Further Jesus said, "Or those eighteen on whom the tower of Siloam fell and killed them, do you think that they were worse sinners than all other men who dwelt in Jerusalem? I tell you no."

Do you remember the story of Job? When Job suffered the loss of his property, the loss of his family, and the loss of his health, what did his friends assume? They assumed Job had to have sinned; why else would all this be happening to him? We, of course, know that was not true. Job was not being punished by God, and through it all, Job never lost his integrity.

Atheists say that if there is a God, why does He allow disease, tragedy, and war to happen? Further, why are young, innocent children dying from disease and tragedies? I don't propose to have all the answers, but I know we cannot blame God. Through sin, death entered the world, as we have observed, and as a result, bad things happen to good people. I do not believe God is in heaven directing calamities to take place.

What is more important is our reaction when bad things happen to the good. This admittedly is a very difficult situation, especially when it occurs to someone to whom we are close, but we simply cannot blame God.

I recently came across a marvelous little book appropriately entitled *When Bad Things Happen to Good People*, by Harold S. Kuscher. His book is not an abstract book about God and theology, but rather, it is a very personal one, as Rabbi Kuscher's son Aaron died early on of a very rare disease called *progeria*, which means "rapid aging." His son looked like a fragile little old man who had lost his hair, as well as being very small in stature, reaching only three feet in height. Aaron died two days after his fourteenth birthday, and Kuscher's book is an attempt to make sense "of the worlds of pain and evil."

I think Kuscher's conclusions merit our attention: "God does not cause our misfortunes. Some are caused by bad luck, some are caused by bad people, and some are simply an inevitable consequence of being human and being mortal, living in a world of inflexible natural laws. The painful things that happen to us are not punishments for our behavior, nor are they in any way part of some grand design of God's part. Because tragedy is not God's will, we need not feel hurt or betrayed by God when tragedy strikes. We turn to him in overcoming it, precisely because we can tell ourselves that God is outraged by it as we are."

Bad things happen to us all, and we can either blame God or try to give meaning to it by realizing God has created a world in which many more good things happen than bad. No doubt time and distance can help put tragedy in its context, especially when we look to eternity. Maybe, in some way, how we handle our individual tragedies can help inspire others when it happens to them.

The world is, indeed, cold and unfair at times, and as we have noted, life is but a vapor, and time and circumstance affect us all. But God's love can help us along our journey to give us strength and hope.

"In the final analysis, the question of why bad things happen to good people translates into some very different questions, no longer asking why something happened, but asking how we will respond, what we intend to do now that it has happened," writes Kuscher.

This brings us back to our purpose on earth, and that is to prepare us for the afterlife mentioned by Peter. Know this, wickedness will not be part of the new heavens and the new earth, only righteousness. It is clear we can only attain that righteousness through Jesus Christ. Jesus said, "I am the way and the truth and the life. No one comes to the Father except through me."[7] Jesus also said, "Therefore whoever confesses me before men, him will I also confess before my Father who was in heaven. But whoever denies me before men, him will I also deny before my Father who was in heaven."[8]

We are, therefore, in a spiritual battle against sin and Satan. The very next verse in the aforementioned quote says, "Do not think I came to bring peace on earth. I did not come to bring peace but a sword." We Christians are to put on the whole armor of God for this battle, so Paul told the Ephesians in chapter 6, in order to stand against the devil. Our war is not against flesh and blood, but against "powers, against the rulers of the darkness of this age, against spiritual host of wickedness in the heavenly places."[9] Paul further says that our armor is to be truth, righteousness, the gospel of peace, the Word of God, and above all, faith.[10]

Faith is so important, because without it, it is impossible to please God, and it does require we believe in certain things we cannot see, such as His very existence, and the existence of those principalities against which we wage war.[11]

But our faith is not blind, as the secularists think. Denis Alexander, a biochemist, in his book, *Beyond Science*, wrote, "The personal relationship with God that may be experienced through Jesus Christ is not mystical in this sense, but rather a rationally based response to Jesus Christ, who rose from the dead as a historical fact, and who is thus alive, if not now in our own world of sense-perception. The revelation of God in Christ is accepted because as a general model of explanation, it 'fits the facts' about the human condition in a way that no other model does."[12] Alexander goes on to say, "Believing in a personal, Creator God as the author of the universe is simply the best explanation for intelligibility of all we see and observe."[13]

Darkness comes in many forms, and for most of us, the best way we can participate in the fight against it is to live quiet, peaceful lives abstaining from sin and honoring God, as well as doing good to our fellow man. We may never have to face the supreme evil we discussed earlier in this chapter, and I certainly hope we don't, but we can make an impact. Deitrich Bonhoeffer once wrote, "Your life as a Christian should make the non-believing question their disbelief in God."[14]

Bonhoeffer practiced what he preached; he was an evangelist in Germany during the horrible Nazi regime, a racist regime bent on evil and eliminating Jews. Though most of his fellow clergymen in Germany failed to notice, Bonhoeffer early on realized the evil being brought upon his country and the discrimination against the Jews. Bonhoeffer sided with others to keep the Nazi Reich out of the affairs of the German church, but unfortunately, out of eighteen thousand clergymen in Germany at the time, only about six thousand would stand with Bonhoeffer and others against the Nazis. As you might expect, Hitler began rounding up many of these clergy who were opposed to his regime and putting them in prisons. Bonhoeffer would not be silenced, though. You might say he was a doer of the Word and not just a hearer.[15] In his book, translated *Discipleship*, Bonhoeffer wrote about faith and works, and though he acknowledged we cannot earn our way into heaven, neither can we get there without good works.[16] Bonhoeffer called this "cheap grace," that is the idea of just going to church on Sundays and confessing our sins, but living a life that is indifferent toward our fellow man.[17] Bonhoeffer, according to Eric Metaxas, in his book *Letter to the American Church*, believed, "If one did not have the guts to speak against the evils being committed against German Jews under Hitler, one had abdicated their right to worship God."[18]

Deitrich Bonhoeffer

So, speak out Bonhoeffer did, and as a result he paid the ultimate price—with his life. Unfortunately, most of Germany chose to either ignore or to be complicit with the Nazi agenda, and the world was thrown into a war where tens of millions of people would die, including Germans themselves, as well as millions of Jews and so-called undesirables, being put to death in concentration camps such as Auschwitz, Bergen-Belsen, Dachau, and so many more.

In Proverbs 24, God tells us, "Rescue those who are being taken away to death; hold back those who are stumbling to the slaughter. If I say, behold we do not know it, does not he who weighs the heart perceive it? Does not he who keeps watch over your soul know it, and will he not repay man according to his works?" It seems as if God was speaking directly about the Nazi era in Germany, doesn't it? Bonhoeffer died at the hands of the Gestapo, being hanged at Flossenbürg, a concentration camp.

But once again, darkness comes from various sources. Although Satan is described as a roaring lion, frequently his tactics are not so obvious. Jesus warned of false prophets who would come in sheep's clothing, but inwardly are "ravaging wolves."[19] Paul told the Corinthian brethren in 2 Corinthians 11:13–15, "For such men are false prophets, deceitful workmen, disguising themselves as apostles of Christ. And no wonder, for even Satan disguises himself as an angel of light. So, it is no surprise if his servants, also, disguised themselves as servants of righteousness. Their end will correspond to their deeds." Paul also told Timothy that a time was coming when "people will not endure sound teaching, but having itching ears, they will accumulate for themselves teachers to suit their own passions."[20] Peter further warned of false prophets and said such will secretly "bring in destructive heresies, even denying the master who bought them."[21] There are other such warnings in the New Testament, but I believe you get the picture. Satan is not always overtly obvious, and his tactics include deceit and persuasion, frequently in the guise of religion.

Today, in our society, dark is light, and bad is good, it would seem. Denying a woman's right to choose, a euphemism for abortion, is considered "evil," but taking an innocent life is acceptable. Some say aborting a living human being in the early stages of gestation is no different or immoral than killing a fish. What is extremely odd is that some would condemn those who kill or exploit animals, but they have no issue with abortion. Alexander Sanger of Planned Parenthood even views abortion as a method of human survival!

Our "woke" society has blurred the definitions of *women* and *men*, and the sanctity of marriage is discarded as archaic. Science in the form of scientism is worshiped more than God and is more "honorable" since it strives to find the "real truth." We supposedly live in a more enlightened world, free from superstition and mythology. I ask, does the world seem more enlightened to you?

Eric Metaxas warns us that it is time to seize the moment. Metaxas writes, "God has ordained that we be born when we were born and that we live now, to do the works now that He has prepared for us in advance to His glory."[22] Metaxas's opinion is that we, meaning fellow Christians, represent God on earth, and it is hard to disagree with him. God thus calls us to do something, but that something is our personal choice to do.

The good news of the Gospel is that people can and do change. The Bible is full of examples, both in the Old and New Testaments, of people

Eric Metaxas

who made a dramatic change in their lives for the better. In the Old Testament, we read about Manasseh, king of Judah, in 2 Kings 21 and 1 Chronicles 33. In those passages, he is described as one of the most evil kings ever, "doing much evil in the sight of the Lord," even sacrificing his son to an idol, making him "pass through the fire." Manasseh also shed "very much innocent blood, till it filled Jerusalem from one end to another." Yet Manasseh changed. After being taken by the king of Assyria, Manasseh "implored the Lord his God and humbled himself greatly before the God of his fathers and prayed to him." We are told that God heard his prayers and brought him back to Jerusalem and to his kingdom, and then Manasseh "knew the Lord was God." As a result, Manasseh took away the idols, repaired the altar to the Lord, made peace offerings and thank offerings to God, and commanded Judah to serve the Lord God of Israel.

Under the New Covenant, the Gospel has the power to change people, as the apostle Paul wrote in chapter 1 of his letter to the Romans. And who would know better than Paul? Paul, who considered himself a Pharisee among the Pharisees, persecuted Christians, even holding the cloaks of those who stoned Stephen, the first Christian martyr. He, however, made possibly the most dramatic change in the history of mankind. Jesus, appearing to Paul, called Saul at the time, on the road to Damascus, told him to go into the city and he would be told what to do. Paul, recounting his conversion in Acts 22, having been blinded by the bright light of Jesus Christ, went to Damascus, where he was led to Ananias, a devout man who told Saul to receive his sight, which he did. Ananias then told him that he [Saul] had been chosen to be a witness to all men of what he had seen and heard. Ananias then called on Saul to "arise and wash away your sins calling on the name of the Lord,"[23] and we know from Acts 9 that Saul's sins were indeed washed away through baptism.

I have quoted many people in this book who have also changed their beliefs and lives and given themselves to Christ. C. S. Lewis was an unbeliever who became not only a believer, but possibly the greatest apologist and defender of Christianity of his time. More currently, William Dembski, Stephen Meyer, James Tour, Eric Metaxas, Michael Egnor, and John Lennox, as well as many others mentioned in this book, made changes in their lives, some of which were very dramatic, and they are now purported to be Christians and defenders of the faith. In fact, all of us who are Christians have had to change our lives—that is, believe and repent—turning away from our past sinful existence.

At this point I would like to digress just a bit and make a few comments about baptism. Notice that Paul's sins were "washed away" with his baptism. For some reason, baptism has gotten a bad rap from many in the Christian world. What I mean by that is many claim that those who believe baptism is essential for salvation believe in "water salvation," as if there is something in the water that literally washes sins away. I personally know of no one that believes that. We are saved by the grace of God, and no one earns salvation through baptism any more than one earns their salvation through belief or repentance or confession. We are all unprofitable servants. Yet if one believes in the inspiration of the Bible, baptism *is* essential for salvation. The apostle Paul says as much in his First Epistle 3:21 and explains it is "not the removal of the filth of the flesh, but the answer of a good conscience toward God, through the resurrection of Jesus Christ."

For those who have trouble understanding this, I would refer them to the story of the leper Naaman found in 2 Kings 5. Naaman, a commander in the Syrian army, could not understand why it was necessary to go wash in the river Jordan seven times to have his leprosy cured as so commanded by the prophet Elisha. This made no sense to him, but when a servant of his persuaded him to do so anyway, he did and was cured. Do you think there was something in the water of Jordan that cured Naaman? Of course not! It was the answer of a good conscience toward God, and Naaman now realized there was no other God in heaven than the God Almighty of Israel.

On the Day of Pentecost, three thousand souls were baptized as they repented and accepted Jesus Christ as their Lord. The Ethiopian eunuch was immediately baptized when Jesus was taught to him by the evangelist Philip. Other examples could be cited from the New Testament, but I would only ask that if it is necessary to have one's sins removed to be saved, doesn't it appear that in these examples, baptism is certainly a part of that process? One doesn't need to make sense of it—only do it.

We know that after Paul's conversion, he became an ambassador for Christianity, preaching the soul-saving grace of the Gospel to all who would listen, especially to the Gentiles. He would write at least thirteen epistles (and maybe the book of Hebrews), and he would make four missionary journeys, establishing churches throughout Asia Minor and Europe and wherever he went. It was not an easy task, to say the least. In 2 Corinthians, Paul writes of his persecutions: being beaten by the Jews with forty stripes minus one five times. He was stoned nigh unto death three times, shipwrecked, imprisoned, starved, left cold and naked, left in peril from robbers, and also suffering weariness of the soul from his toil for the sake of Christ.

And yet Paul counted it all joy! He told the Roman Christians, "For I consider the sufferings of this present time are not worthy to be compared with the glory that will be revealed to us."[24] Further, he wrote, "We hope for what we do not see, we eagerly wait for it with perseverance." Likely toward the end of his life, Paul wrote to Timothy that he had "fought the good fight" and "had finished the race and kept the faith."[25] He then wrote, "Finally there is laid up for me the crown of righteousness, which the Lord, the righteous judge, will give to me on that day, and not to me only but also to all who have loved His appearing."[26] Does this sound like a man who believed in a fable or fairy tale? Historically, we are told that Paul died a martyr's death. Sadly, most people—past, present, and future—will not have "loved his [Christ's] appearing."

The Bible is replete with many others who changed their lives. They changed their lives because Christ offered something no one else could—a hope for a life hereafter—but not only that, a life here on earth much more fulfilled and with promise. As a result, Christianity eventually thrived despite persecution "turning the world upside down."[27]

Jesus said, "Ye are the light of the world. A city that is set on a hill cannot be hidden. Nor do they light a lamp and put it under a basket, but on a lampstand, and it gives light to all that are in the house." He further said, "Let your light so shine before men, that they may see your good works and glorify your Father in heaven."[28] Could our purpose on earth be any clearer?

THE INELUCTABLE MODALITY OF THE VISIBLE

In science, we are only reading the notes to a poem; in Christianity we find the poem itself.

—C.S. Lewis

If everything was reducible to how descriptions of quantities interacting according to mathematical principles, what would be left to the why explanations that carry the fundamental dimensions of human agency, such as truth? Consciousness? Free will? Love? Good? Evil?

—David R.C. Deane

"Is it chance or dance moves the world? Is the world blind and dumb or bloom, festal? A vain gest, or holy feast?" So wrote poet Eugene Warren.[1] In Thomas Howard's short masterpiece, based on this poem, he puts it this way: "The myth sovereign in the old age was everything means everything. The myth sovereign in the new age is that nothing means anything."[2] This represents a good summation to the purpose of this book. Using dance as a metaphor, much like Garth Brooks did in his hit song "The Dance," Warren is asking, Is there any purpose in life? Are we just here by pure chance, living lives with no purpose, with our only expectation being death? Or is there a purpose, and should we not seize the day, enjoying our lives on earth in preparation for an even greater journey in the hereafter?

Henry David Thoreau wrote in "Walden" that the "mass of men 'live lives in quiet desperation'," a sentiment echoed by Willy Loman, the protagonist of Arthur Miller's play *Death of a Salesman*. That is because today, in our materialistic world, a person's value is determined largely by how much money he or she makes or what their net worth is. In Miller's play, Loman is locked into this paradigm, never realizing the potential freedom available to him. "The secular world is one in which significance seems to have disappeared," writes Howard.[3] He further writes, "We live by story. This is how we understand ourselves, who we are and where we are going. We want a story that makes sense of the world and helps us to find our place in it, a story to justify our decisions, comforts us in the time of suffering, and helps make sense of life."[4]

Denis Alexander has written, "One of the paradoxes of modern science is that while on the one hand it appears to give man God-like powers, on the other hand it appears to reduce man to another rather puzzling animal in a puzzling universe. There appears to be no limits to man's ingenuity and creativeness in comparing himself with animals."[5]

Reading Alexander, I can't help but think of my experience this past summer at the Smithsonian Museum of Natural History in Washington, D.C., as previously discussed. Time after time we are shown in the museum how much we are like our "ancestors, the mammals," with the sign hanging over the Hall of Mammals reading, "Come Meet Your Relatives." How absurd!

If Warren is right, and I think he is, life is, indeed, meant to be "festal." What does that mean? *Festal*, an old term, means "joyful or happy in a celebratory way." Life is not meant to be drab and melancholy, and this is even a biblical concept. Paul told the Philippians to "rejoice in the Lord always; again I say, rejoice."[6] Again, Paul tells the Roman brethren, "May the God of hope fill you with all joy and peace as you trust in him, so that you may overflow with hope by the power of the Holy Spirit."[7] Jesus said, "No one will take away your joy."[8] Finally, Paul also wrote that the Kingdom of God "is righteousness, peace and joy in the Holy Spirit."[9]

Once upon a time, there lived a great and powerful king, considered the wealthiest and the wisest man in history, Solomon. Solomon wrote the book of Ecclesiastes, a book devoted to studying the purpose of life. It seems prudent to look at the words of Solomon, inspired by the Holy Spirit, and see what He had to say about this subject.

Solomon—or "the preacher," as he refers to himself—begins his book on a rather somber note, writing, "Vanity of vanities, says the preacher; all is vanity. What profit has a man from his labor in which he toils under the sun? One generation passes away and another generation comes; but the earth abides forever. The sun also arises and the sun hastens to the place where it arose."[10]

If we stop reading here, it would appear that Solomon had a materialistic view of the world, but he did not stop writing. In chapter 3 of Ecclesiastes, he wrote, "He (God) has made everything beautiful in its time. Also He has put eternity in their hearts, except no one can find out the work that God does from beginning to end."[11] Further Solomon wrote, "I know that nothing is better for man than to rejoice and to do good in their lives, and also that every man should eat and drink and enjoy the good of all of his labor—it is the gift of God."[12] But Solomon also warns, "God will judge the righteous and the wicked, for there is a time there for every purpose and every work."[13]

Time and again in Ecclesiastes, Solomon writes that we are to "rejoice in our works";[14] "enjoy the good of all [our] labor";[15] "in the day of prosperity be joyful; in the day of adversity consider, surely God has appointed the one as well as the other";[16] "live joyfully with a wife whom you love all the days of your life which He has given you under the sun;"[17] and "whatever your hand finds to do, do it with your might."[18]

It seems to me, Solomon is telling us to enjoy our lives "under the sun," but to not forget our Creator. In chapter 9, he wrote, "I returned and saw under the sun that the race is not to the swift, nor the battle to the strong, nor bread to the wise, nor riches to men of understanding, nor favor to men of skill. But time and chance happen to them all."[19] Eventually, either circumstance or time will overtake us all, and death is inevitable.

Solomon ends his great book with this: "Let us hear the conclusion of the whole matter: fear God, and keep his commandments, for this is man's all. For God will bring every work into judgment including every secret thing, whether good or evil."[20] The previous quote is from the New King James Version. Other versions interpret "man's all" as "applies to every man" (the New American Standard Version); "the whole duty of man" (the American Standard Version); "the whole of man" (Darby's version); and "what he expects of all human beings," taken from the New International Reader's Version, which I think conveys the point precisely.

As we have noted previously, man was created with the freedom of choice. It is for us to choose to heed Solomon's advice or not, but know this, nothing will go unseen, and this passage, as well as others we have cited, clearly show that accountability is a fact of our lives.

Life, then, has purpose, one of which is to actually enjoy it! Howard writes, "Experience doesn't hold off while we are at work and begin when the whistle blows. The *whole thing* is the 'real stuff',," and the irony is that "unless we take ourselves by the scruff of the neck and make ourselves reflect on it, we allow it to tumble past us helter-skelter and never grasp any as real."[21]

Children live their lives in the moment; adults not so much. As a young man, I was told by the elderly to appreciate my youth because life goes by so quickly. James wrote in chapter 4, verse 14 of his book, "For what is your life? It is even a vapor that goes for a little time and then vanishes away."[22] Peter, quoting Isaiah, wrote, "All flesh is like grass and all its glory like the flower of grass; the grass withers and the flower fades off, but the word of the Lord endures forever."[23] Now in the seventh decade of my life, I appreciate these sentiments even more. Every day is truly a gift of God. I have learned and continue to learn to embrace the "humdrum," as Thomas Howard calls it, the everyday things of life. "We can't spend every day contemplating the cosmos; we have neither the time nor the stamina," writes Howard in *Chance or the Dance*.[24]

Most people live an empty life caused by unfulfilling work, lack of leisure time, and misguided values, like money, possessions, or accolades. But we, I, need to appreciate the "humdrum." Enjoy a beautiful sunrise, the beauty of a Labrador retriever, the taste of a good cup of coffee in the morning, the changes in the seasons, a good ball game, a delightful meal with people you love, and even work itself. Everything does mean everything; nothing is insignificant.

It's easy to say that life is a big lottery, and after all, we are only here by chance. I like the word *concatenations*. It is used in chemistry to explain chemical reactions that occur one after another, but it also means a series of interconnected things or events that produce a result in a particular event or effect, kind of like a domino effect. Our births are concatenated, when you think about it. It took a long series of interrelated events for you and me to get here. Our mothers and dads had to get together, as did our grandparents, and for that matter, all our ancestors. One change in the link for any reason would have resulted in our not being born. This is the butterfly effect we saw when we discussed chaos theory. It is thus extremely unlikely that you and I would even be here, yet we are. From my perspective, it's not chance that I am here. For whatever reason, God has intended for me to be here, as I believe He has for you. Let us take this wonderful blessing to fulfill our purpose toward God. As Solomon wrote concerning our lives, "It is the gift of God."[25] We are either "grinding tediously towards entropy, or dancing towards the dance."[26] I prefer the latter!

Of Faith and Hope

Two words that are commonly misused or misapplied by secularists are *faith* and *hope*, especially as they apply to Christianity. The faith of a Christian is frequently described as a blind faith by the secularists, but that is far from the truth. The faith of the Christian is based on evidence, and it is not blind. Believing in Jesus Christ, including His resurrection, is, therefore, a factual faith. The Christian weighs all the evidence and concludes that Jesus was a person of history, performed miracles, and was crucified and buried, and then was raised after three days from the dead. It is not the same as believing in Paul Bunyan or Santa Claus or the Tooth Fairy.

Christianity is not mystical—or at least, it should not be. I have a personal relationship with Christ because I believe in His physical resurrection. As Denis Alexander writes, "It fits the facts,"[27] and the world has been changed as a result. Light entered the world, and the Light illuminates by His Word, which abides forever.

I'm not downplaying the importance of faith. Faith is extremely important, so much so that the Hebrew writer even states, "And without faith it is impossible to please God, because anyone who comes to Him must believe that he exists and that he rewards those who earnestly seek him."[28] But a blind faith is not what God wants. He wants us to believe because He has given us ample evidence of not only His own existence, but that of His Son, as well.

This brings us to hope. The hope of a Christian is not just a fanciful wish, but an earnest expectation. For many, the word *hope* conveys a notion of an unlikely event, such as I "hope" to go to Mars someday, or I "hope" to be president of the United States. But once again, the Hebrew writer gives us some insight: "Now faith is the substance of things hoped for, the evidence of things not seen."[29] What evidence? Is it not examining the facts or information as to whether a belief is true or valid? There are many things we believe to be true, yet none of us have seen them. A prime example would be gravity. We are confident gravity exists, but have you ever seen it? You have certainly experienced it, and you have certainly experienced the consequences of it. And we also know there is such a thing as gravitational fields, but science cannot see gravity, nor its fields, yet we can be certain of its existence. I know, or at least am reasonably confident, that George Washington was a real individual, but I don't know that from experience—only from the evidence.

I also have faith in the future. We wake up, go through our daily activities, and go to bed with the expectation that there is going to be another sunrise, another day. But we don't know that, do we? We have faith it is going to happen, not discounting death. David Berlinski, in *The Devil's Delusion*, gives a pretty good definition of this type of faith: "We can make no sense either of daily life *or* the physical sciences in terms of things that are seen. The past has gone to the place where the past goes; the future has not yet arrived. We remember the one; we count on the other. If that is not faith, what then is it?"

Hope, then, stems from evidence. As a noun, *hope* is a desire accompanied by expectation or a belief in fulfillment, says *Merriam-Webster Dictionary*. As a verb, it is looking forward to with desire and reasonable confidence. I may say I hope to win the US Open Golf

Tournament, but there is zero chance of that happening. It is then a fantasy, not a hope.

The Christian hope lies in an expectation and an anticipation of eternal life. We talked about the joy Christians are to have in this life, but that joy is predicated on a life hereafter, the resurrection of Jesus Christ being the primary evidence for such. This is the reason the apostle Paul could be joyful even in his many persecutions.[30] Paul told the Roman Christians to "rejoice in hope, persevering in tribulation."[31] Jesus said, "Rejoice and be glad for your reward in heaven is great; for in the same way they persecuted the prophets who were before you."[32]

Peter warned Christians to expect persecution, but to "keep on rejoicing, so that also at the revelation of His glory you may rejoice with exaltation."[33] Historically, we are told that Christians went to their deaths singing songs and rejoicing, but why?

God has made a promise, and it is impossible for Him to lie.[34] That promise is heaven, eternal life. The Hebrew brethren were told that this hope could, therefore, be fully assured, and it was an "anchor of the soul, both sure and steadfast."[35] Jesus told His disciples in John 14, "Let not your heart be troubled; you believe in God, believe also in me. In my Father's house are many mansions; if it were not so, I would have told you. I go to prepare a place for you. And if I go to prepare a place for you, I will come again, and receive you to myself, that where I am, there you may be also. And where I go, you know, and the way you know."[36]

I ask you, what was Jesus talking about? If He wasn't talking about heaven, I am quite unsure of to what else He could be referring.

We as humans are familiar with four dimensions, height, width, length, and time (or space-time). Our day-to-day interactions are familiar with these dimensions and no others. Yet, there is at least one other dimension—a dimension evangelist and chemist Larry Dickens likes to refer to as the "first dimension."

Dimensions are things we like to measure, such as length and time, but they are not dependent on our ability to measure them. When the universe was created, these dimensions became the fabric of the universe, long before man's ability ever existed to measure them. But what existed before these dimensions were created? I can tell you with certainty, science cannot answer this question. The question can only be answered by revelation! This dimension, then, is in the realm of the eternal and is spiritual in nature, and you and I cannot have access to it while we remain in this physical body.

Beginning in the book of Genesis, we see the plurality of the Godhead, which existed before the universe was created.[37] We have already noted that this universe was created by "the Word," and that "Word" was Jesus Christ.[38] I find it interesting that Jesus is called "the Word." In Greek, *logos* is the word, and words indicate information. That "word" eventually became a real physical Person, or like John Lennox writes, it "demonstrates fully that the ultimate truth behind the universe is personal and thus God the creator encoded himself in humanity."[39]

But until that time, Christ existed in a realm not seen, touched, or felt by humankind, the realm of God and His angels, a realm of eternity. We understand angels were created beings; therefore, they were not there initially, and the prophet Nehemiah indicates they were created by God.[40] We have discussed previously how the devil, or Satan, seems to have been a created being as well, and very likely was a fallen angel.[41] Humans certainly are born with a soul that is eternal, but we currently belong in this world of four dimensions.

We are not, while physically alive, part of that spiritual world, or the "first dimension." That occurs after our physical death.

Now comes a very key concept to grasp, and that is that God's plan for man's salvation was there before the creation and was thus part of that "first dimension." How do I know that? Paul told the Ephesians in his epistle that they were "chosen in Him before the foundation of the world" and that Christians are "predestined" according to the good pleasure of His will.[42]

There is a lot of misunderstanding of what this "predestination" is, but from the context and other passages, what is predestined is God's plan for man's salvation; thus those who obey that plan can, in a sense, be said to be predestined. We know God is not a respecter of persons,[43] and He wishes all to be saved.[44] It is thus His plan that was predestined before the world was ever created.

How is that done? Through the preaching of the Gospel! The Gospel was preordained in the "first dimension" as the vehicle for salvation. "Faith cometh by hearing and hearing by the word of God."[45] Paul was not ashamed to preach the Gospel "because it is the power of God that brings salvation to everyone who believes."[46]

Those who were/are saved thus become added to the Church, both then and now.[47] Recall that Jesus told Peter, after his confession of His deity, that "on this rock I will build my church."[48] The Church, therefore, is not an "afterthought of a failed messiah who intended to establish his kingdom (as pre-millennial doctrine supposes)," writes Larry Dickens.[49] It was planned *before* the creation of the earth, and Paul refers to this as God's "eternal purpose" whose headship is Christ.[50] We are thus "His workmanship, created in Christ Jesus for good works, which God prepared beforehand, that we should walk in them," so wrote Paul in Ephesians 2:10. And understand this:

These good works will follow us to heaven,[51] and we will be judged by them.[52]

Heaven—and yes, even hell—are, therefore, part of this unseen dimension.[53] Heaven is not a reconstructed earth. It is not of this world, but beyond it. Sometimes we think of heaven as being "up" and hell as being "down," but in reality, this view is incorrect. They are in different dimensions, and the Hebrew writer says that our salvation in heaven is eternal.[54]

The purpose of God is for all of us to get to heaven, though unfortunately, most will miss out, not because they cannot obey, but because they will not obey. In the gospel of Matthew, Jesus told His followers to "enter the narrow way, because the broad way leads to destruction and the narrow way to life." Christ warns, "Not everyone who says to me, 'Lord, Lord,' shall enter the kingdom of heaven, but he who does the will of my Father in heaven. Many will say to me in that day, 'Lord, Lord,' have we not prophesied in your name, and done many wonders in your name?' And I will declare to them, 'I never knew you; depart from me, you who practice lawlessness.'"[55]

It seems to me that just saying, "Lord, Lord," is not enough. We must do His will! The Christian hope is not in this life, but in that "first dimension." This earth, and indeed this universe and all that is in it, are not eternal and will be destroyed by fire, writes the apostle Peter in 2 Peter 3:3–4. But Peter also writes that God is "longsuffering towards us, not willing that any should perish but that all should come to repentance."[56] With this in mind, we should be looking forward, not with dread or despair, but with joy, to that day when He comes with promise to take us where the righteous will dwell forever!

Chapter
15

EPILOGUE

"Those who declare they have no mind, are not intelligent, conscious or free are hardly in a position to reason about any topic, let alone about the state of the mind they deny having.

—Michael Behe

"Faith backed by knowledge is much stronger than faith based on an emotionally driven gossamer hope, whether that faith be secular or religious."

—Gerald Schoeder

"AND YOU SHALL KNOW THE TRUTH AND THE TRUTH SHALL MAKE you free," said Jesus to His disciples in John 8:32. Later in the gospel of John, Jesus told Pontius Pilate that He had come into the world to "bear witness of the truth," and that everyone who is "of the truth hears my voice."[1] You may recall Pilate's likely sarcastic reply, "What is truth?"—a question Jesus responded to with silence. In these contexts, the truth Jesus was referring to was that of His own deity. Those responding to that truth, through faith and obedience, would be set free of sin, meaning they would no longer be under its bondage.[2]

Today, the truth is under attack. We are told truth is relative, and what is true for you may not be true for me. I may believe Jesus is the Son of God, but for someone else, that might not be true, so we are told. Of course, that is nonsense. Jesus is either the Son of God, or He is not. He was either resurrected from the dead in three days, or He was not. These facts cannot be just relative to some and not to others.

Some want to say Jesus was a good man with a kind heart, possibly a prophet, who spoke of peace and love, but He certainly was not the Son of God. Christianity is nice and meaningful for some, but not others. But these statements are absurd. Jesus claimed deity—that is, equality with God. Therefore, He cannot be a good man, because such a claim, if it were not true, would make Him either a liar or a lunatic. Further, C.S. Lewis once wrote, "Christianity if false, is of no importance, and if true, of infinite importance. The one thing it cannot be is moderately important." Jesus said, "Whoever is not with me is against me."[3]

It thus becomes the most important decision a person can make to determine the truth of Jesus Christ. Or not. This side of heaven we cannot know for certain, but at least it ought to cause someone to examine the evidence, doesn't it?

The Bible is under attack, as well. I have unashamedly quoted many Scriptures in this book because I find the Bible to be, indeed, the inerrant Word of God, and I further believe we have the words recorded by His prophets, disciples, and apostles faithfully preserved for us today. Paul told Timothy, "All scripture is given by inspiration of God, and is profitable for doctrine, for reproof, for correction, for instruction in righteousness, that the man of God may be perfect, thoroughly furnished unto all created works."[4] I know it is circular to "prove" the Bible by the Bible, and it is not in the scope of this book to give all the evidence of biblical inspiration, of which there are many, but I would be remiss not to mention just a few. Josh McDowell's monumental work

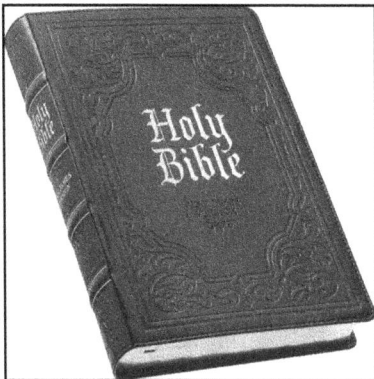
Holy Bible

The New Evidence That Demands a Verdict is still the best compilation of evidence of biblical inspiration, and it is highly recommended for those seeking a more in-depth analysis.

The Bible is indeed the most unique book in the world that has ever been written, penned over the course of 1,500 years by more than forty separate authors, written in different times and places and in different styles, yet it is cohesive and tells the tale of man's fall and then his ultimate redemption through Jesus Christ. Lewis S. Chafer said, "The Bible is not such a book a man would write if he could, or could write if he would,"[5] and I think this is a truthful statement.

The Bible, unlike other so-called religious books, focuses on reality, not fantasy, and "deals frankly with the sins of its characters."[6]

Both the New Testament and the Old Testament are historically accurate, and much of the New Testament was written by eyewitnesses of Jesus Christ and of His resurrection.

For me, though, the most profound indication of the Bible's inspiration is found in its fulfillment of biblical prophecy, especially as it pertains to Jesus Christ. There are at least sixty-one prophecies concerning the Messiah that Jesus perfectly fulfilled—prophecies with high levels of specificity and prophecies Jesus could not have self-fulfilled, such as the place of His birth and other events surrounding His birth. Peter Stoner has calculated the likelihood that any man might have fulfilled just eight of these prophecies being 1 to 10^7, which is 1 in 100,000,000,000,000,000.[7] Furthermore, the chances of fulfilling forty-eight of the prophecies jumps to 10^{157}. This probability is so low, the chance of fulfillment becomes impossible.[8]

Some have attacked Christianity itself by comparing it to other religions, implying and even stating that all religions are basically the same. "If you consider the major successful religions on the planet that have each survived the test of time and been significant players in the development and success of major cultures, they have remarkable similarities in their rules, in the moral code they have discovered to be true. In fact, at a very basic fundamental level, they are all virtually identical."[9] What an absolutely absurd statement. It is either the height of ignorance to say this or due to the need for some type of self-gratification, because it is far from true.

Surely, one must consider pagan religions of animus cults who offer human sacrifices to appease the nature gods to guarantee good crops. Are these religions virtually identical with the religion of the apostle Paul and Peter, or for that matter, the religion of Martin Luther King and Albert Schweitzer? I certainly think not.

It is true that a few religions other than Christianity espouse something similar to the Golden Rule—that is, to love your neighbor as yourself—but no religion that I am aware of says to love your enemies, as does Christianity. Jesus, in His mountain sermon, said, "You have heard that it was said, 'You shall love your neighbor and hate your enemy.' But I say to you, love your enemies, bless those who curse you, do good to those who hate you, and pray for those who spitefully use you and persecute you." Can you imagine radical Muslims doing this? I don't see Christianity calling for some type of jihad, do you, and it was not Christians who flew into the Twin Towers and the Pentagon, was it?

Furthermore, the remains or ashes of virtually every religious leader can still be found. For example, the remains of the prophet Muhammad are kept at the mosque in Medina, the ashes of Buddha are found scattered around eight different countries in Asia, kept in gold bottles. Confucius's remains are kept in Qufu City, and Joseph Smith is buried in the Smith Family Cemetery in Nauvoo, Illinois.

Where is the body of Jesus? Of course, there is no grave where His remains are kept, because Christianity is based on His resurrection. No body of Christ has ever been produced since His death and resurrection. If someone had wished to destroy Christianity, they could have begun by simply producing the body of Christ.

Of course, there are many, many other differences between Christianity and other religions, but to say all religions are basically the same borders on the ludicrous.

The truth is also under attack by the scientific community because of a priori belief in materialism. Science is supposed to be about the search for the truth, not validating preconceived concepts. Evolution has been the paradigm of origins for scientists for at least 150-plus years now, even though the truth is that there is virtually no evidence for macroevolution. William Dembski wrote in *The Comprehensive Guide to Science and Faith*, "A theory can be beautiful but untrue. Science is a fallible enterprise with many pitfalls. It has gotten some things astoundingly wrong (e.g., alchemy, phlogiston, phrenology, luminiferous aether, etc.)." Unfortunately, evolution's lasting importance was the banishment of purpose in life. Yet the lie persists. Science should instead follow the evidence of the best explanation, and the best explanation we have for our origin is an intelligent designer. It seems odd to me that people like atheist Richard Dawkins can declare that God is not real by virtue of its improbability, yet they never seem to acknowledge how utterly impossible it is for the existence of our universe and life to have spontaneously appeared.

We are further told that life has no purpose, a lie I hope we have somewhat dispelled at this point. We are also told today that gender is relative and men can have children! Some cannot even bring themselves to define what *male* and *female* mean in reality. We are also told the lie that life doesn't begin until birth.

The fact is, truth is not inclusive; rather, on the contrary, it is exclusive—that is, it excludes that which is not true. As we have seen, two plus two equals four. This excludes any other number. Black is not white, and Boston is not Houston. Josh McDowell writes, "The same is true about Christianity. If the claims of the Christian faith are true—and many people accept them as true—

these people are no more intolerant for their belief than those people who accept Washington, DC, as the capital of the United States. They are either correct or mistaken about how God has revealed himself in the world. If they are right, there really is no other way to God but through Christ. If they are wrong, then Christianity is false. The question of tolerance isn't the issue. The question of truth is."[10]

This book has been about purpose—our purpose in the universe and God's purpose for us. During this process, we have encountered several people historically who have lived lives of purpose: such people as William Wilberforce and John Newton, who sought for decades to abolish the slave trade in Great Britain; Johannes Kepler, who saw purpose in mathematics and believed it revealed the mind of God; and Deitrich Bonhoeffer, who tried to save the Jews from Nazi Germany.

Then there was the apostle Paul, who gave his life for Christ, establishing churches throughout Asia Minor and Europe, and writing at least thirteen epistles.

The writer of the book of Hebrews, in chapter 11, spoke of many who have lived lives of faith, fulfilling their purpose here on earth, such people as Abel, Enoch, Noah, Abraham, Sarah, Moses, Gideon, Samson, and Rahab, as well as others. These all received "good testimony through faith." But Hebrews mentions others who are unnamed, people who were scourged, mocked, stoned, tormented, afflicted, caused to wander in the desert, and slain for the cause of Christ.

The vast majority of us will live our lives quietly, with little fanfare or notoriety, and be forgotten within two generations. Think about your great-grandparents. Did you know them or anything about them? I certainly can tell you virtually nothing about mine. My grandparents, yes. But my great-grandparents, no. This will be the way for you and me, most likely.

Yet, what we do on this earth can have a lasting impact, even if we never become famous. Remember that word *concatenation*? Who is to say, three or four generations from now, what our legacy may be? Hopefully it will be for the good.

If you will indulge me, I would like to tell you of someone who impacted my life and who continues to impact generations of lives as well. My point is to illustrate how one person can make a difference and have a positive effect, thus fulfilling a grand purpose in life. One such person was Dr. Curtis Torno, my mentor while I attended undergraduate and graduate school. I worked for "Dr. T," as I like to call him, for five years doing lab work, taking x-rays, assisting in his occupational medicine clinic, and assisting him in surgery.

Dr. T was an "old-fashioned general practitioner" who did his own obstetrics for most of his career, as well as most of his own orthopedic work. I like to say Dr. T never saw a fracture he could not reduce, my left radius being one when I was eleven years old. But he was also a very good diagnostician, as well as a surgeon, being trained after medical school by local surgeons who were overwhelmed with cases and glad to teach GPs. I was privileged to "scrub in" and first assist on hundreds of surgeries with Dr. Torno long before I ever stepped a foot in medical school. Dr. T was a very good surgeon, and in my more than forty years since, having worked with many other surgeons, I can honestly say no one had better hands than him. Dr. T mentored many students during his career, with all those going on to careers in medicine, either as nurses, physicians, or physician's assistants.

In my time with him, I felt like a family member, and he treated me as such, as I am sure he did with all the others who worked with him. Dr. Torno was gregarious, funny, generous, and energetic. He had a zest for life and never met a person he didn't like. In many ways, he was bigger than life. Most mornings, before surgery at around 6 am., we would meet at Denman's Cafe, where he would buy me breakfast. We would discuss many topics, including politics, sports, and medicine, but we would also discuss religious topics as well. You see, Dr. Torno was not only a fantastic physician, but he was also a warrior for Christ, and he freely shared the Gospel with anyone and everyone, including my father and my mother, who became Christians because of him, and as a result, so did I and my five siblings.

Dr. T was an elder in the church, as well as a Bible teacher and at times a preacher, but most of his work was done in personal evangelism. He was personally responsible for converting hundreds to the cause of Christ, and his legacy lives on to this day in untold numbers, including my own family and his who are still dedicated Christians.

Dr. T led a purposeful life, dedicated to Jesus Christ. He was by no means perfect, as none of us are save one, but he had a compassion for his fellow man, not just for his physical health, but for his spiritual health, as well. The world is a better place because of his life, and though he's gone now, his influence will live on for many generations, I am sure.

But there is one Person who walked on the earth who had more purpose than any of us, Jesus Christ. Think of this: He gave up the splendor of heaven to come to the earth He created in order to save us from our sins. The writer of the book of Hebrews tells us that Jesus "was made a little lower than the angels, for the suffering of death, crowned with glory and honor, that He by the grace of God might taste death for everyone."[11] This verse explains it all. Jesus, mightier than the angels, became a man so that He could die and redeem mankind. But notice, the writer said He "tasted death." Death did not conquer Him, because He overcame it through His resurrection.

Jesus repeatedly testified that He came to this earth "to do the will of Him who sent me."[12] He was to do God's will and not necessarily His own.[13]

Is it not amazing that Jesus, our supreme example of obedience, knew the will of God and did it, yet some people think they are better, and therefore, they refuse to do His will, though the mystery is revealed to us and thus we are without excuse.

Some people think Jesus failed on the earth and will one day return again to fulfill His ministry, but they are mistaken. Paul told the Ephesians that Jesus was now seated with God in heavenly places "far above all principalities and power and might and every name that is named, not only in this age but also in that which is to come."[14] Furthermore, He also put all things under His feet and gave Him to be head of all things to the Church, which is His body, the fullness of Him who feels all in all.[15]

Jesus fulfilled His eternal purpose, as we have noted. When He comes again, it will be for the final time. There will be no new kingdom set up on earth. This earth will pass away, and those whom God calls His own will see no more death, sorrow, or crying. They will experience no pain either, because the "former things have passed away."[16]

Paul told the Corinthians about the people still alive at Jesus' Second Coming, how they will be changed in a "twinkling of the eye," meaning the physical body will take on a spiritual body at the Second Coming of Christ.[17] This is when "death will be swallowed up in victory."[18] Thus Paul says we are to be "immovable, always abounding in the work of the Lord, knowing that your labor is not in vain in the Lord."[19]

Conclusion

The preacher wrote: "To everything there is a season, a time for every purpose under heaven; a time to be born, a time to die; a time to plant, and a time to pluck what is planted; a time to kill, and a time to heal; a time to break down, and a time to build up; a time to weep, and a time to laugh; a time to mourn, and a time to dance;

a time to cast away stones, and a time to gather stones; a time to embrace, and a time to refrain from embracing; a time to gain, and a time to lose; a time to keep, and a time to throw away; a time to tear, and a time to sew; a time to keep silence, and a time to speak; a time to love, and a time to hate; a time for war, and a time for peace."[20]

It would seem there is a proper time for everything, and it would behoove us to discern when that time is. As I write this, I am now three years retired from my family practice. In July 1983, I began my more than thirty-six years as a family practitioner. For the last three years, I have been a hospice director, a job I gain satisfaction in and for and for which I seem to have a personality for doing.

In 1983, the AIDS epidemic was gaining momentum. Of course, early on there were no antivirals for HIV, thus a diagnosis of AIDS was essentially a death sentence, and I treated my share of those patients. We treated them with antibiotics for the host of opportunistic infections that came to them, but eventually antibiotics were not enough, and all my patients succumbed to their disease. These were all previously healthy, young people in the prime of life, yet their bodies could not overcome this dreadful virus. Now, fortunately, we do have antivirals, and patients with HIV can and do live lives of relative normality.

At the close of my family practice, we began treating patients with an aggressive respiratory virus that eventually became known as COVID-19. As in the case of the HIV virus, early on we had no antivirals that were effective against COVID-19. Though most patients survived, many did not, especially those with comorbid conditions and the elderly. We did all we could with antibiotics, and then later some other supportive measures, to keep people alive long enough for their bodies to overcome the virus, but unfortunately, sometimes it just wasn't enough. Now, three years later, the mortality rate of COVID-19 has declined significantly, with medications and with the natural loss of virility that viruses develop over time.

During my three and a half decades in family medicine, I treated a wide variety of illnesses, both from infectious diseases and degenerative diseases, as well as traumatic diseases and even some conditions that were self-inflicted, such as alcoholism, illicit drug use, and tobacco use. My purpose was always to cure the disease, if possible, to prolong life and give my patients the best quality of life as it pertained to their condition. I treated all my patients like they were family and like I would want myself to be treated, but I came to realize that no matter what I did, sometimes it simply was not going to be enough. The mortality rate of life is 100 percent. Nonetheless, death is always difficult to deal with, especially when it occurs suddenly or unexpectedly, and I shed many a tear with grieving family members.

Now, as a hospice director, my purpose has changed in treating my patients. By definition, all my patients have terminal conditions, which means their life expectancy is less than six months. I am very aware I am no longer trying to "cure" their condition. The purpose now is to make their journeys end as peacefully and comfortably as I can, with the help of my team, as well as helping families deal with their grief. It is a challenge at times, but it also can be fulfilling, for I know we are doing all we can to help the dying patient ease into their next journey.

I believe with all my heart that something in us keeps on going after this life. Death is not just the body giving up life, but rather a separation of the soul from the body. The Bible certainly teaches us this.

When Jesus was hanging on the cross, do you remember what He told one of the thieves hanging beside Him who believed in Jesus? In Luke 23:43, Jesus told Him, "Today you will be with me in paradise." And who was present at the Transfiguration of Jesus? Was it not Moses and Elijah? How could that be if they had ceased to exist after death?

I have had patients who were resuscitated after cardiac arrest and survived. These patients were essentially dead, with no vitals and no heartbeats. They all had different experiences, but universally they were henceforth changed forever, as you might imagine. What was common with them all was a loss of the fear of death.

I recently saw the movie *After Death*, in which dozens of patients were interviewed with what has come to be called "near-death experiences." Also in this movie, several doctors who have studied these patients with near-death experiences were interviewed. Some anecdotes are interesting, such as people sensing themselves hovering above the room where their "death" occurred and describing in detail accurately things that were happening during this time. But once again, what seemed universal among all those interviewed was a loss of the fear of death after this experience. Now, I am not saying this film, with these fortunate individuals, proves life after death, and I would still be committed in my personal belief without these testimonials, but it certainly does give one pause. If we do go on existing after life on earth, does it at least make us concerned about our actions here on earth? Will we be held accountable for what we do and what we have done? Jesus said we would. In Matthew 12:36–37, He said, "But I say to you that every idle word man may speak, he will give account of it in the day of judgement. For by your words you will be justified, and by your words you will be condemned."

Jesus also said, "I am the resurrection and the life. The one who believes in me will live even though they die."[21] The Hebrew writer wrote, "And it is appointed unto men once to die, but after this the judgment."[22]

The theme of this book has been about purpose—God's purpose and ours. God created us in His own image and appointed man to be "fruitful and multiply; fill the earth and subdue it."[23] He then sent His Son to redeem us: "For we are His workmanship, created in Christ Jesus for good works, which God prepared beforehand that we should walk in them."[24] We—that is, Christians—are a "chosen generation, a royal priesthood, a holy nation, His own special people."[25]

Our purpose on earth should be to do good, to obey our Lord and Savior, striving to emulate His life. This world is full of hate, strife, envy, jealousy, and pride. It ought not to be that way! Oh, if the world only loved God like He loves us! It would truly be a more wonderful place to live, would it not? But alas, such is not the case. John wrote, "Beloved, if God so loved us, we ought to love one another."[26] And, "He who does not love does not know God, for God is love."[27] Further, John tells us that God so loved us that He "sent his son to be the propitiation for our sins."[28]

Do you think God doesn't understand our sorrows? He sent His own Son to die on the cross. I end with a plea—to choose a good, purposeful life. God would have us all to be saved, and He is patient toward us, but it is our choice.[29]

"Blessed are the poor in spirit for theirs is the kingdom of Heaven. Blessed are those who hunger and thirst for righteousness, for they will be filled."[30]

"You are the light of the world, a city that is set on a hill cannot be hidden; nor do they light a lamp and put it under a basket, but on a lampstand, and it gives light to all who are in the house. Let your light so shine before men, that they may see your good works and glorify your Father in heaven."[31]

APPENDIX

Why did it take so long to abolish slavery in the United States and Great Britain? Greed, of course, was the major driving factor for slave owners to keep slaves, but it is also true that some, especially in the American South, tried to justify slavery from a biblical perspective. Sadly, some so-called Christians still think slavery is condoned by God. They are wrong! Two passages were primarily used in the argument for slavery—Ephesians 6 and the book of Philemon. Ephesians 6:5 (NASB) states, "Slaves be obedient to those who are your masters according to the flesh with fear and trembling in the sincerity of your heart as to Christ, not as men pleasers, but as slaves of Christ, doing the will of God from the heart." In the book of Philemon, verse 16, Philemon's servant is referred to as a "slave" (NASB). In the book of Philemon, the apostle Paul urges Philemon to send Onesimus, the servant, back to Paul, though clearly Philemon has the right to keep him. It should be noted that the Greek word *doulos*, rendered "slave" by the New American Standard Bible, is translated "bondman" by Darby, "servant" in the King James, "servant" in the American Standard Version, and in Ephesians 6:5, "bond servant" by the New King James Version.

Slavery in New Testament times was an extraordinarily common practice, with some estimates being that 20 to 50 percent of the entire population of the Roman Empire were slaves. Two-thirds of these slaves became slaves by conquest, with the alternative of being put to death, and one-third were bond servants. Bond servants were those who sold themselves into bondage, usually in order to pay off some sort of debt incurred by either themselves or their family members. It also should be noted, God can allow something without approving it. For example, polygamy was permitted under Old Testament law, but it was never the intention of God, as witnessed in Mark 10:5–8 and in 1 Timothy 3: 2. Divorce for any reason was also permitted under Old Testament law, but God clearly hated divorce, as seen in Malachi 2:16, and God no longer allowed divorce for simply any reason in the New Testament, as seen in Matthew 19:8–9. Slavery, as practiced in Great Britain and America during the seventeenth, eighteenth, and nineteenth centuries was a quite different animal from the slavery seen in Roman times. In Great Britain and America, slaves were rounded up like cattle, separated from their families, and treated as a subspecies. Those condoning slavery must ignore a lot of plain teachings of the Bible. Kidnapping, murder, and brutality have never been condoned in Scripture. In the Old Testament, a kidnapper who sold his victim or even kept him or violently dealt with him was to be put to death (Exodus 2:16; Deuteronomy 24:7). In 1 Timothy 1:9–10, kidnappers are lumped in with lawless sinners, the ungodly, and the profane. Abraham Lincoln once said, "If slavery is not wrong, nothing is wrong," and with that I concur. One must conclude that Onesimus was more than likely a "bond servant" of Philemon's, and Ephesians 6:5 is better translated as "bondman" or "servant" than "slave," as in the New American Standard Bible.

For those who think slavery no longer exists in our modern times, think again. Human trafficking persists to this day primarily for sexual slavery, but also to populate sweatshops in places like Russia, Nigeria, Egypt, the Congo, and Indonesia. Recently, the movie *Sound of Freedom* documented the sex trafficking that is happening in our own hemisphere at this present time. Estimates vary widely, but between twenty-one and forty-one million people are trapped in some form of slavery today, obviously illegally, as no country openly permits it. It is nonetheless practiced by some countries, whether it be the result of domestic servitude, sex trafficking, forced labor, bonded labor, or child labor.

ENDNOTES

Quotes

[1]Gonzalez, Guillermo. Signs In The Sky: The Wonder of our Solar Eclipses. SALVO. Issue 68, Spring, 2024. Page 44.
[2]Eph. 2: 10

Introduction

Intro Quotes

Schrödinger, Erwin. *Nature and the Greeks and Science and Humanism*. Cambridge University Press, 1954. Reprinted in 1996. Page 95.

Deane, David R.C. "Is Science the Only Means of Acquiring Truth" in *The Comprehensive Guide to Science and Faith*. Dembski et al. Harvest House. Page 422.

End Notes

[1]Feynman, Richard. BBC television special YouTube.
[2]Feynman Richard. *The Strange Theory of Light and Matter*. Princeton University Press, 1988. Page 10.
[3]TIME LIFE. The ages of God-Kings. Time Life Books. Publisher Joseph P Ward. 1987. Page 10.
[4]Lennox, John C. *God's Undertaker*. Page 43.
[5]Dawkins, Richard. The Blind Watchmaker. Page 1.
[6]Deane, David R.C. "Is Science the Only Means of Acquiring Truth" in *The Comprehensive Guide to Science and Faith*. Dembski et al. Harvest House. Page 423.
[7]Ibid. Page 426.
[8]Ibid. Page 420.
[9]Churchill, Winston. From the "American Rhetoric" in a speech delivered to the US Congress, December 26th, 1941.
[10]Baugh, Carl. *Against All Odds*. Page 11.
[11]Zucker, Charles. Found in *The Comprehensive Guide to Faith and Science*. Page 389
[12]Evans, Glen. Found in *The Comprehensive Guide to Faith in Science*. Page 389.

[13]Goodman, Morris. Found in *The Comprehensive Guide to Faith and Science*. Page 389.
[14]Alexander, Denis. *Beyond Science*. Page 141.
[15]Ibid. Page 141.
[16]Psalm 14:1.
[17]Romans 1:20.
[18]Dembski, William. Found in *The Conference Guide to Science and Faith*. Page 27.

Chapter 1

Intro Quotes

Axe, Douglas. *Undeniable*. Page 103.

Deane, David R. C. "Is Science the Only Means of Acquiring Truth?" *Found in the Comprehensive Gude to Science and Faith*. Page 428.

End Notes

[1]Chernow, Ron. Alexander Hamilton. Page 33.
[2]Aitken, Jonathan. John Newton. Page 54.
[3]Ibid. page 103.
[4]Ibid. page 112.
[5]Ibid. page 124.
[6]Hague. William Wilberforce, page 125.
[7]Ibid. page 125.
[8]Ibid. page 132.
[9]Ibid. page 90.
[10]Ibid. page 140.
[11]Ibid. page 141.
[12]Ibid. page 187.
[13]Aitken. John Newton, page 315.
[14]Hague. William Wilberforce, page 273.
[15]Ibid
[16]Ibid. page 275.
[17]Ibid. page 354.
[18]Ibid. page 354.
[19]Ibid. page 354.
[20]Lincoln on abolition in England and the United States, 1854. From the Gilder Lehrman Institute of Human History.
[21]Hague, William. William Wilberforce. Page 508.

Chapter 2

Intro Quotes

Carroll, Sean. In *Return of the God Hypothesis.* Meyer, Stephen C. Page 218.

Lennox, John C. *God's Undertaker.* Page 210.

End Notes

[1]Dembski William et al. The Comprehensive Guide to Science and Faith. Page 25.
[2]Ibid, page 27.
[3]Bertrand, Russell. Mysticism and Logic.
[4]Ibid.
[5]Oxford Reference. David Hume.
[6]Internet Encyclopedia of Philosophy. Friedrich Nietzsche.
[7]Dawkins, Ricard. A River out of Eden: A Darwinian view of Life. Page 133.
[8]Greenblatt Swerve Page 11
[9]Ibid, page 13.
[10]Pederson, Ken. Modern Science Proves Intelligent Design. Page 31
[11]Hawking, Steven; Mlodinow, Leonard. A briefer History of Time. Page 69.
[12]O'Leary, Denise. "Is Evolutionary Psychology a legitimate way to understand our humanity". Found in The Comprehensive Guide to Science and Faith. Dembsky, p 373.
[13]Ibid. p 374.
[14]Ibid. p 374
[15]Ibid. p 376
[16]Berlinski, David. The Devil's Delusion. P 33.
[17]Ibid. p 34.
[18]Jerimiah 10:23..
[19]Epicurus. The Art of Happiness.
[20]Matthew 12, 30 - 31.
[21]Dembski, William, et al. The Comprehensive Guide to Science and Faith. Pages, 545- 553.
[22]Berlinski, David, The Devil's Delusion. Page 21.
[23]Ibid, page 22.
[24]Berlinski, David. Human Nature. Page 153.
[25]Berlinski, David. The Devils Delusion. Page 25.
[26]Metaxas, Eric. Is atheism dead? Page 281
[27]Ibid, page 281.
[28]Ibid, page 349.

[29]Ibid, page 349.
[30]Ibid, page 278.
[31]Berlinski. The Devil's Delusion. Page 26.

Chapter 3

Intro Quotes
Hoyle, Fred. "The Universe: Past and Present." Annual review of Astronomy & Physics. 2016. 1982.

Axe, Douglas. Undeniable. Page 185.

End Notes
[1]Denton, Michael. *The Miracle of Man*. Page 23.
[2]Ibid. Page 29.
[3]Carroll, Sean. *Dark Matter, Dark Energy: The Dark Side of the Universe*. Pages 88, 89.
[4]Wallace, J. Warner. *God's Crime Scene*. Page 218.
[5]Ibid. Page 219 From BBC-TV's "Parallel Universes, 2002."
[6]Khan, Fouad. "Scientific American". April 2021.
[7]Tyson, Neil deGrasse - from multiple YouTube videos including interviews with Larry King and James Corden.
[8]Meyer, Stephen C. *Return to the God Hypothesis*. Page 335.
[9]Meyer. *Return of the God Hypothesis*. Page 339. "Return of the God Hypothesis"
[10]Dawkins, Richard. Featured in "Strong", Richard Dawkins.
[11]Meyer. *Return of the God Hypothesis*. Page 345.
[12]Lewontin, Richard. *Billions and Billions of Demons*. January 9, 1997.
[13]Ross, Hugh. *The Creator and the Cosmos*. Page 159.
[14]Hawking, Stephen C. *A Brief History of Time*. Page 127.
[15]Ross, Hugh. *The Creator and the Cosmos*. Page 165
[16]Denton. *The Miracle of Man*. Page 42.
[17]Ibid. Page 47.
[18]Ibid. Page 47.
[19]Ibid. Page 53.
[20]Ibid. Page 61.
[21]Ibid. Page 91.
[22]Ibid. Page 204.
[23]Ibid. Page 23.
[24]Ibid. Page 206.
[25]Lennox, John C., *God's Undertaker*. Page 147.
[26]Lennox, John C., *2084*. Page 123
[27]Denton. *The Miracle of Man*. Page 208.
[28]Meyer. *Return of the God Hypothesis*. Page 153.
[29]Ibid. Page 154.
[30]Ibid. Page 156.

[31] Ibid. Page 156.
[32] Ibid. Page 149.
[33] Ibid. Page 116.
[34] Strobel. *The Case for the Creator*. Page 133.
[35] Ibid Page 133
[36] Ibid Page 134
[37] Ross, Hugh. *Found in God's Undertaker*. Lennox, John. Page 71.

Chapter 4

Intro Quotes

Einstein, Albert. Physics and Reality (1936). "In Ideas and Opinions". Bargmann, Sonja. Page 292.

Proverbs 25: 2.

End Notes

[1] Wolfson, Richard. *Simply Einstein*. Page 30.
[2] Feynman, Richard. *Six easy pieces*. Page 32.
[3] Wolfson. *Simply Einstein*. Page 110.
[4] Ibid. Page 110.
[5] Ibid. Page 110.
[6] Feynman. *Six Easy Pieces*. Pages 117-138.
[7] Ibid. Page 129.
[8] Ibid. Page 138.
[9] Carroll, Sean. *Mystery of Time*. Page 53.
[10] Feigenbaum, Mitchell. Found in *Chaos*. Gleickman, James. Page 185.
[11] Ibid. Page 1.
[12] Feynman. *Six Easy Pieces*. Page 2.
[13] Planck, Max. www.goodreads.com.

Chapter 5

Intro Quotes

Coyne, George and Hiller, Michael, "A Comprehensible Universe: the Interplay of Science and Theology." In "Thinking God's Thoughts." Travis, Melissa-Cain, page 237.

Feigenbaum, Mitchell. Found in "chaos". Gleick, James. Page 187.

End Notes

[1] Lorenz, Edward, found in "The Fractal Foundation". Website.
[2] Gleick, James. Chaos. "Page 7"
[3] Haim, H. Bau and Shachmurove, Yochanan "Chaos Theory and its Applications."

[4]Gleick, James. Chaos. Page 329.
[5]Ibid. Page 23
[6]Ibid. Page 23.
[7]Ibid. Page 68.
[8]Ibid. Page 112.
[9]Ibid. Page 110.
[10]Ibid. Page 171.
[11]Ibid. Page 180.
[12]Oestreicher, Christian. "A History of Chaos Theory."
    National Library of Science
[13]Gleick. Chaos. Page 182
[14]Ibid. Page 183
[15]Oestreicher, Christian. "A History of Chaos Theory."
    National Library of Science **
[16]Gleick. Chaos. Page 267.

Chapter 6

Intro Quotes

Axe, Douglas. *Undeniable*. Page 166.

Bechly, Günter. "Does the fossil record demonstrate evolution?" *In The Comprehensive Guide to Science and Faith*. Dembski et al page 348.

End Notes

[1]Nirody, Jasmine. "Journal of General Physiology" September
    23rd, 2020, "ATP synthase: Evolution, energetics, and
    membrane interaction."
[2]Denton, Michael. *Children of Light*. Page 78.
[3]Axe, Douglas. *Undeniable*. Page 168.
[4]Ibid page 75.
[5]Denton, Michael. *Children of Light*. Page 23.
[6]Ibid page 23.
[7]Ibid page. Page 75.
[8]Goodsell, David. "Molecule of the Month". December 2005.
[9]Ibid.
[10]Behe, Michael J. "Darwin's Black Box". Page 39.
[11]Ibid page 39.

Chapter 7
Intro Quotes
Laufmann, Steve and Glicksman, Howard. *Your Design Body*. Page 159-160.

Ibid. p. 378

End Notes
[1]Denton, Michael. The Miracle of Man. p. 83
[2]Ibid, p. 88.
[3]Ibid, p. 90.
[4]Ibid, p. 90.
[5]Ibid, p. 94.
[6]Ibid, p. 94.
[7]Laufmann, Steve and Glicksman, *Howard. Your Designed Body*. P. 95.
[8]Denton. *Miracle of Man*. p. 28.
[9]Laufmann and Glicksman. *Your Designed Body*. p. 99.
[10]Ibid. p. 103.
[11]Ibid. p. 103.
[12]For a fuller discussion, I would recommend *The Designed Body* by Laufmann and Glicksman.
[13]Denton. *Miracle of Man*. p. 150.
[14]Ibid. p. 151.

Chapter 8
Intro Quotes
Laufmann, Steve and Glicksman, Michael. *Your Designed Body*. Page 444.

Lewontin, Richard. Found in "Do Fossils Demonstrate Human Evolution". Luskin, Casey. *The Comprehensive Guide to Science and Faith*. Page 357.

End Notes
[1]Behe, Michael. "Darwin Devolves". Page 85.
[2]Ibid page 10.
[3]Ibid page 10.
[4]Ibid page 88.
[5]Ibid page 90.
[6]Wells, Jonathan. *Icons of Evolution*. Page 164.
[7]Behe. *Darwin Devolves*, page 264.
[8]Tour, James. "The Mystery of Life." YouTube video.
[9]Metaxas, Eric. *Is Atheism Dead?*, page 90.
[10]Ibid page 104.

[11]Laufmann, Steve and Glicksman, Howard. *Your Designed Body*. Page 415.

[12]Ibid page 416.

[13]Ibid page 421.

[14]Ibid page 422.

[15]Ibid page 422.

[16]Darwin, Charles. *On the Origin of Species*. Dover Thrift Edition. Page 133.

[17]Cassell, Eric. *Animal Algorithms*. Page 133.

[18]Ibid page 99.

[19]Darwin. *On the Origin of Species*. Page 153.

[20]Einstein, Albert. *Physics and Reality*. 1936.

[21]Eberlin, Marcos. *Foresight*. Page 35.

[22]Ibid page 36.

[23]Cassell. *Animal Algorithms*. Page 42.

[24]Eberlin. *Foresight*. Page 101.

[25]Ibid page 102.

[26]Cassell. *Animal Algorithms*. Page 43.

[27]Ibid page 54.

[28]Ibid page 57

[29]Churchill, Winston, Radio address 1939.

[30]Cassell. *Animal Algorithms*. Page 86.

[31]Ibid page 85.

[32]Ibid page 96.

[33]Ibid page 98.

[34]Ibid page 99.

[35]Ibid page 99.

[36]Ibid page 99.

[37]Darwin. *On the Origin of Species*. Page 124.

[38]Ibid page 124.

[39]Cassell. *Animal Algorithms*. Page 125.

[40]Ibid page 60.

[41]Ibid page 60.

[42]Ibid page 61.

[43]Ibid page 125.

[44]Melville, Herman. *Moby-Dick*. The Northwestern-Newberry Edition. Pages 134 to 145.

[45]Kirkwood, Milton. *The Evolution Delusion*. Page 97.

[46]Wells, Jonathan. *Zombie Science*. Page 100.

[47]Ibid page 100.

[48]Ibid page 100.

[49]Ibid page 103.

[50]Ibid page 107.

[51]Ibid page 109.

[52]Ibid page 114.

Chapter 9

Intro Quotes

Kepler, Johanne. In "Is Christianity at war with Science?" Keas, Michael N. in *The Comprehensive Guide to Science and Faith*. Dempsky, et al. p 63.

Richards, J.W. "How Can We Use Science in Apologetics?" in *The Comprehensive Guide to Science and Faith*. Dempsky, et al. p 130.

End Notes

[1] Lisle, Jason. *Fractals*. Page 6.
[2] Ibid page 7.
[3] Travis, Melissa Cain. *Thinking God's Thoughts*. Pages 63 to 64.
[4] Paul. "Roman Letter, Chapter 1," *The New King James Bible*.
[5] Lennox, John. *God's Undertaker*. Page 24.
[6] Ibid page 60.
[7] Ibid page 61.
[8] Ibid page 63.
[9] Ibid page 63.
[10] Wigner, Eugene. "The Unreasonable Effectiveness of Mathematics in the Natural Sciences." In Communication in Pure and Applied Mathematics, Volume 13. Number 1. As quoted in *Fractals*, Jason Lisle.
[11] Lennox. *God's Undertaker*. Page 45.
[12] Wigner. "The Unreasonable Effectiveness of Mathematics in the Natural Sciences."
[13] Travis. *Thinking God's Thoughts*. Page 5.
[14] Ibid page 5.
[15] Berlinski, David. *Science After Babel*. Page 33.
[16] Ibid page 34.
[17] Kitts, David. "Evolution" Volume 28, September 1974 (page 467).
[18] Berlinski. *Science After Babel*. Page 36.
[19] Ibid page 39.
[20] Dembski, William A. et. al. *The Comprehensive Guide to Science and Faith*. The previous 6 paragraphs utilized information and articles written by Casey Luskin and Jonathan Wells.
[21] Psalm 46:10 *The New King James Bible*.
[22] Isaiah 46:10 *The New King James Bible*.
[23] Lisle. *Fractals*. Page 133.
[24] Berlinski, David. *The Devil's Delusion*. Page 218.

Chapter 10
Intro Quotes
Ward, Keith. In *Thinking God's Thoughts*. Travis, Thomas, Melissa Kane Travis. P 239.

Schroeder, Gerald L. *The Science of God*. Page 66.

End Notes
[1]Berlinski, David. *Science After Babel*. Page 233.
[2]Ibid. Page 234.
[3]Aristotle "Metaphysics." From Good Reads.
[4]Travis, Melissa-Cain. *Thinking God's Thoughts*. Page 50.
[5]Ibid page 68.
[6]Ibid page 91.
[7]Paul. Romans 1:20. *New King James Bible*.
[8]Berlinski. *Science After Babel*. Page 234.
[9]Ibid. Page 41.
[10]Ibid. Page 41.
[11]Gödel, Kurt. "Harmonis." December 5, 2009.
[12]Lennox, John. "The Question of Science and God Part 1", Socrates in the City with Eric Metaxas, January 12, 2018.

Chapter 11
Intro Quotes
Kepler, Johannes. From A Sayer. 1623. In *Thinking God's Thoughts*. Travis, Melissa Cain. P. 127.

Lennox, John. *God's Undertaker*. P. 61.

End Notes
[1]Gleick, James. *Chaos*. Pages 215 to 222.
[2]Lisle, Jason. *Fractals*. page 8.
[3]Gleick. *Chaos*. page 98.
[4]Ibid. page 114.
[5]Lisle. *Fractals*. page 125.
[6]Ibid page. 125.
[7]Ibid page. 126.
[8]Gleick. *Chaos*. Page 240.
[9]Ibid page 110.
[10]Berlinski, David. *Science After Babel*. Page 234.
[11]Hebrew writer. Hebrews1:3. *New King James Bible*.
[12]Lisle, Fractals. page 211.

Chapter 12

Intro Quotes

Haines, David and Correa, Frank. "Can a Christian be a Scientist (and vice versa)? In Dempsk, et al *The Comprehensive Guide to Science and Faith*. Page 95.

Axe, Douglas. "Is Our Intuition of Design in Nature Correct?". In Dempski, et al *The Comprehensive Guide to Science and Faith*. Page 151.

End Notes

[1] Stroble, Le. *The Case For A Creator*. Page 41.
[2] Ibid page 74.
[3] Ibid page 77.
[4] Ibid page 111.
[5] Ibid page 123.
[6] Ibid page 141.
[7] Ibid page 111.
[8] Ibid page 111.
[9] Ibid page 81.
[10] Ibid page 81.
[11] Ibid page 327.
[12] Ibid page 284.
[13] Ibid page 113.
[14] John 3:16 *New King James Bible*.
[15] Stokes, George. In Dempski, et al. *Comprehensive Guide to Science and Faith*. Page 517.
[16] Stroble. *The Case For A Creator*. page 249.
[17] McDowell, Josh. *The New Evidence That Demands A Verdict*. Page 271.
[18] Ibid page 271.
[19] Ibid page 271.
[20] Davies, Norman. *Europe*. Page 203.
[21] Hebrews 11:1. *New King James Bible*.
[22] Romans 10:17. *New King James Bible*.
[23] Travis, Melissa-Cain. *Thinking God's Thoughts*. Page 5.
[24] Genesis 2:16. *New King James Bible*.
[25] Acts 5:3-4. *New King James Bible*.
[26] Dembski, William et. al. *The Comprehensive Guide to Science and Faith*. Page 204.
[27] Ibid page 202.
[28] Ibid page 209.
[29] Ibid page 209.
[30] Ezekiel 18:20-21. *New King James Bible*.
[31] Matthew 22:27. *New King James Bible*.

[32]Matthew 22:28 New King James Bible.
[33]John 14:15; 1 John 5:2-3.
[34]Galatians 6:10.
[35]James 1:22.
[36]Matthew 5:16.
[37]Philippians 3:20.
[38]James 4:14.
[39]Colossians 4:5; Ephesians 5:14-15.
[40]Philippians 1:23.
[41]1 Peter 2:11.

Chapter 13

Intro Quotes

West, John G. "How Has Darwinism Negatively Impacted Society?" in Dembski, et al. *The Comprehensive Guide to Science and Faith*. Page 395.

Behe, Michael. *Darwin Devolves*. Page 269.

End Notes

[1]New York Times. August 18th, 2023
[2]NIH "Drug Overdose Rates." June 2023
[3]Genesis 3:1 and 4
[4]Ezekiel 28:12-18
[5]Revelation 20:7-10
[6]Revelation 21:1
[7]John 14:6
[8]Matthew 10:32-33
[9]Ephesians 6:12
[10]Ephesians 6:14-18
[11]Hebrews 11:6
[12]Alexander, Denis. Beyond Science. Page 147
[13]Ibid. page 154
[14]Bonhoeffer, David. Good Reads Quotes
[15]Metaxas, Eric. *Letters to the American Church*. Page 59
[16]Ibid. page 71
[17]Ibid. page 72
[18]Ibid. page 72
[19]2 Timothy 4:3
[20]2 Peter 2:1
[21]2 Peter 2:1
[22]Metaxas, Eric "Letter to the American Church." Page 129
[23]Acts 22:16
[24]Romans 8:18
[25]2 Timothy 4:8

[26]2 Timothy 4:8
[27]Acts 17:6
[28]Matthew 5:14-16

Chapter 14

Intro Quotes

Lewis, C. S. Found in *The Comprehensive Guide to Science and Faith*. Page 578.

Deane, David R. C. "Is Science the Only Means of Acquiring Truth". In *The Comprehensive Guide to Science and Faith*. Page 423.

End Notes

[1]Warren, Eugene. *Christographia*. Chance Or The Dance.
[2]To Howard, Thomas. *Chance or the Dance*. Page 2.
[3]Ibid. Page 134.
[4]Ibid. Page 134.
[5]Alexander, Denis. *Beyond Science*. Page 44
[6]Paul. Philippians 4-4.
[7]Paul. Romans 15: 13
[8]John 12: 22.
[9]Paul. Romans 14: 7.
[10]Solomon. Ecclesiastes 1: 2-5.
[11]Ibid. 3-11.
[12]Ibid. 3-12.
[13]Ibid. 3-17.
[14]Ibid. 4-3.
[15]Ibid. 5-1.
[16]Ibid. 7-14.
[17]Ibid. 9-9.
[18]Ibid. 9-10.
[19]Ibid. 9-11.
[20]Ibid. 12-13.
[21]Howard. *Chance Or The Dance*. Page 44.
[22]James: 4-4.
[23]1 Peter 1: 24.
[24]Howard. *Chance Or The Dance*. Page 119.
[25]Solomon Ecclesiastes. 3-16.
[26]Howard. *Chance or the Dance*. Page 132.
[27]Alexander, Denis *Beyond Science*. Page 181.
[28]Hebrews 11: 16.
[29]Hebrews 11: 1.
[30]Paul. Colossians 1:24.
[31]Paul Romans 12: 12.

[32]Matthew 5: 12.
[33]1 Peter 4: 12-13.
[34]Hebrews 6: 18.
[35]Ibid. 6-19.
[36]John 14: 1-4. 7 Genesis: 1-3.
[37]Genesis 1:1-3
[38]John 1: 1.
[39]Lennox, John. *God's Undertaker.* Page 205.
[40]Nehemiah 5: 6.
[41]Luke 10: 18; Revelation 12: 7-9.
[42]Ephesians 1: 3-7.
[43]Acts 10: 34.
[44]1 Timothy 2: 1-4.
[45]Romans 10: 17.
[46]Romans 1: 16.
[47]Acts 2:47.
[48]Matthew 16: 18.
[49]Dickens, Larry. From sermon "The First Dimension".
[50]Ephesians 1: 22.
[51]Revelation 14: 13.
[52]Ibid. 20: 12-13.
[53]2 Thessalonians 1: 7-9; Matthew 25: 46; Matthew 18:8;
    John 14: 1-3.
[54]Hebrews 5: 9.
[55]Matthew 7:13-14
[56]2 Peter: 3-9.

Chapter 15

Intro Quotes

Behe, Michael. *Darwin Devolves.* Page 258.

Schroeder, Gerald L. *The Hidden Face of God.* Page 94.

End Notes

[1]John 18:37.
[2]John 8: 33.
[3]Matthew 12: 30.
[4]1 Timothy 3: 16.
[5]Chafer, Lewis S. From Josh McDowell's. *The New Evidence That Demands A Verdict.* Page 12.
[6]McDowell, Josh. *The New Evidence That Demands A Verdict.* Page 13.
[7]Ibid. Page 193:
[8]Ibid. Page 194.

[9]Pederson, Norman. *Modern Science Proves Intelligent Design.* Page 227.
[10]McDowell. *The New Evidence That Demands A Verdict.* Page 1.
[11]Hebrews 2: 9.
[12]John 4: 34.
[13]John 5: 30.
[14]Ephesians 1: 20-21.
[15]Ephesians 1: 22-23.
[16]Revelation 21: 4.
[17]1 Corinthians 15: 53.
[18]1 Corinthians 15: 54.
[19]1 Corinthians 15: 58.
[20]Ecclesiastes 3: 1-8.
[21]John 1: 25.
[22]Hebrews 9: 27.
[23]Genesis 1: 28.
[24]Ephesians 2: 10.
[25]1 Peter 2: 9.
[26]1 John 4: 10,
[27]1 John 4: 8.
[28]John 2: 2.
[29]2 Peter 3: 9.
[30]Matthew 5: 1.
[31]Matthew 5: 14-16.

Bibliography.

1. Aitken, Jonathan. John Newton. Crossway Books, 2007.
2. Alexander, Denis. Beyond Science. A.J. Holman Company, 1972.
3. Douglas. Undeniable. Harper Collins, 2016.
4. Baugh, Carl E. Against All Odds? Bible Belt Publishing, 1999.
5. Behe, Michael. Darwin's Black Box. Touchstone, 1996.
6. Behe, Michael. The Edge of Evolution. Free Press, 2007.
7. Behe, Michael. Darwin Devolves. Harper One, 2019.
8. Berlinski, David. The Deniable Darwin. Discovery Institute, 2009.
9. Berlinski, David. The Devil's Delusion. Basic Books, 2009.
10. Berlinski, David. Science After Babel. Discovery Institute Press, 2023.
11. Berlinski, David. Human Nature. Discovery Institute Press, 2019.
12. Bethell, Tom. House of Cards. Discovery Institute Press, 2017.
13. Carroll, Sean. Mysteries of Modern Physics: Time. The Great Courses, 2012.
14. Carroll, Sean. Dark Matter, Dark Energy: The Dark Side of the Universe. The Teaching Company, 2007.
15. Cassell, Eric. Animal Algorithms. Discovery Institute Press, 2021.
16. Chernow, Ron. Alexander Hamilton. Penguin Books, 2004.
17. Churchill, Winston. From "American Rhetoric" speech to U.S. Congress. Dec. 26, 1941.
18. Darwin, Charles. On the Origin of Species. Dover Thrift Editions, 2006.
19. Darwin, Charles. The Descent of Man. Pacific Publishing Studio Edition, 2011.
20. Davies, Norman. Europe: A History. Oxford University Press, 1976.
21. Dawkins, Richard. The God Delusion. First Mariner Books, 2008.
22. Dawkins, Richard. The Blind Watchmaker. W.W. Norton & Company, 1996..

23. Dean David R.C. "Is Science the Only Means of Acquiring Truth". In *The Comprehensive Guide to Science and Faith*. Dembski, et al. Harvest House.
24. Dembski, William A; Ruse, Michael. Debating Design. Cambridge University Press, 2006.
25. Dembski, William A. The Design Inference. Cambridge University Press, 1998.
26. Dembski, William A., Luskin, Casey and Holden, Joseph M. The Comprehensive Guide to Science and Faith, Harvest House Publishers, 2021.
27. Dembski, William A. and Ewert, Winston. The Design Inference, Second Edition Revised and Expanded, Discovery Institute Press, 2023.
28. Denton, Michael. Children of Light. Discovery Institute Press, 2018.
29. Denton, Michael. The Wonder of Water. Discovery Institute Press, 2017.
30. Denton, Michael. The Miracle of Man. Discovery Institute Press, 2022.
31. Dickens, Larry. The First Dimension. Sermon from August 22, 2023, unpublished.
32. Eberlin, Marcos. Foresight. Discovery Institute Press, 2019.
33. Feynman, Richard. BBC Television Special. YouTube.
34. Gonzalez, Guillermo; Richards, J.W. The Privileged Planet. Regency Publications, 2004.
35. Feynman, Richard P. Six Easy Pieces. Basic Books, 1995.
36. Feynman, Robert. *The Stange Theory of Light and Matter*. Princton University Press. 1988.
37. Goodsell, David. "Molecule-of-the-Month". Dec. 2005.
38. Greenblatt, Stephen. The Swerve. W.W. Norton & Company, 2011.
39. Greene, Brian. The Elegant Universe. W.W. Norton & Company Inc., 1999.
40. Hague, William. William Wilberforce. Harcourt, Inc., 2007.
41. Hawkins, Stephen C. *A Brief History of Time*. Bantam Books 1988.
42. Hoyle, Fred. "The Universe: Past and Present". Annual Review of Astronomy and Physics. 1982.
43. Gurtler, Joshua. Unraveling Evolution, Revised, Second Edition. Publications, 2018.

44. Hague, William. William Wilberforce. Harcourt, Inc., 2007.
45. Hawking, Stephen. A Briefer History of Time. Bantam Dell, 2005.
46. Hedin, Eric. Cancelled Science. Discovery Institute Press, 2021.
47. Howard, Thomas. Chance or the Dance. Ignatius, 2001.
48. Isaacson, Walter. Einstein. Simon and Schuster, 2007.
49. Joyce, James. Ulysses. Dover Edition, 2009.
50. Khan, Fouad. "Scientific American". April 2021.
51. King, Daniel H. Sr. God Does Exist! Truth Publications, 2020.
52. Kirkwood, Bo. The Evolution Delusion. Truth Publications, 2016.
53. Kushner, Harold S. When Bad Things Happen to Good People. Schocken Books, 1981.
54. Laufmann, Steve; Glicksman, Howard. Your Designed Body. Discovery Institute Press, 2022.
55. Lennox, John. 2084. Zondervan Reflective, 2020.
56. Lennox, John. Seven Days That Divided the World. Zondervan Reflective, 2021.
57. Lennox, John. God's Undertaker. Lion, 2009.
58. Lewis, C.S. Mere Christianity. Harper Collins Edition, 2001.
59. Lisle, Jason. Fractals. Masters Books, 2021.
60. Lisle, Jason. Understanding Genesis. Masters Books, 2019.
61. Lisle, Jason. Introduction to Logic. Masters Books, 2018.
62. Lisle, Jason. The Ultimate Truth of Creation. Masters Books, 2009.
63. Lisle, Jason. The Physics of Einstein. Bible Science Institute, 2018.
64. Melville, Herman. Moby-Dick or The Well. 150th Anniversary Edition, 1988.
65. Metaxas, Eric. Is Atheism Dead? Salem Books, 2021.
66. Metaxas, Eric. Letter to the American Church. Salem Books, 2022.
67. Meyer, David M. Experiencing Hubble: Understanding the Greatest Images of the Universe. The Great Courses, 2011.
68. Meyer, Stephen C. Darwin's Doubt. Harper One, 2013.
69. Meyer, Stephen C. Return of the God Hypothesis. Harper Collins, 2021.
70. McDowell, Josh. The New Evidence. Thomas Nelson Publishers, 1999.
71. Mukherjee, Siddhartha. The Song of the Cell. Scribner, 2022.

72. Nirody, Jasmine. "ATP Synthase: Evolution Energetics and Membrane interaction". Journal of General Physiology. Sept. 23, 8080.

73. Oluniyi, Olufemi. Darwin Comes to Africa. Discovery Institute Press, 2023.

74. Pederson, Ken. Modern Science Proves Intelligent Design. Archway Publishing, 2019.

75. Ross, Hugh. The Creator and the Cosmos. Naupress, 2001.

76. Schrodinger, Erwin. *Nature and the Greeks ad Science and Humanism.* Cambridge University Press. 1954. Reprinted 1996.

77. Schroeder, Gerald L. Genesis and the Big Bang. Bantam Books, 1992.

78. Schroeder, Gerald L. The Science of God. Free Press, 1997.

79. Schroeder, Gerald L. The Hidden Face of God. Touchstone, 2001.

80. Shumacher, Benjamin. Impossible: Physics Beyond the Edge. The Great Courses, 2010.

81. Smith, Daniel. How to Think Like Einstein. Michael O'Mara Books Limited, 2014.

82. Strobel, Lee. The Case for a Creator. Zondervan, 2004.

83. Strobel, Lee. The Case for Christ. Zondervan, 1998.

84. Travis, Melissa Cain. Thinking God's Thoughts. Roman Rhodes Press, 2022.

85. Wallace. J. Warner. *God's Crime Scene.* David C. Cook Publishing. 2016.

86. Wells, Jonathan. Zombie Science. Discovery Institute Press, 2017.

87. Wolfson, Richard. Physics in Your Life. The Teaching Company, 2004.

88. Wolfson, Richard. Simply Einstein. W.W. Norton & Company, 2003.

To Order Additional Copies of

A
Purpose Driven
GOD

Visit your local bookstore, online bookstores
or
Amazon.com

Other quality books available by Bo Kirkwood:
Unveiling the Da Vinci Code
The Evolution Delusion

www.ingramcontent.com/pod-product-compliance
Lightning Source LLC
Chambersburg PA
CBHW060558100426
42742CB00013B/2610